MARILYN MONROE:

PRIVATE AND UNDISCLOSED

MARILYN MONROE:
PRIVATE AND
UNDISCLOSED

MICHELLE MORGAN

CONSTABLE • LONDON

I would like to dedicate this book to two very special ladies:
to my beautiful daughter, Daisy Elizabeth Pearl, who sees every day as
a new adventure and has taught me to do the same. Since she came
into my life, my dreams have all come true.
And, to the memory of my dear friend, Cathy Smith, the bravest
person I have ever known. She was such a huge supporter of my
writing that I'm sure if there are bookshops in heaven, she'll be the
first person to buy this book.

Constable & Robinson
3 The Lanchesters
162 Fulham Palace Road
London W6 9ER
www.constablerobinson.com

First published in the UK in 2007 by Constable, an imprint of Constable & Robinson Ltd

A copy of the British Library Cataloguing in Publication Data is available from the
British Library.

ISBN-13: 978-1-84529-524-0

10 9 8 7 6 5 4 3 2 1

CONTENTS

AUTHOR'S NOTE

Writing this book has given me the tremendous opportunity of corresponding with many of the people who met Marilyn. This has been a source of great joy and enabled me to write a thorough and original account of her life.

I should like to hear from anyone who either met or knew Marilyn and for their memories or photos to appear in future editions of this book. If you did ever meet Marilyn, or know anyone else who did so, please contact me at:

michelle@michellemorgan.co.uk

or please visit my website:

www.michellemorgan.co.uk

ACKNOWLEDGEMENTS

Writing a biography of Marilyn Monroe has been a huge labour of love for me and would not have been possible without the help and support of a network of friends, family and contacts. To that end I would like to thank the following people for assisting me during the four years I have been working on this book.

First I would like to thank my dear friends Eric Woodard, David Marshall and Roy Turner, who opened their personal archives to me, and also visited museums and universities on my behalf. Not only did they become huge contributors to my research but also extremely good listeners too. This book would not have been half as much fun without you!

A big thank you to Greg Schreiner, Stacey Eubank, Jill Adams, Tony Plant, Linda Weevers, Brian Beard, Brian Meech, Merja Pohjola, Rebecca Staley, Heather Williams, Suus Marie, Walt Dixon, Shaney Evans, Rita Oliveira, Shar Daws, Dawn Jones, Sally Wilson, Andrew Porteus, Valerie Samuel, Jenniffer Jones, Angelika Bartuseviciute, Andrea Pryke, Tara Hanks, Robert Ward, Bill Niles, Jeremy Markowitz, Gary Vitacco-Robles, Rachel Stockdale, Graham Dixon, Tiffany Ball, Karen Inskip-Hayward, Christelle, Priscilla Smits, Mary Sims, Suzie Kennedy, Mas Christine, Carol Summers, Cynthia Becht, Betsy Brett, Molly Schwartzburg, Edward Cunningham, Lasse Karlsson, Cheryl Plummer, John Necich, Lisa Bramen, Nikki Mensah, Geenie Stevens and Alberto for supplying articles, research and assistance.

For inspiration and encouraging emails, I'd like to thank biographers David Stenn and Lee Server. If my book is as well received as yours, I'll be a very happy lady.

Special thanks to John Porter who was a huge help to me during the research for this book. His knowledge of Marilyn and his knack of being able to find important internet resources was a great help. He also helped me try to locate the copyright holders of rare photos, for which I'm very grateful.

Darren Julien from Juliens Auctions helped me locate important sources and answered my questions.

Carla Orlandi trawled through the Twentieth Century Fox archives for me when I was not able myself to travel to Los Angeles; she also set up an interview with her friend Stefan Gierasch and personally made sure everything ran smoothly. Thanks, Carla.

The members of my Marilyn fan club, The Marilyn Lives Society, were extremely patient and supportive during the writing of this book, and I am eternally grateful to them.

I am indebted to Don Obermeyer and his daughter Kristen for their friendship and support. Don very kindly allowed me to use his Korea photos in this book – all of which were unpublished until now. Don is selling copies of those photos to raise money for Breast Cancer, and I encourage all readers of this book to invest in his beautiful photos and support such a worthwhile cause. Please email michelle@michellemorgan.co.uk if you would like to purchase copies of Don's photos.

The many archives, libraries and universities who helped me research and confirm particular events in Marilyn's life. (A list appears in the Sources section of this book.) Your assistance made my job all the easier. Thank you.

To all the newspapers, theatres, museums and organizations who helped during my quest to piece together Marilyn's trip to England in 1956.

To the newspapers in the USA and UK that printed my letters and allowed people to contact me with their Marilyn memories.

To Bill and Mac Pursel, who not only shared memories, but also friendship and hospitality to both myself and my family. You are both very special people, and I think the world of you.

To Paul 'Wes' Kanteman who became a friend as well as a source. You're one in a million – thank you.

To Bill Pursel, Joshua Greene, George Finch, Evan Finch, Horace Ward, Greg Schreiner, George Bailey, William Carroll, Stars and Stripes, Hollywood Bowl Museum, Alan Young, Paul Kanteman, Win Rosette, Albert Wimer, Gus Zernial, April and Jim Dakis, Don Loraine, Bob Vannucci, Andrea Pryke, Melissa Melgosa, William Davies, and all the photographers I have tried (and failed) to locate, for allowing me the use of photos from their personal collections.

To all the members of Immortal Marilyn and Forever Marilyn who answered my questions and undertook research for me. I am sorry I can not thank each and every one of you personally, but I hope you know how very grateful I am for all the help and support you gave me.

To my wonderful agent, Robert Smith, for sharing my vision and supporting this book from day one. Thanks so much, Robert.

To Pete Duncan, Nick Robinson and everyone at Constable & Robinson for making this book a reality.

To Helen Armitage, who went through this book with a fine-tooth comb and came up with some terrific questions and suggestions.

This book would be nothing without the memories shared by the vast amount of people who knew and met Marilyn over the years. To that end I am extremely grateful to the following for sharing their own memories and those of their family: Nancy Bolender Jeffrey, Bill Fredendall, Berniece Baker Miracle, Mona Rae Miracle, John Gilmore, Jeanne Chretien, Jim Dougherty, Nelson Cohen, Stanley Rubin, Kathleen Rubin, Richard Baer, Charles H. Page, Nanciele Finnegan, Dale Robertson, Gus Zernial, Mayor Johnny Grant, A. C. Lyles, Howard Sheehan, James Haspiel, Dick McKay, Bob Cornthwaite, Henry Swain, Joseph L. Jacob, Lisa Truax, Pat Brennan, Alan Young, Harry Carey Jr, Timothy Henderson, Win Rosette, Joe Franklin, Nancy Thome, Elliott Reid, Hal Schaefer, Joe Coudert, Kenny Kingston, Don Loraine, Bob Vannucci, Earle Hyman, Patricia Rosten, Edith Shaw Marcus, Peer J. Oppenheimer, Mark Weston, Karla Jones, Samantha Corner, Dolly Stiles, Beryl Belmont, Norman Wisdom, Sir John Gielgud, PC J. Packham, Colin Clark, Wolf Mankowitz, Colin Wilson, Vera Day, Frank Williams, Allan R. Pemberton, Donald W. J. Foot, Brenda Porter, Mr G. Pearson, Daphne Anderson, Jean Kent, Gerald Searle, Joyce Jackson, John Casson, Bryan Godfree, Margaret Gillon, Carl Schlesinger, Peggy McGuiggan, Vanessa Steinberg, Kae Turner, Bob Banas, Tobias M. Van Buren, Curtice Taylor, Angela Allen, Howard Sheehan Jnr, John Damiecki, Douglas Kirkland, Michael Selsman, Lynn Pupello, Eric Skipsky, Tony D'Antonio, Jim Gough, Allan Abbott, Ron Hast, Stephanie Baloghy and Maureen McArdle.

Marilyn had very few female friends during her lifetime, but I am blessed to have had the same group of friends for the past 26-plus years. Through good times and bad we have somehow managed to remain close and to that end I would like to thank Claire, Mandy, Helen, Loraine, Sharon and Katharine for their friendship throughout the years. Thanks also to Loraine for answering questions on Freud and 'false memory'!

Writing a book about Marilyn made me realize what a wonderful family I have, and I would like to thank Mum, Dad, Paul, Wendy and Angelina for all the support and happiness they give me, and particularly Mum and Dad for giving me the best start in life – the love and foundation that Marilyn never knew from her own parents. I feel truly privileged to be your daughter; thank you so much for everything.

To my best friend and sister, Wendy, who sends me long, gossipy emails and makes me laugh on a regular basis. I miss working opposite you every day, but know that one of these days we'll work on a writing project together!

Finally my biggest word of thanks must go to my dear husband, Richard, and our beautiful little girl, Daisy, who was born during the writing of this book. You both bring such light and laughter into my life – this book could never have been written without your help.

And to anyone I may have forgotten – I'm sorry for the oversight, but thank you too!!!

PREFACE

About 20 years ago, I first saw a photo of Marilyn in a gold-lamé dress, blowing a kiss to the camera, and I felt immediately drawn to her. I wanted to find out more about her. On a trip away with my family, I bought a book about her as a holiday read, and I became inspired by her hope, her individuality and her courage. Through reading about her life and watching her films, I began to admire her talent and felt that she was (and is) badly underestimated not only as an actress but as a person too. Unfortunately, so much has been said and written about her, as an icon, a legend and a sex symbol, that the real person has been lost in a maze of scandal, intrigue and drama.

I began *Marilyn Monroe: Private and Undisclosed* with the intention of writing about Marilyn Monroe as a human being, as opposed to a celluloid invention; to do this I interviewed almost 100 people who had known her or worked with her, were related to her or had met her during the course of her everyday life. Especially exciting is the large number of people who have come forward from her childhood and early years, details of which, until now, have remained mysterious and patchy.

This book celebrates Marilyn Monroe as a talented and worthwhile woman and explains why, 45 years after her death, she continues to attract the admiration and fascination of both new and established fans.

Michelle Morgan, 2007

PART ONE:

'SPRING'

1926—1952

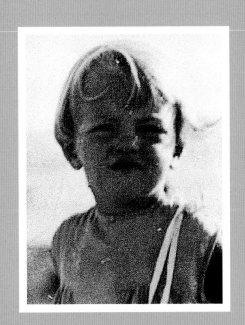

1

'I'M NOT YOUR MAMA'

When Gladys Pearl Monroe was seven, her father died in the California State Hospital for the mentally ill. Although it was later revealed that the cause of death was syphilis of the brain, the family believed Otis Monroe, the grandfather of the woman who would become Marilyn Monroe, had died insane, thereby sparking the fear of a legacy of madness that would come to haunt the Monroes.

Born in 1902, to Della and Otis Monroe, Gladys had one brother, Marion Otis. Their childhood was one spent on the move, although she settled, aged 14, when she married John Newton Baker, a man twelve years her senior. Baker was a tyrant, who ruled with his fist and with whom she had two children, Jackie (Robert Jasper) and Berniece. The marriage was not a success, and they were divorced in 1921, although, after the separation Baker continued to see the children, until, one day he vanished, taking them with him. Gladys felt devastated and spent time and all her savings trying to get the children back; tracking them down to Kentucky, she found work as a housekeeper for Harry and Lena Ramm Cohen (and looked after their three-year-old daughter, Norma Jean). But her efforts were in vain; by the time she returned to California she was alone.

Gladys found work at Consolidated Film Industries in Los Angeles, where she became friends with Grace McKee, a colleague, with whom she went out dancing, and where she earned herself something of a reputation among the male employees. By 1924, Gladys was married again, this time to Martin Edward Mortensen, who worked as a meter man for the Los Angeles Gas and Electric Company. Mortensen loved his wife, but his love was not reciprocated. Gladys soon strayed, falling for one of the bosses at Consolidated, Charles Stanley Gifford, 'a real likeable guy,' remembered one friend; another describing him as 'well-dressed and who always drove a pretty nice car'. Gifford himself was newly divorced and enjoying the single life too much to settle down, but Gladys was determined to become the next Mrs Gifford and, in May 1925, walked out on a bewildered Mortensen.

A stylish Gladys Pearl Baker, née Monroe - Norma Jean's mother

At a New Year's party at Gifford's family home, Gladys broke the news of her pregnancy to Gifford. It was an immediate source of tension within the family; Gifford's sister Ethel was particularly displeased and issued the ultimatum: 'Either marry the woman or do something.' According to relatives, Gladys was never to be seen at the Gifford home again. Some months later, on 1 June 1926, she gave birth to a daughter, whom she decided to call after little Norma Jean in Kentucky. For the sake of respectability, she gave her daughter the surname of her second husband, Martin Edward Mortensen, and so the woman whose life would become a legend started out as Norma Jeane Mortenson (Gladys had added an 'e' to Norma Jean and changed Mortensen to Mortenson on the birth certificate). Subsequently, Gladys changed her mind and she and her daughter would use the surname Baker (from her first marriage). Embittered by Gifford's reluctance to marry her, Gladys refused to let him have anything to do with his daughter, and Gifford's minister, Dr Liden, claimed that '[Gifford] felt the mother had been unfair ... She had cut him off and didn't allow him to see the child.'

Gladys and Norma Jeane lived first in an apartment at 5454 Wilshire Boulevard, but within days Gladys made the trip to East Rhode Island Avenue, where her mother, Della, lived. She knew about the Bolenders who lived opposite, Wayne, a postman, and his wife, Ida, who fostered children and had done so since just before the start of the Depression (and continued for the next 35 years). Gladys deposited Norma Jeane with the Bolender family at no. 459, a two-acre plot in Hawthorne, an agricultural area, with lots of space, dairies and farms. A quiet and friendly community, it was the ideal place to raise children, and they opened their home to any who needed their help.

Contrary to popular belief, Gladys did not abandon Norma Jeane at the Bolenders; instead she moved in with them and left her in their care while she commuted to and from her job at Consolidated (and subsequently at another major film company, RKO). However, the long journey to and from work and the responsibilities of single-motherhood soon became too burdensome, and Gladys took the difficult decision to resume her old life in Hollywood on her own. But she did not neglect Norma Jeane entirely, paying $25 a

Los Angeles General Hospital: birthplace of Norma Jeane Baker, June 1926

418 East Rhode Island Street, home of grandmother Della Monroe

month to the Bolenders and often staying with them at weekends and involving herself in family life. And, indeed, Gladys's own mother, Della, lived near by, although her presence was, ultimately, to prove less than supportive, as Marilyn recalled latterly, describing the occasion she awoke from a nap to find her grandmother trying to smother her with a pillow. As she had only just reached her first birthday, it is unlikely that Marilyn would have actually remembered the event, though her recollection is explainable as 'false memory' (not recalling a direct experience but rather an amalgam of other people's recollections of it). What happened can only be guessed at, but presumably Della was interrupted and, certainly, banned from visiting, although this didn't always stop her. As Ida Bolender recalled: 'She did come over one day for no reason I know of. She just broke in the glass of our front door, and I believe we called the police.' This sequence of events led to Della Monroe's admission to the Norwalk Mental Hospital, diagnosed with manic-depressive psychosis. She was there until her death in 1927, thus adding to the fearful legacy of mental illness that dogged the Monroe family.

The Bolenders tried their best to ensure some sort of normal life, not just for Norma Jeane but also for their other foster child, Lester (so like each other, they were called the Twins). When the family decided officially to adopt Lester, they hoped to do the same with Norma Jeane, but Gladys was against the idea (having already lost her two older children). Instead, she continued to visit Norma Jeane at the weekends, a source of confusion for Norma Jeane, who, when she once referred to Ida Bolender as 'Mama', was immediately told otherwise. 'But [Wayne] is my daddy,' exclaimed Norma Jeane, to which Ida replied that he was not, after which Marilyn later recalled that she became afraid to call anyone mummy or daddy, as not even Gladys referred to her as a daughter.

Gladys told Norma Jeane that her father had died in a car crash, either before she was born or when she was a baby – the story changing with Gladys's mood. The story contained some kernel of truth, as in 1929 Edward Mortensen had been killed in a car crash (though, confusingly, and unbeknown to Gladys, it later transpired he had not and was alive and well and living in California). Since she had named Mortensen as Norma Jeane's father on the birth certificate, she was undoubtedly referring to Mortensen when she spoke of Norma Jeane's father having died. Mortensen

As a toddler (left) on the beach with mother, Gladys (behind)

himself would later claim that he was Norma Jeane's real
father, although it is unlikely – and certainly was not
Gladys's belief. And, Norma Jeane had her own vision of
her father. As a young child, she would occasionally visit
her mother's home in Hollywood, where a photo of C.
Stanley Gifford hung on the wall. He bore a striking
resemblance to Clark Gable, and from that moment on,
Norma Jeane always considered Gable something of a

Giving a friend a ride, c. 1928

surrogate father. But the photo was one of the few things that Norma Jeane enjoyed
about her visits to her mother, where she spent most of her time hiding in the closet
or being chastised for turning the pages of a book 'too loudly'.

· · · · ·

Norma Jeane's time with the Bolenders has been enhanced over the years with
stories concocted latterly by the film studios and the media to present her subsequent life as Marilyn as something of a Cinderella story. Such economy with the
truth may have provided a great deal of public sympathy for Marilyn the star, but
according to her foster sister Nancy Bolender, it gave her parents nothing but
heartache: 'Mother and Daddy always felt bad about the things written about
Marilyn Monroe's young life that said she was brought up in poor homes and not
loved or taken care of.'

In later years, Ida Bolender, very upset at how Norma Jeane's life was
continually misrepresented, told reporters: 'We treated her like our own child
because we loved her.'

Unfortunately, this affection didn't protect them from the rumours that have
circulated ever since; yet while Norma Jeane's early years weren't exactly the best,
life with the Bolender family was not one of hardship and destitution but 'safe,
secure and comfortable', remembered Nancy, 'with plenty of playmates. [Our
parents] truly loved us and protected us and nurtured us with all of their hearts.'

The family did have strict values and religious beliefs, and, certainly, 'Idle
hands are from the devil' was something Lester Bolender frequently told his foster
siblings. However, while Ida was very schedule-oriented and hardly ever known to
laugh, there is some explanation of this in her deafness, a result of a childhood bout
of scarlet fever that had left her with hearing loss in one ear. Subsequently she
required hearing aids in both ears and learned to lip-read in order to communicate.

Life had been hard for Ida and looking after a team of children in the 1920s
was not easy, although her mother did live next door and often helped out. The children always had clothes, made for them by Ida, and most of the food was grown

on their land; an abundant supply of apples, tomatoes, corn, watermelon and string beans. Trips to town to buy flour, butter, sugar and coffee were family occasions. They would pile into Wayne Bolender's Model T and travel to the store, where Ida would do her shopping while the children stayed in the car with Wayne, playing guessing games, singing songs and telling stories.

On some occasions Norma Jeane even enjoyed pretending to drive the car while sat on her foster-father's lap. Wayne loved her as one of his own, considering her his baby. She spent a lot of time with him, sitting on a stool while he shaved and asking him questions such as: 'Who is God?', 'Where does he live?' and, 'How many people live in the world?'

For Norma Jeane, there were happy times with the Bolenders. Days were spent at nearby Redondo beach or climbing the apple tree outside her bedroom window, with Lester in tow. The two would drag blankets up into the branches to make a fort, looking down on the chickens, rabbits and a goat (bought because some children were allergic to cow's milk) running free in the yard below. Norma Jeane had a small dog, Tippy, of whom she was inordinately proud, and with whom she spent hours playing; afternoons were sometimes spent playing hopscotch on the pavement with Nancy. Going to the cinema was frowned upon (although Marilyn later remembered that she snuck into a movie theatre once or twice), although there was a radio and Norma Jeane had her favourite shows, *The Green Hornet* and *The Lone Ranger*. There was always music in the house, too, as Ida loved listening to symphonies on the radio, and the family would often sing together when they got home from church. Norma Jeane even learnt to play the house piano, a passion she never lost throughout her life.

The Bolenders' religious beliefs also featured in Norma Jeane's upbringing, and, according to Nancy Bolender, she was taught about God; that he was trustworthy and bigger than any situation she might face. This aspect of her life with the Bolenders has been exaggerated, with stories of the family being so consumed by religion that they had no time for the children, with Norma Jeane forever criticized for what they considered to be sinful acts. However, this is certainly not how Nancy remembers it: 'I never heard [my parents] criticize or talk badly about anyone. They accepted people for who they were and loved them unconditionally.'

Norma Jeane remained with the Bolenders for a number of years, and was there when she started school on 14 September 1931. Nancy remembered watching 'the Twins' skipping to the Washington Street School that day, followed by Tippy the dog. They were to stay there until the Los Angeles earthquake of 10 March 1933, after which they were relocated to the 5th Street School (now the Ramona School), where music teacher Evelyn Gawthrop recalled Norma Jeane as a timid child who loved to sing and got on well with the other children. Her singing skills were put to good use when she was chosen for the children's chorus in the Easter sunrise services at the Hollywood Bowl, an event at which the chorus, dressed in black capes, stood in the shape of a cross. As the sun rose over the bowl, as instructed, the children removed their capes to reveal their white clothes beneath. Marilyn later lamented that she became so engrossed in checking out everything else going on around her that she

Children's cross at the Easter Sunrise Service, Hollywood Bowl

forgot to take off her cape. However, the mistake must have soon been rectified, since none of the photos of the childrens' cross taken around that time shows any 'black dots' that might be her.

Norma Jeane's settled existence with the Bolenders came to an abrupt halt in 1933. Just prior to her departure, there was great upset when Tippy the dog died, killed, it is said, by a neighbour after a particularly noisy barking session. Tippy was never forgotten; later Marilyn named another dog, the one in her last, unfinished film, after him. Norma Jeane left the Bolenders' care because Gladys no longer wanted to live apart from her daughter. She was going to buy a house for them both. The Bolenders were shocked by the news but could do nothing about it. When the day of Norma Jeane's departure dawned, she and the other children in the Bolender household hid in a closet in the hope of not being found. Norma Jeane's going was felt as a loss. The Bolender family never forgot the little girl who had been part of their lives for so long and had touched their hearts: 'It was a sad time for mother and daddy,' says Nancy Bolender, 'because they truly loved her. They had raised her from infancy to eight-plus years of age. That's a long time and when so much of yourself is put into training, nurturing and loving a child it is like losing your own flesh and blood.'

But for Norma Jeane, it was a chance to live with her own flesh and blood, though how successfully would have to be seen.

2

'NORMA JEANE, STRING BEAN'

Norma Jeane (on the right) with Gladys (behind her), during a rare visit, late 1920s

Gladys had reclaimed her daughter, but she now had to find a place for them both to live. For the moment she lodged Norma Jeane with an English couple, the Atkinsons, and their daughter, Nellie, in Afton Place. George and Maud Atkinson were bit players in the movies – George often worked as a stand-in for the British stage-turned-screen actor George Arliss. Living with the Atkinsons was completely different to the upbringing Norma Jeane had experienced with the Bolenders. According to Marilyn, the English couple were 'happy, jolly, and care-free'. They introduced her to card games and taught her to dance, buying her a little hula skirt so she could practise her steps. However, the Atkinsons' happy-go-lucky existence confused her: 'They liked to drink a little, smoke, dance and sing and play cards – all of the things that I had been taught were sinful. And still they seemed like very nice people to me.' She spent hours praying for them and feeling guilty whenever she enjoyed their company and their stories of their acting life.

During the months that she lived with the Atkinsons, Norma Jeane would often visit Grauman's Chinese Theatre and try to fit her hands in the prints. She would spend hours at the movies, watching the actors and actresses on the screen, and then imitating them back home in her bedroom. She fell in love with the cinema and dreamt of being a famous actress like her new screen idol, Jean Harlow, a wisecracking platinum blonde.

Gladys announced one day that she was going to build a home for them both. With the dream that she and all her children would eventually live together under one roof, she took out a mortgage on a small house on Arbol Drive, near the

Hollywood Bowl. Grace McKee begged her not to take on such an onerous responsibility, but all requests for caution went unheard. As Gladys couldn't afford the house on her own, it was agreed that the Atkinsons would move in too and continue to care for Norma Jeane.

In September 1933, Gladys and Norma Jeane moved into their first home together. Marilyn later described Arbol Drive as 'a pretty little house with quite a few rooms. But there was no furniture in it, except for two cots that we slept on, a small kitchen table, and two kitchen chairs.' However, for Norma Jeane, having her mother to herself for the first time in her life more than made up for the lack of material items. Gladys did her best to provide a stable upbringing, with trips to movies and at one point even enjoying an outing to nearby Catalina Island, where Norma Jeane stayed past her bedtime and watched her mother dancing at the Catalina Casino. It was at this time that Gladys first talked to her daughter about Christian Science and tried to involve her via occasional 'healings'. Gladys had been interested in Christian Science since the mid-1920s, and her curiosity had grown over the years. Unfortunately, the fascination was later to develop into an obsession, to the point at which it was the only thing that glued her life together.

Materially, things began to look up; Gladys bought a white piano, a Franklin Baby Grand, said to have belonged to Oscar-nominated film actor Fredric March. It became the focal point of the house; one day, Gladys told Norma Jeane, she would warm herself by the fire and listen to her daughter framed against the window, playing the baby grand. Unfortunately, events that followed ensured that this was never to be. Unbeknown to Gladys, shortly before she had removed Norma Jeane from the

Bolenders' care, Gladys's grandfather, Tilford M. Hogan, had committed suicide. A local newspaper described how, on the afternoon of 29 May 1933, while his wife was out shopping, he'd hung himself in the barn. If that weren't bad enough, a couple of months later, on 16 August 1933, Gladys's son, Robert 'Jackie' Baker died of tuberculosis of the kidneys. He was only 15; his death the end of a life plagued by misfortune. News of the deaths struck Gladys like a thunderbolt and in her grief she hit out at her young daughter: 'Why couldn't it have been you?' she screamed at her over and over again. Already emotionally fragile, Gladys spiralled down into a

The white piano from her childhood that she kept all her life

depression plagued by anxiety. While the house move had been intended as a new start for her and Norma Jeane, Gladys found herself increasingly unable to cope with the responsibility of working and caring for her daughter.

Throughout 1934, Gladys's worsening mental health was continually evaluated at Los Angeles General Hospital. Grace McKee tried to care for both Gladys and Norma Jeane, but it was a losing battle. Norma Jeane was often left to her own devices, playing outside the house, setting up a stall pretending to sell old whiskey bottles and cigarette packets to passers-by. She began to feel increasingly unwanted: 'I was a mistake. My mother didn't want to have me. I guess she never wanted me. I probably got in her way. I wish – I still wish – she had wanted me.'

But Gladys was not able to show love to anyone, not even to herself, and eventually her emotional problems reached a climax, when, in early 1935, she tipped over the edge into a complete breakdown. Norma Jeane was eating breakfast, when she heard her mother yelling as the Atkinsons tried desperately to calm her down. When she came back from school that day, her mother had gone, and she was told: 'Your mother is very sick – you won't be able to see her for a long, long, time.' On 15 January 1935, Gladys was declared insane and committed to the state institution at Norwalk.

· · · · · ·

Grace McKee took over the responsibility of caring for Norma Jeane and looking after Gladys's affairs. On 25 March 1935 she filed a petition to be guardian of the estate, and thereafter began the long task of logging and assessing Gladys's possessions and debts. It was decided it would be best for Norma Jeane to stay on in the Arbol Drive house with the Atkinsons; she liked them, and it seemed pointless to uproot her again. But her mother's illness affected her deeply and in some unexpected ways. One day when she was running round the block just for the fun of it, some boys stopped to ask what she was doing. Before she could answer another child snapped: 'Don't bother her. She's just like her mother – crazy.' It was comments like those that led Norma Jeane to deny her mother's existence, often declaring that she was dead – something she continued to do throughout her life.

In the many biographies of Marilyn's life, one tale often crops up from around this time concerning her molestation aged nine or ten. As Marilyn told it, a Mr Kimmell (Marilyn may have changed the name Kinnell to Kimmell, for legal reasons) lived in a house where she was staying. One day he called her into his room, locked the door and indecently assaulted her. The consensus is that she was sexually assaulted though not actually raped. When the ordeal was over she ran to her foster mother who responded by slapped her face for telling lies. Some biographers dismiss this as a Marilyn fabrication, while others, such as Donald Wolfe, insist that the incident happened when she lived on Arbol Drive; that it was her mother who did the slapping. Wolfe also names Murray Kinnell, a character actor who gave Bette Davis her big break in Hollywood, as Norma Jeane's molester. Ironically,

Kinnell had also worked with Norma Jeane's idol, Jean Harlow in various films, including *The Public Enemy* (1931), *The Secret Six* (1931) and *The Beast of the City* (1932).

Marilyn never suggested that she was molested while in Gladys's care, which could just be an attempt to cover up for her mother or it could be true. We do know that the attack took place while she was living somewhere that took in boarders, and if so, it is possible that she was molested at the Arbol Drive house after Gladys was admitted to Norwalk. George Arliss, for whom George Atkinson worked as a stand-in, was a friend of Kinnell. They had worked together in a number of movies, including *Cardinal Richelieu* (1935), filmed in March 1935, when Norma Jeane was still with the Atkinsons. As George Atkinson was Arliss's stand-in on *Richelieu*, he almost certainly knew Murray Kinnell, though to what degree is unclear. Whether or not Kinnell ever stayed with the Atkinsons is not clear either. In any case, from then on Norma Jeane began to stutter when faced with difficult, public situations, such as reading aloud in class. Marilyn later recalled a 'terrible' moment when she had to read the minutes of a class meeting, only to find herself constantly tripping over the words.

There has been much debate about why Norma Jeane left the Atkinsons' care at this point. Was it because the couple mistreated her (unlikely given Marilyn's later memories of the family)or, as some claim, because the family were about to move back to England. In any case on 27 May 1935 Grace McKee put Arbol Drive and its contents up for sale to pay off Gladys's debts. A 1933 Plymouth Sedan (for which Gladys was still paying) was listed on the sales inventory, along with the Franklin Baby Grand and a small radio. Grace kept detailed records of her expenditure, and court records show that, on 22 May 1935, five days before the house went on sale, a payment of $25 was made to Mrs Atkinson for care of Norma Jeane. There were no further payments, and the house was sold on 12 June. Years later, driving through the area with her sister-in-law Elyda Nelson, Norma Jeane pointed out

As a teenager (right) with two friends, late 1930s

the home she had shared with her mother. 'I lived there once,' she said, 'before mother was ill. It was beautiful. The most wonderful furniture you can imagine; a baby grand piano and a room of my own. It all seems like a dream.'

* * * * *

After Arbol Drive, Norma Jeane was placed in the care of Elsie and Harvey Giffen at 2062 Highland Avenue. Grace kept a close eye on her, as she did on Gladys. With Gladys's sister-in-law Olive Monroe, she visited the state institution at Norwalk and spoke to her friend's doctor. In a letter dated 15 August 1935, Grace wrote to a friend, Mrs van Hyming: 'He [the doctor] explained to me that Gladys's type of insanity is the hardest case to do anything with. Her brain did not develop like an ordinary person's [sic]. They examined her brain with a floroscope [sic], and it proved to be about one third the size of a normal human being's.'

The doctor added that Gladys might have gone on living a normal life if she'd been worry free and had someone able to take care of her; as things were, however, her condition was incurable. Although it was possible that she might be able to leave the institution eventually, any upset would return her, 'worse than ever'. Gladys knew nothing of this, and believed that one day she would be able to return to her job at RKO. She'd been popular with her fellow workers, loved and respected, and, as Grace later recalled, 'honest, hard-working, thrifty, dependable and kindly to everyone'. Her bosses at the studio did not see it that way; they would never allow her to return under any circumstances.

With Gladys now permanently residing in the state institution, somewhere had to be found for Norma Jeane to live. The Bolenders wanted her back, but Grace could not allow this, although they did, on occasions, take Norma Jeane to see her mother at Norwalk, as Nancy Bolender Jefferies remembers:

> *'Many Sunday afternoons were spent picking her up at one of the homes she was at and taking her over to visit her mother at the Norwalk Mental Institute. We would sit on the lawn and eat and visit and watch Norma Jeane and her mother play together. The Bolenders wanted to make sure that their relationship as mother and daughter was not interrupted any more than could be helped. She was always glad to see us and to go with us to see her mother.'*

While Grace was happy for Norma Jeane to live with her and her new husband Erwin 'Doc' Goddard; (who had been married previously and had three children; two daughters and a son) in their home on Barbara Court, it was a legal requirement for her to be placed in a children's home until Grace's guardianship was fully approved. As a result, on 13 September 1935, Grace took the reluctant step of placing Norma Jeane in an orphanage, until she was in a position to look after her again.

Los Angeles Orphans Home, where Norma Jeane was taken in 1935

The Los Angeles Orphans Home was a red-brick building in the heart of Hollywood, close to Grauman's Chinese Theatre and the Hollywood Roosevelt Hotel. As Norma Jeane was led up the front steps, she started screaming: 'I'm not an orphan.' The label, orphan, was something she had been railing against for a while. Arriving at Selma Avenue School to enrol, shortly after first going to live with the Atkinsons, Marilyn recalled, in an interview with reporter Liza Wilson in 1952, how all the other children were there with their parents. When one well-meaning teacher asked if her parents were dead, confused, she had replied, 'Yes, ma'am, I think so,' at which one of the other students pointed at her, exclaiming, 'Look, Mummy. That girl's an orphan.' Marilyn said she 'leaned against a wall and bawled'.

There was no one to save her this time either. Despite her desperate plea to Grace to take her home, she found herself in Girl's Cottage, in the south wing of the building, a space she shared with twelve other girls. 'It seemed very big,' Marilyn told woman's magazine *Redbook* reporter Jim Henaghan in 1952, 'but maybe it wasn't. Maybe I just remember it as big.' Of the two dormitories – one large, one small – the smaller one was seen as more desirable: 'I don't know why,' Marilyn recalled, 'because, after all, it was still the orphanage.' Her bed stood beside the window with a view of RKO, a source of heartache for the little girl who knew her mother had once worked there. It was a heartache that never left her, evidenced in the unpleasant stories she told about the orphanage throughout her life.

Grace McKee, now Goddard, visited almost every week, taking her presents and clothes, on trips to the hairdresser or the occasional movie. She continued to be responsible for Norma Jeane and took an active interest in her welfare; when she discovered how upset she was after a visit from Mrs Bolender, Grace contacted the superintendent of the home, Sula Dewey. In a letter dated 5 December 1935, she asks that nobody should be allowed to 'see or talk to little Norma Jeane Baker, unless you have my written permission to do so'. She especially did not want her to be visited by Ida Bolender, as 'her visits seem to upset the child'. Concerned that she should be consulted about any future visitors, Grace included a list of people who were allowed to see Norma Jeane: Elsie and Harvey Giffin; Maude, George and Nell Atkinson; Norma Jeane's aunt, Olive Monroe; and Olive's mother, Mrs Martin. On 6 December 1935, Mrs Dewey wrote a reply to Grace, on Los Angeles Orphans Home Society letterhead:

> Dear Mrs Goddard
> When Mrs Bolender was here I told her she should not talk to Norma about her mother.
>
> The physicians have said Mrs Baker would not get well – that means the child must have first consideration.
>
> Will you please give a letter to each person you want Norma to see and go out with. This would be an extra check. If I just tell the ones who are on duty the names of the ones to see Norma there might be a slip.

Norma is not the same since Mrs B. visited with her. She doesn't look as happy. When she is naughty she says, 'Mrs Dewey, I wouldn't ever want my Aunt Grace to know I was naughty.' She loves you very much.

I'll do as you request. We want to do all we can to make Norma happy, and to please you.

Sincerely yours

(Mrs) S. S. Dewey

Although Marilyn would later tell nightmarish tales of her treatment in the orphanage – often on a par with the story of *Little Orphan Annie* – the care of the children in the Institution actually seemed to be very good. Each child received five cents pocket money every Saturday and candy. There was a garden for playing, trips to the home's beach house in the summer and Christmas parties. Indeed, in December 1935, three months after Norma Jeane's arrival, the Los Angeles chapter of the National Association of Cost Accountants took the children to the Army and Navy Club, at 1106 South Broadway, for a mammoth Christmas party. On a typical Christmas Eve the children, some chosen to sing carols, would attend the Vine Street Methodist-Episcopal church; on Christmas Day there were more carols in the auditorium above the dining room, before gifts of clothes – sweaters, underwear, shirts and trousers or skirts. The orphanage was decorated with Christmas trees, each one containing toys and gifts for the children.

Bill Fredendall arrived at the orphanage in March 1934, 18 months before Norma Jeane. He has many memories of the place and of Christmas time in particular:

'At Christmas we had several special trips out to large parties. One year I remember I attended a party where Joe E. Brown was the master of ceremony. You will remember him as Jack Lemmon's boyfriend in Some Like It Hot. *We would receive gifts at these occasions and one Christmas my brother and I were taken out and given complete outfits; suits, shirts, ties, shoes. We wore these clothes when we left the Home for good in 1940 …*

The Fire Department favoured the home at Christmas. They would arrive with the sirens going with a truckload of gifts. That was exciting! That happened each year. Christmas was a big deal at the Home and is another example of how they made it a swell place to be – remember this was in the depths of the Depression and in that regard we were quite fortunate.'

Halloween party, Los Angeles
Orphans Home, during Norma
Jeane's time there

The girls at the orphanage all had a younger boy whom

they 'mothered', and this practice went on until the home finally closed its doors in 2005. Norma Jeane was asked to look after Bill, as he was younger than her, and the staff most likely thought it would do her good to care for someone other than herself. 'My time with Norma Jeane would have been after meals in the yard,' remembers Bill. 'On the swings with other kids of similar ages; I remember very clearly the swings, slide and holding hands, and she would give me a peck goodnight when it was time to go in.'

Although Norma Jeane craved the outside world, there was plenty to do in the home to keep her busy. The day started with breakfast, after which there was teeth-cleaning and tongue-brushing, the latter all part of the orphanage nurse's regular tongue inspection for the slightest hint of a 'coating', which resulted in an unwelcome dose of castor oil. Then it was time for Vine Street School, wearing uniform gingham dresses. The school was close to orange groves, protected from frost by burning pots of oil. This meant smoky skies on cold winter's days, clearly visible from the school yard. Marilyn later recalled that her school attendance was probably the hardest thing she had ever done in her life. This was not helped by the other pupils, who every so often would whisper and point at them: 'They're from the home.' She became friendly with three boys in her class; when they found out their new friend was from the orphanage the relationship floundered, sending Norma Jeane further into her shell. 'I was always shy and scared,' she later recalled. Luckier in that respect, Bill remembers only one occasion when he was taunted by someone about being from the home. He even recalls the time the orphanage kids were treated to a ride to school in a fire truck, sirens blaring, making them the envy of the other children.

Outside the orphanage around the time Norma Jeane lived there

After school it was back to the home and play until dinner, followed by time to listen to the radio or read a book from an extensive library. One of the matrons was a relative of actor Oliver Hardy (famous as the larger half of the comedy duo Laurel and Hardy), who was very generous with donations of books, along with furniture and toys too. At the weekend there was Sunday School at the Vine Street Methodist Church, where each child was given a penny to put into the collection. Some of the children got wise to this, however, and started hiding their pennies in their clothes – particularly the boys' neckties – so that they would not be found when required.

But the weekends weren't just about going to church. There were trips to the park and such places as the Ringling Brothers Circus, Tom Mix Circus, Griffith Park

Observatory and Le Brae Avenue Tar Pits. Bill Fredendall also recalls a birthday party for child star Shirley Temple, held at a film studio, along with movies at the nearby RKO studio, held at least once a month. These outings would often result in autographs and presents for the children, along with the odd penny or two from actors on the RKO lot; there were also several movies made at the home, some of which included the children as background players.

When the children were old enough, they were given the opportunity of working in the laundry or the kitchen to earn money, and it is here that much of the controversy about Marilyn's memories of the home and her role within it occurs. She would later complain to interviewers that she often had to wash and dry hundreds of dishes, but Bill Fredendall remembers it a little differently:

> 'Dishes and chores: Marilyn was talking about the job of kitchen help. We were paid, and this was obviously the type of chore that needed doing daily. We had lots of help and we made lunches too. We all took our lunch to Vine Street school, so it would be a mass production to prepare 75 or 80 lunches. I recall the fun of spreading butter, and peanut butter on a huge layout of sliced bread, and then slapping on a leaf of lettuce and putting it into a bag together with apples and oranges. There was another chore we enjoyed and that was polishing the floors. We had an abundance of rags [underwear etc] and we would wrap our feet and race and slide along the dorm rooms on the second floor, which were large – about 15 beds per side, with the open space in the middle.'

So what about Marilyn's tales of hundreds of dishes and chores? Bill says:

> 'I am sure her comments about the dishes were coloured by her biographers. Part of the poor, unhappy child routine. I would guess there were fewer than twenty staff, including matrons, cooks, hospital and laundry staff, but we were loved, protected, trained and cared for.'

Sula Dewey, superintendent,
Los Angeles Orphans Home

One of the people responsible for caring not just for Norma Jeane but for the other children too was Sula Dewey, a kind woman who tried to give each individual child the love and attention they craved. When Bill Fredendall burnt his hand with a firecracker, during a trip to the beach house, Mrs Dewey came personally to take him to the emergency room. Another time his clothes were wet through after an unfortunate accident at a lake, and it was she who brought him dry clothes. When he was old enough to become interested in music, she made sure that he had the drumsticks he needed to practise.

Unhappy orphanage tales abound, but how many are true? One of the more outlandish was the large cake produced on birthdays, around which everyone sang 'Happy Birthday'. It was no ordinary sponge; apparently made of wood with only a tiny slice of real cake secreted inside for the birthday girl or boy. Afterwards it went back in the cupboard till the next birthday. However, like many of the orphanage stories, this is probably not true; certainly not something that Bill Fredendall remembers: 'A wooden cake? I doubt it. I never saw it. It sure sounds like one of those 'tales'. I don't remember any birthday celebrations. But almost for sure Mrs Dewey would take the opportunity to give one a few pieces of candy, at least … She dispensed justice, but she was so kind.'

When he lied about a firecracker accident, he was punished by being grounded in Hollywood for two weeks, while the others visited the Manhattan beach house.

Out of all Marilyn's later orphanage memories, perhaps the only happy ones concerned the time Mrs Dewey allowed her to apply a little make-up to her cheeks and, on another occasion, being allowed to pat Mrs Dewey's little dog. Mostly, though, she just kept herself out of trouble and tried to settle in as best she could; her grades were good, she was quiet and well-behaved and participated in all the activities. But there were times she found herself getting into scrapes, just like any other ten year old. Years later, Marilyn admitted that she had once tried – and failed – to run away by climbing over a hedge, egged on by some of the 'tough' children.

But when she did leave eventually, it was because it was thought she would benefit more from a stable home environment than life in an institution. Since Grace Goddard was now in a position to look after her, by late 1936, Norma Jeane moved in with the Goddards at 3107 Barbara Court then, shortly afterwards, at 6707 Odessa Avenue in Van Nuys. So how long had she actually lived at the orphanage? Most sources agree that she was there for two years or so, from 1935 to 1937. However, court records show that the last payment Grace made to the orphanage was on 21 June 1936; she had certainly removed Norma Jeane from the orphanage by October 1936, by which date she had begun to charge for her care.

Norma Jeane when she lived with Grace Goddard in Barbara Court, Los Angeles

After the orphanage, Norma Jeane no doubt revelled in family life and the chance to settle down into some kind of normality, and Grace loved having her around. Grace bred cocker spaniels, and Norma Jeane liked spending time with them. Grace was also a huge fan of Jean Harlow and began to mould her young charge into her screen idol, taking her to Columbia Studios, where she worked in the film library, and showing her off to her fellow workers. One of them, Leila Fields, later told Marilyn biographer Maurice Zolotow that Grace adored Norma Jeane and took her everywhere with her, convinced she would one day be a movie star. Fields gave Grace all the credit for Norma Jeane's subsequent success, observing: 'Grace had an obsession about her.'

Just when it all seemed to be going well, Grace approached Norma Jeane's aunt Olive Monroe and asked her to consider taking her niece to live with them. Why she did so is not clear. Some sources claim that Grace found Doc making a fumbled pass at her one night when drunk. But, almost 60 years later, his daughter Eleanor 'Bebe' Goddard, disputed this. As she told the All About Marilyn fan club: 'The fact is that my father never touched Marilyn. He was a real lady's man, in that he loved women and they loved him, but that was only a big show, and I never encountered a more faithful man than my father was to his wives.' This is supported by the fact that Norma Jeane returned to the family some time later; she kept in touch with Doc and Grace for years.

The more likely explanation for Norma Jeane's departure is that Grace and Doc just couldn't afford to look after her anymore. Money was extremely tight, and on more than one occasion Grace stood in line with Norma Jeane queuing for stale bread. 'Daddy was not a very dependable type of character when it came to bread-winning,' said Bebe.

· · · · ·

In 1937, Olive Monroe was living with her mother, Ida Martin, and her three children, John 'Jack', Ida Mae and Olive Elizabeth. Her husband, Marion Otis Monroe, Gladys's brother, had disappeared in 1929, shortly after the birth of his youngest child and had never been seen since, despite the family's best efforts to find him. He left his wife and children struggling financially, and so perhaps when Grace Goddard approached Olive about Norma Jeane the idea of the $30 per month that she would be paid for caring for her niece was welcome.

Norma Jeane arrived to live with the Martin–Monroe family at 12000 Block Oxnard Avenue, Lankershim, in December 1937. From the start it was tricky, with three generations of women and a boisterous twelve-year-old boy all under one roof. When Marilyn described a foster home presided over by a 100-plus-year-old great-grandmother, she may have exaggerated the age, but she was probably referring to Ida Martin. Her memories of this time were entirely negative; of bath times where she was last in line and had to bathe in putrid, black water and of a dress that she was falsely accused of tearing. The truth about it is hard to establish with all the nonsense printed over the years, and the raft of stories and rumours have hurt the family to such a degree that Jack Monroe refuses all requests for interviews.

Whatever the reality, life with the Martin–Monroe family wasn't all hardship. Norma Jeane became friends with Ida Mae, who recalled how the two of them would get into all kinds of mischief, including a plan to run away to San Francisco, where Marion Monroe had been spotted. She also mentioned the sexual assault she had experienced before moving to the orphanage, clearly comfortable enough around her cousin to confide in her and describe how, after it, she had bathed for days afterwards.

With the move came a new school, the Lankershim School on Bakman Avenue. It was here that Norma Jeane began to create an imaginary world for herself: 'I remember a vacant lot that I used to cross on my way home from Bakman Avenue school in North Hollywood. It was just a dirty old lot overgrown with weeds, but from the moment I stepped on to it, it became a magic and private place where I could be all of the people I had been thinking about all day in the classroom.'

On 3 March 1938, a great flood hit Los Angeles. Newspaper reports estimated damage at $25 million; homes were without power and thousands fled for their lives. The Martin–Monroe family were no exception. Court records show Ida Martin was paid expenses for Norma Jeane until August 1938; however, Eleanor 'Bebe' Goddard, in an interview with the All About Marilyn fan club, claimed that Norma Jeane moved out of the Martin home after the flood. She went to live temporarily with Grace's brother, Bryan Atchinson, his wife, Lottie, and their daughter, Geraldine, at 1826 East Palmer Avenue. It is likely that the Martin–Monroe family continued to receive the care payments to help them financially after the disaster. The move meant a change of schools, a brief return to Vine Street, before, in September 1938, Norma Jeane went to live with Ana Lower, arguably one of the people whose influence would be most powerful on her life.

Edith Ana Lower (known to everyone as Ana) was Grace's paternal aunt and 58 years old when Norma Jeane went to live with her. She had been married to Edmund H. 'Will' Lower, but by 1938 they were divorced. She supplemented the income she made from property bought during her marriage by working as a Christian Science practitioner. Ana's home was a two-storey duplex at 11348 Nebraska Avenue, where she occupied the upstairs apartment and rented out the unit below and the house next door. Every morning she could be seen on the sidewalk, sweeping up the fruit that had fallen from the abundance of fig trees outside her property.

Nebraska Avenue, where Norma Jeane lived with her beloved 'Aunt' Ana Lower

However, from the moment Norma Jeane walked through the door of Ana Lower's apartment, her world shifted; in Ana she was to discover 'a wonderful human being' who changed her life and gave her more confidence. Aunt Ana, as she called her, provided Norma Jeane with kindness and love; something she had rarely experienced, and she revelled in her devotion to her new aunt. Ana believed whole-heartedly in Christian Science and passed on what she could to Norma Jeane, taking her with her to Christian Science services. As her mother had practised the religion too, it wasn't totally unfamiliar, though Marilyn was later to say: 'I've read Mrs Eddy [founder of Christian Science and author of *Science and Health, with key to the scriptures*] and tried to put some of her ideas into my life, but it doesn't work for me.'

Norma Jeane's arrival at Ana Lower's coincided with her puberty. Her periods were so painful that she would often lie on the floor, sobbing, in agony. Aunt Ana did her best to help. With painkillers not an option because, as a strict Christian Scientist,

Crouched beside the woman said to be foster mother Ana Lower

Ana did not rely on conventional medicine, Ana turned to her religion to bring relief. 'Aunt Ana used to pray with me, but it seems I had such a strong belief in pain that she couldn't overcome it,' Marilyn was to recall. It was the start of a lifetime of the painful periods and endometriosis that ruled Marilyn until the day she died.

Life was otherwise fairly settled and calm; Norma Jeane worshipped Ana, from whom she got the love and protection she had so often sought. But school was a problem, especially because she stuttered quite badly; her limited wardrobe was also something the other children loved to make fun of. Attending the seventh grade at Sawtelle School, Norma Jeane made few friends and felt alienated: 'In school I was very quiet. I was never the life of the party. Everyone talked so glibly; they all knew the latest slang and the smartest stories, and I'd stand around like an idiot – never knowing what to say.' Furthermore, she was tall and skinny – somewhat cruelly nicknamed 'Norma Jeane, String Bean' – and extremely hurt when one boy in her class told her, 'I hope some day your legs fill out.' Dismissed as dumb and with no personality, at least she had a sympathetic ear, something she had rarely experienced in the past.

In early 1939, not long after she'd gone to live with Ana, Norma Jeane was shocked to hear from Grace that she had a half-sister, Berniece. Grace, of course, had known about Berniece and her brother, Jackie, now dead, for many years, but hadn't felt it was her place to tell Norma Jeane. But Grace had received a letter from Berniece to inform her that Gladys had been in touch from Agnew State Hospital, to where she had moved, and had told her all about her half-sister Norma Jeane (and begged her eldest daughter to get her out of the hospital). This prompted

Berniece (who had had no idea she had a half-sister and believed her mother had died) to contact Grace, who passed her letter on to Norma Jeane.

Emerson Junior High School, which Norma Jeane attended as a teenager

As a child who craved the stability of a family of her own, Norma Jeane was thrilled to discover she had a sister. Berniece was married, to Paris Miracle, and lived in Pineville, Kentucky, now pregnant with her first child. Grace wrote to Berniece, passing on news of her half-sister and of Gladys's dream one day to have had all her children with her. Norma Jeane then wrote too, enclosing a photograph. It was the start of an important new relationship that was to last a lifetime. With Berniece in the picture, Grace wondered whether Norma Jeane might move in with her sister. But Gladys had always vetoed any idea that Norma Jeane might leave California, and in any case Berniece had neither the money nor room to take her in.

A year after she'd arrived at Ana's, Norma Jeane moved to Emerson Junior High. Although she flunked arithmetic, and even admitted to hating the subject, she did well in English and literature, and once wrote a paper on Abraham Lincoln that was judged best in the class. This small achievement was a boost for her confidence; suddenly she didn't feel so 'dumb' anymore. Added to that, her once skinny body had begun to fill out, which began to attract attention: 'The boys didn't have cars; they had bikes. They'd come by the house and whistle or they'd honk their little horns. Some had paper routes and I'd always get a free paper.'

Some attention was unwanted, however, from an older boy who regularly stood on the corner, shouting obscene remarks. The problem was eventually sorted out with the help of a friendly store-keeper and a local policeman. 'The fellow was let go with a stern warning,' her future sister-in-law, Elyda Nelson, recalled.

Soon boys were walking Norma Jeane home from school and would often end up talking outside Aunt Ana's. Occasionally a large crowd would gather and be ushered into the house by Aunt Ana, joking about how they were 'starting to resemble a mob'. The attention encouraged Norma Jeane's first crush, on a 22-year-old man from across the street, but, still only 13, she had no idea how to deal with her new feelings. One day, with permission from Aunt Ana, she accepted his invitation to the movies and set off in his car on what she thought would be a romantic date. 'I was gawky, I was giggly, I was stupid,' she said years later about her failed attempt at sophistication. It is generally believed that her first crush was soon-to-be

With the girlfriend of Ana Lower's nephew, Max Ritchie

leading man and singer, the actor Howard Keel, whom, as Marilyn, she dated in the late 1940s.

Norma Jeane's confidence took a dip after that, not helped by some of the girls at school commenting on how her clothes weren't as pretty and up-to-date as theirs. One day she returned home in tears, and Aunt Ana sat her down to console her: 'It doesn't matter if other children make fun of your clothes or where you live,' she said. 'It's what you are that counts. You just keep being your own self, that's all that matters.'

Aunt Ana's inspirational talks – not to worry about what others thought of her, live each day, take things as they come and work hard at what she wanted to accomplish – slowly but surely helped to inspire confidence in Norma Jeane. Before long, she was wearing make-up to school (making her look, she thought, at least 17), and started to accept when schoolmates asked her out: 'And that way I sort of slid painlessly into going out,' she later said. She was at the age for role models and became drawn to the actress, comedienne and dancer Ginger Rogers, deciding that she wanted to be just like her. To her amazement, Aunt Ana not only tolerated the idea but also encouraged her to read lines aloud, never criticizing her fledgling talent. 'She was most tolerant of my big ambition of being an actress,' Marilyn later said.

Unfortunately, Aunt Ana was in failing health. 'She was a gentle woman in her sixties, very dignified and wise,' recalled Marilyn. 'She had heart trouble but she never told me about it.' Instead Ana continued her inspirational talks, but began adding theories on how loneliness wasn't the worst thing in the world and urging Norma Jeane always to be herself and stand on her own two feet. 'I didn't realize that she was preparing me for her death,' Marilyn later said.

·　·　·　·　·　·

However willing Aunt Ana's heart was, her body wasn't up to the strains of raising a child. While the Bolenders had continued to visit, it was not possible for Norma Jeane to go back to live with them, and so, instead, in February 1940, she moved in again with guardian Grace Goddard and husband, Doc. By the time she arrived at the Goddard home at 14743 Archwood Street, Doc's daughter Bebe had moved in too. Like Norma Jeane, Bebe had endured a mentally unstable mother and a childhood of foster homes, so the two girls had much in common.

14743 Archwood Street: home as a teenager, with foster mother Grace Goddard

Grace promised Norma Jeane that she would never again have to worry about having stability in her life; there would always be a home for her with them. Grace spent hours intently – and non-judgmentally – listening as Norma Jeane poured out her heart. As Norma Jeane's trust grew, she became close to the entire family and enjoyed many Goddard family get-togethers, spending time with Grace's brother Harold, her sister Enid, and Enid's husband, Sam Knebelkamp. In years to come, Marilyn would play down her relationship with the Goddards, as she did with her sister, Berniece. She would imply that Grace was just one in a long line of

With friends at Green Valley Lake, February 1940

foster-mothers and say she had nothing in common with Berniece, that they lived different lives. However, all of this was designed to protect the lives of those she loved; in reality she stayed in touch all her life with Berneice and with Grace until she died in 1953.

Norma Jeane, who had never been at the height of fashion, started to develop a keen interest in her hair and clothes, and Grace helped her with make-up and grooming. With Bebe, she would spend hours designing clothes and hairstyles; some of the designs she sent to Berniece, and others Bebe kept (for the rest of her life). Her social and school life were beginning to settle down too. She had joined the Emerson Girls Glee Club, taking a day out, on 25 February 1940, with friends Bob Stotts, Betty Duggen and Bill Heisonat to Green Valley Lake, where they were photographed playing in the snow.

When archivist Roy Turner interviewed Marilyn's Emerson Junior High contemporaries, most remembered their classmate Norma Jeane in a positive light. But apart from memories of her 'plain clothes' and the 'powder-blue suit that she wore often', one comment kept recurring: 'I did not see her too often in school,' remembered Marian Losman, 'but when I did she seemed alone.' To Ron Underwood, 'She was somewhat shy and withdrawn, and seem-ingly had few friends,' while Tom Ishii recalled, 'She was alone most of the time.'

With the Goddards, though, she was not alone, and through them she was to meet the Dougherty family, whose house backed on to theirs. The two families were close; Ethel Dougherty could often be seen chatting over the back fence with Grace, and the two women liked to gossip and make plans. The Doughertys' son, Jim, was a strapping young man, some five years older than Norma Jeane, who considered himself 'happily footloose', way ahead of Bebe and Norma Jeane, whom he dismissed as boring kids.

During 1941, however, the Goddards moved into a larger,

A coloured-in print of a teenage Norma Jeane

6707 Odessa Avenue: home with the Goddards, 1937 and 1941

more dilapidated house at 6707 Odessa Street. Grace and Doc set about doing up the place, and their photos show a home comfortably furnished with a large dining table, rocking chair, china cabinet and floor-length mirrors plus lots of books and a piano. While the rooms were probably spruced up for the photos (the dining room is almost stage set with large candlesticks, streamers and feathers), it is clear that Norma Jeane was hardly living in squalor. The new house proved popular with the rest of the family, and there was often a crowd at weekends for get-togethers and celebrations; Aunt Ana would visit, as did Uncle Harold and others. The only unwelcome visitor was Bebe's mother, determined to regain control of her daughter's life, but during her visits, Norma Jeane and Bebe would hide outside up trees, or Bebe would call on a neighbour until danger had passed. Life was otherwise stable and fun.

In September 1941, Bebe and Norma Jeane enrolled as students at Van Nuys High School. The journey to school was not an easy one, so Grace, who was still in constant contact with Ethel Dougherty, asked if Jim might run the girls home from school in his car each evening. Rather reluctantly, Jim agreed – it was conveniently en route to his job on the graveyard shift at Lockheed – and so Bebe and Norma Jeane started to walk from their new school to the Doughertys, from where Jim would bring them home. The first day of the new arrangement, Jim was still sleeping prior to his night shift when the girls arrived, somewhat boisterously, and woke him up. Jim was won over, though, by Norma Jeane's apologies; from then on she always got to sit in the middle seat in the car, chatting so much with Jim that Bebe often felt left out. She must have felt a total gooseberry when Norma Jeane coquettishly touched Jim's knee as she laughed at his jokes: 'There was quite a flirtation when Jimmy was bringing us home from school,' she later told All About Marilyn.

Encouraged by Grace and Ethel, this flirtation led to a first date at the Christmas party of Doc's company, Adel Precision Products. As they danced, Jim surprised himself by having a good time; Norma Jeane seemed happy too as she leaned in close during the slow dances. They began to see each other regularly, but although they liked each other and enjoyed dating, Jim worried about the difference in their ages. The relationship had reached the point at which it was about to fizzle out when the Goddards announced they were leaving for West Virginia. Norma Jeane would not be going with them.

UNSEEN PHOTOGRAPHS

1926–1941

ABOVE AND RIGHT

Despite being fostered for most of her childhood, Norma Jeane did live with
her mother from time to time, and they enjoyed trips out, on this occasion
most likely to Santa Monica beach. Here she is seen (opposite, on the right)
on a rare seaside outing with her mother, Gladys (above, second from the
left in the row of heads in the sand), and friends.

ABOVE

Living in a rural community with foster parents the Bolenders, as a young
child Norma Jeane would be taken to visit her mother in Hollywood. Seen
here, right, in the dotted and flounced dress, outside her Hollywood home,
Gladys didn't help to make the visits much fun, chastising her daughter
(here holding a toy) for turning the pages of a book 'too loudly', ensuring
that she spent a large portion of the visit hiding in a closet.

Easter Sunrise Services. 30,000 at Hollywood Bowl. California

ABOVE

The Hollywood Bowl Easter Sunrise Service, 27 March 1932, where Norma Jeane was chosen to appear as part of the children's cross. As the sun rose over the bowl, the children, standing in the form of a cross, took off their black robes, as instructed, to reveal their white clothes underneath. Norma Jeane was so captivated by the crowds that she forgot to remove her dark outer robe and became momentarily a black spot in an otherwise white cross, though obviously not at the moment at which this photograph was taken.

A willowy Norma Jeane (right) with two younger children. Her unsettled childhood often made it hard for her to allow herself to get close to other children, particularly following her mother's committal, in 1935, to a mental institution. On one occasion when a boy tried to engage her in conversation, his friend warned, 'Don't bother her. She's just like her mother – crazy.' Cruel comments like these resulted in Norma Jeane often pretending her mother was dead.

An apparently rural idyll for Norma Jeane, photographed just after she left the orphanage, aged about ten, during the time she lived in Barbara Court with foster mother Grace Goddard, who bred cocker spaniels. She liked being with the animals and enjoyed her life with the Goddards, a time cut short by the family's financial problems.

LEFT

Norma Jeane crouches down next to a woman believed to
be foster mother 'Aunt' Ana Lower, whom she would come
to describe as 'a wonderful human being'. A key person in
her future screen career, Ana encouraged Norma Jeane to
read lines aloud and never stunted her fledgling talent: 'she
was most tolerant of my big ambition of being an actress'.

ABOVE

A coloured-in photo of a radiant Norma Jeane as a
teenager c. 1940–43, quite at ease in front of the camera.
It was in her teens that she discovered the existence of her
older half-sister, Berniece, then married and living in
Kentucky. Never having had any real family and craving
the stability that could bring, the relationship became an
important one that lasted a lifetime.

LEFT

When, in September 1938, Norma Jeane moved into Aunt
Ana's home at 11348 Nebraska Avenue, where these
photos were taken, a whole new world opened up for her.
She felt very much loved by Ana Lower and gained
confidence, as can be seen by her fooling around in one of
the photos. She also began to make friends, among them
Ana's nephew, Max Ritchie, who took these photographs.

ABOVE

Norma Jeane, front left, with friends Bob Stotts, Betty
Duggen and Bill Heison, during a snowy outing to
California's secluded Green Valley Lake resort in the San
Bernardino mountains, on 25 February 1940. With her
figure beginning to fill out, she was starting to attract the
attention of the opposite sex; boys on paper rounds would
ride their bikes past her house and give her free papers in
an attempt to gain ground and her attention.

3

MRS DOUGHERTY

Marriage to Norma Jeane was not something that had ever occurred to Jim Dougherty, so when his mother discussed it with him, he was surprised, to say the least. For a start, he felt she was too young, and, anyway, he wasn't sure he was quite ready to settle down. But when Ethel Dougherty told him Grace Goddard was worried Norma Jeane would have to return to the orphanage when they moved east, he began to consider things differently. When Ethel announced, 'Let's set it up for June,' he went along with it and was pleased to realize that he felt good about the prospect. So was the courtship and marriage a set-up between Grace and Ethel or a love match? Paul Kanteman, Jim's nephew, recalled that Jim had a very definite answer to that:

> 'The idea of an arranged marriage almost made him vomit! Yes, there was an introduction and maybe a little push in that direction, but he would not allow anyone to push him into anything, let alone marriage. Believe me, he would never have gotten married to her if he hadn't had great feelings for her. He wasn't the worst-looking guy on the block and could get just about any body he wanted or pursued.'

Indeed, Jim later admitted that he enjoyed the idea of being Norma Jeane's knight in shining armour; yet when Marilyn spoke of the marriage latterly, she never mentioned Jim in those terms. 'Instead of going back into a boarding house or with another set of foster parents, I got married.' The fact was that Norma Jeane felt let down and abandoned by the Goddards (the family couldn't afford to take her with them) and despised the idea of going back to the orphanage, so marriage was the better option. However, Jim would insist that they were happy and fell more in love each day. If Norma Jeane felt differently, she kept it to herself though she did admit to worrying that her future husband was only marrying her out of a sense of obligation.

Out shopping for a ring, Jim was surprised at Norma Jeane's insistence on something less expensive than the one he'd selected. When they returned to the Doughertys and broke the news of their engagement to the family, Norma Jeane appeared happy. Nevertheless, on a family picnic at Lake Sherwood, she seemed unusually pensive, despite Jim trying to serenade her out of it on his guitar. 'Her only contribution to the fun was a quiet smile of pride – and six lemon pies,' recalled sister-in-law Elyda Nelson.

Jim and Norma Jeane began dating regularly, going to the beach, hiking in the Hollywood Hills, boating at Pop's Willow Lake and fishing at Lake Sherwood. It was at the lake that she first spent time with Jim's nephew, Paul Kanteman, then around eight years old: 'I thought she was very pretty and nice. We had a row boat, and Norma Jeane rowed while we fished. She did do a good job of rowing, and we caught some nice bass!'

When Norma Jeane told her social-studies teacher that she was leaving school to get married, he said it would ruin her life and insisted that she didn't even know what love was. Her decision to quit before graduation was to plague Marilyn for the rest of her life. She would lie about it in interviews, claiming she graduated after her marriage, and forever try to catch up, attending courses and paying for private tuition. But in summer 1942, she wanted nothing to distract her from becoming Mrs Dougherty.

The wedding preparations were hasty but lavish. The ceremony was to be held at the 432 South Bentley home of Chester and Doris Howell, chosen because Norma Jeane loved the idea of using its large, winding staircase. Aunt Ana made her dress; she picked out the wedding rings herself, and notices appeared in the local paper. Even younger members of the family like Paul Kanteman had lots to do for the big day:

> '*A couple of weeks before the event my mother and I went to Shulman's men's store in Van Nuys to buy me clothes that would be fitting for a ring bearer; a new pair of black pants, white shirt and black, shiny shoes. I remember going to school and telling all the kids that my uncle was going to marry the most beautiful girl in the world and that I was to be their ring bearer. We had a rehearsal and I was taught how to do the hesitation step and how to hold the pillow that would have the ring pinned to it. I practised that step all the time so that it would be just right and my Uncle Jim would be proud of me. If my mother asked me to do something, it was always to the hesitation beat — I'm sure everyone was glad when it was all over and my productivity level returned to full time!*'

Once married, Norma Jeane had been keen to live with her in-laws, but on 8 June 1942 the couple found and leased a furnished apartment at 4524 Vista Del Monte, where according to Paul Kanteman, they were the first residents: 'It was small but nice. It had a small bedroom, living room, bathroom and a tiny kitchen; so tiny that if you were to turn around too quickly, you might stick your own finger in your eye!'

Tiny or not, it would be home for Mr and Mrs Dougherty, and they took pride in it; in the new sofa from their landlord, the Murphy pull-down bed and the pile of wedding presents. Watching Norma Jeane so enjoy preparing her new home made Jim realize just how much he loved her. 'I sometimes thought my heart would burst. She was everything to me,' he later wrote.

On 19 June 1942, at 8.30 pm, Norma Jeane swept down the grand staircase to be given away by Aunt Ana. She looked every bit the blushing bride, shaking with nerves in an embroidered lace gown with long sleeves, full skirt and sweetheart neckline; her veil was white lace and she carried a bouquet of white gardenias. Neither Gladys nor the Goddards were in attendance, but Mrs Bolender was there, at the insistence of the bride. Jim's sister Elyda remembered her as 'a docile and subdued little person, her pride and devotion cast a glow of warmth over the whole event'. Jim's brother Marion was best man and Lorraine Allen, a school friend from University High, was Norma Jeane's maid of honour. A Goddard family friend, Reverend Benjamin Lingenfelder, officiated, while Aunt Ana played music and Florence Andre sang. There was a small celebration at the home of the Howells afterwards, a source of some tension just days before the big day, as Elyda Nelson recalled:

> 'Someone brought up the question of who would give the reception after the wedding. Norma Jeane spoke up promptly and said, 'The bride's parents are supposed to take care of that.'
> 'I know, dear', one of the catty, feminine neighbours said, 'but you have no parents.'
> The look of sadness Norma Jeane gave me I'll never forget, and to this day I detest the thought of that offending woman.'

After the reception, Jim's brother Marion thought it would be fun to kidnap Norma Jeane and take her and Jim to the Florentine Gardens, a nightclub on Hollywood Boulevard. It didn't go well; a waiter spilt soup over Jim and he was persuaded to dance on stage with a chorus girl, much to Norma Jeane's chagrin. Years later, Jim reflected on the evening and decided that his new wife might have been looking for a reason to argue with him, as she was not looking forward to their wedding night. Plagued with insecurities, she had asked Grace Goddard if it were possible to 'just be friends' with her husband, and she had ploughed her way through an educational book from Aunt Ana. Neither the talk nor the book helped her confidence,

Florentine Gardens nightclub, Hollywood Boulevard, where the Doughertys celebrated their nuptials

however, and on the wedding night she spent a long time locked in the bathroom.

Although Norma Jeane tried cooking and experimented on her new relatives, her lack of culinary skills soon became apparent. She made the mistake of putting salt in Jim's coffee and, famously cooked carrots and peas just because she liked the colour. She wasn't helped by an offer from Jim's brothers, Tom and Marion, as Paul Kanteman remembered:

> 'They decided stocking the cupboards would be a great wedding present, as Uncle Jim and Aunt Norma would surely appreciate this. These guys were practical jokers and took all the labels off every item on the shelf. A lot of cans look alike as far as size is concerned, especially when they are undressed. Aunt Norma asked me to have lunch with her at the new house, and it was like a treasure hunt, shaking this can and that can until we found one that sounded right. We were going to have tuna-salad sandwiches that day, but the can of tuna turned out to be water-chestnuts, and the peas turned out to be fruit cocktail! So when I say the lunch was different it really was, but Aunt Norma kept a stiff upper lip and laughed about it.'

Aged 16, Norma Jeane had gone from footloose girl to responsible married woman in just a few, short months. She was a quick learner, but the emotional upheaval was huge. Neither Jim nor she knew how to react in an argument (she once went tearing out of the house in her nightclothes after a fight, only to be followed by a stranger). Another time she hit Jim over the head with a rubbish bin, after he'd criticized her for mistakenly feeding him raw fish. Jim tried to cool her off under the shower, but this made her even more irate, and he left to walk the streets until she had calmed down. Norma Jeane also struggled with a certain lack of life skills: she divided a bottle of scotch among four people; threw a cup of coffee over a sparking electrical socket; and didn't like or understand jokes told by Dougherty's friends. Jim made the mistake of mocking her naivety and later reflected: 'I think my teasing was the one thing that made her unhappy during our marriage. I was young myself and didn't know very much about how to treat a woman.'

Yet the marriage did provide Norma Jeane with a stable and secure relationship, and she clung to it ferociously, calling her new husband 'Daddy' and dramatically threatening to jump from Santa Monica pier if things ever went wrong. Her insecurities ran high, and when Jim worked the graveyard shift at Lockheed, he never told her how dangerous the job was, for fear of how it would affect her. As it was, if he ever forgot to kiss her goodbye she would worry she had upset him, or if she forgot to slip a billet-doux in his lunchbox, she would apologize profusely when he returned. She liked to place her husband's interests above her own, and although she never enjoyed fishing or hunting, she went along with Jim on expeditions, learning to shoot a rifle he had given her as a present.

She also bonded well with Jim's family, and although Marion Dougherty was too much of a tease for Norma Jeane, Paul Kanteman remembered that they 'got along just fine and she thought he was pretty funny'. She loved Jim's brother Tom and adored Jim's father; Jim later remarked that she thought his father 'the greatest guy in the world'. Paul Kanteman agrees:

> 'When Grandpa met Norma Jeane he thought she was a treasure and the feelings were mutual. From their first meeting there was an attraction for each other that made a bond that was as if they had been together since birth. Maybe she was like a granddaughter to him and her feelings seemed to be the same towards him. She looked up to him and respected all that he said. They were great friends from the first meeting.'

Norma Jeane also spent time with Jim's sister Elyda, who later said: 'She was the most beautiful little creature I had ever seen … Not only did she have beauty, but everything else it takes to make a lady. I loved her from the beginning.' Jim would always take Norma Jeane to visit his sister on Sundays, and as time went on, Jim's young wife and Elyda became friends:

> 'During the first year, Norma Jeane came to my home many times, to play with my son, Larry. 'My first baby has to be a boy,' she told me. She was wonderfully kind and patient with me while I was carrying my little Denny, who was two weeks overdue. At the time I was staying with my mother in Van Nuys, so Norma Jeane stayed with me during the day, and Jim picked her up at night.'

When the baby was born, Norma Jeane helped look after him, and as a result she became extremely fond of all Elyda's children, as Paul Kanteman remembered:

> 'Aunt Ana was a Christian Scientist, and Marilyn went along with their teachings and practices … my brother who, at the time was a baby about ten or eleven months and had become very ill with scarlatina and bronchial pneumonia. He was in very bad condition and Aunt Norma and Aunt Ana both went to work on him in prayer and what ever else they do, and he recovered. He is now retired and is about 6ft 3in so I guess something worked.'

The first Christmas as a married couple was almost certainly spent at the home of Jim's parents, the biggest of all the Dougherty homes and the place for family get-togethers and holidays. A haven of fun and music. Paul Kanteman remembered:

'My grandfather played the fiddle, guitar, banjo and chorded piano, while my mother played the fiddle and a little violin and sang. Aunt Norma would just sit there with her eyes glued on Uncle Jim when he would sing a love song to her or some cute holiday song that was directed to her. She would occasionally join in and sing a little but as I recall would rather just watch. She did enjoy the get-togethers and was always there to help in the clean-up … like table clearing and washing dishes etc. She didn't just sit and let everyone else do the work.'

In January 1943 the lease on the Vista Del Monte apartment ran out while Jim's parents were out of town. The couple moved into the Dougherty family home, which they shared with Jim's brother Tom. It was here that Norma Jeane received news that was to change the course of her life, as Jim Dougherty recalled: 'Her mother told Grace that Stanley Gifford was her father, and Grace told my mother, who told Norma Jeane.'

Never having known her father, and barely knowing her mother, Norma Jeane was amazed by this news, and on 16 February 1943 she wrote to Grace about her plan to visit Mr Gifford. The discovery had made a new person of her, she said, and she told Grace: 'It's something I have to look forward to.' In the orphanage she used to daydream of her father rescuing her, and she was determined that he would be pleased to see her now; her anticipation heightened when a friend read her fortune, predicting that they would successfully meet. But when she found the confidence to phone her father, according to Jim Dougherty: 'He hung up on her. It took a lot of tender loving care to bring her out of the disappointment.'

＊ ＊ ＊ ＊ ＊

In spring 1943, the couple moved into a new house at 14223 Bessemer Street. One day Dougherty arrived home to find his wife encouraging a cow into the house for shelter that had been standing out in the rain. Would he help? It took quite a lot of persuasion for her to drop the idea. Wet cows aside, it was a settled time, until World War II prompted Jim to leave Lockheed and enlist with the merchant marines. He did his basic training in San Diego, moving to Catalina Island to take up the post of Physical Instructor at the Maritime Service Training Station. Norma Jeane joined her husband in a $35-a-month hillside apartment – probably 323 Metropole Avenue, Avalon.

Hillside apartment, reputedly where the newly wed Doughertys lived on Catalina Island

'We had a very normal life,' Jim recalled. 'Norma cooked and cleaned, and I was the breadwinner.' Her

Beside the penguin pool, Wrigley
Bird Park, 1943

chores done, she liked to indulge herself, washing her hair and making-up her face, and fussing over Muggsie, her dog: 'She spent hours bathing him, grooming him, teaching him tricks,' said Elyda Nelson. 'They were inseparable when Jim was not home.' She wrote to her sister, Berniece, urging her to move to the island, to share the evenings, on the porch and their plans for the future. Jim would play guitar and sing; friends came over to dance to music from their new record player. At weekends they went horse-riding and fishing, and a visit to Wrigley Bird Park was recorded in a photograph of Norma Jeane holding a rare hornbill. Trips to the beach were not so frequent as Norma Jeane attracted too much attention in her swimsuit – a pleasure for husbands but not for their wives.

At Christmas 1943, there was a dance at the Catalina Casino Norma Jeane had visited years before, during a rare outing with her mother. The evening was not a success. Jim became understandably worn down by the many comments and dance requests Norma Jeane received from male admirers. The last straw was when he wanted to leave and she didn't. If she left, she said, she'd come back later once he had gone to sleep. Jim made his feelings clear; come home with me or not at all, and they returned home.

They'd been married for a year or so, and although Jim was keen to start a family, Norma Jeane did not share his enthusiasm. She quizzed her sister-in-law about child-rearing, said she wanted a baby one day, but becoming a parent terrified her. Jim remembered her as lukewarm about parenthood, becoming hysterical when her period was late one day, and she feared she might be pregnant. Yet when Jim was told he was leaving for the war, scared of being alone, she pleaded with him to make her pregnant. This time, though, it was Jim who said no, worried that if he didn't return, she would have to raise a child on her own.

In 1943, with unknown
friend and baby, Catalina
Island

Concerned about leaving his young wife alone, Jim arranged for her to stay with his parents while he was away. On the day he left, Norma Jeane presented him with an expensive watch (which she had used their entire savings to buy), before going to visit her sister-in-law Elyda. As she walked up the path to her house, an admirer in a convertible wolf-whistled at her: 'Move on, old man,' she yelled, furious. 'Go pick on somebody nearer your own age.'

With Jim gone, not able to bear the idea of endless hours of inactivity, Norma Jeane asked Ethel if she could get her a job at

Radioplane, a company that made target planes for Air Corps gunnery practice, where Ethel worked as a nurse. On 18 April 1944, Norma Jeane started work there, but Ethel was not pleased about it. Elyda recalled: 'Mom bawling her out for working in the paint shop. "Honey," she said, "You'll ruin your beautiful hair – and all those fumes – it's just not good for your health." But Norma Jeane persisted, even though she came home looking a wreck.'

Norma Jeane worked ten hours a day, on her feet the entire time and was a popular and trusted member of the team. She was rated above average by her managers and admired by her male co-workers. In July 1944 she was even crowned Queen of the Radioplane picnic, winning a $50 war bond and a mention in the 15 July edition of the *Radioplane Static*. She was mentioned there again on 31 August on winning a gold button for useful suggestions about how the plant operated. But despite her popularity, she remained faithful to her husband, as Elyda later wrote: 'Naturally Norma Jeane was aware that other wives and sweethearts dated while their men were away, but she never did. Furthermore, she never gossiped about these situations nor would she listen to gossip.'

At the annual Radioplane picnic in the 1940s

Although living with her in-laws couldn't have been the easiest of situations, Norma Jeane seemed to accept life at the Hermitage Street house and would often have morning coffee with her mother-in-law then go out shopping with her later. Still close to her new nephews, Norma Jeane must have been pleased when she heard that Paul was coming to visit, and he still remembers the week with great affection:

'*We hadn't seen each other for a while and I really did miss her. Grandma asked me if I would like to spend a week or so with them and Aunt Norma. Well my response obviously was yes, and it was good to see her again as she was my buddy and I wanted to spend some time with her. She asked me a few days later if I would like to have lunch with her and I replied: 'Yes, as long as you aren't cooking.' She said: 'There is a great hamburger place on the west end of the Valley called The Hangman's Tree.' I thought that sounded great as I certainly loved hamburgers, so off we went.*

The food looked really good and I ordered a Bar-B-Q cheeseburger with a coke and she ordered just a regular burger with all the trimmings and a lemon coke. The orders came but her coke was cherry not lemon as she had ordered. She called the waiter over and reported the oversight, he checked his order and said, 'You did order a cherry coke.' She really didn't want to make a scene but she did want the lemon coke. The manager heard the commotion and came over to the table to see what the problem was with this pretty lady. She told him she wanted a lemon coke, in no uncertain terms, or we would leave and go someplace else. I'm thinking, this burger sure looks good and, boy, was I hungry. She stood her ground and they made the right coke, and it was a good lunch. Aunt Norma could be one tough lady if provoked.'

She could be extremely late too, which caused problems with her in-laws, as Paul also witnessed:

'A couple of days after the coke incident, Grandma asked if we would like to go out for dinner and a movie that evening. We all thought it would be a great idea and all we had to do was pick the movie. Well, evening came and it was time for dinner, but Aunt Norma wasn't quite ready. We waited a little while and then decided to go to dinner without her. When we came back to pick her up for the movies, Grandma went in to see if she was ready yet and came back out of the house alone, telling Grandpa that Norma Jeane was still wandering around without a stitch on! Grandma sounded a little perturbed, and we went to the movies without her.'

Posing for husband Jim Dougherty,
Catalina Island, 1943

Ethel later lamented, 'I just love that girl. I never knew anyone more unselfish, but she is so lost in her own world that she frightens me.'

· · · · ·

In autumn 1944, Norma Jeane felt the need to reconnect with her foster family and establish a link with her blood relatives. She cleared out her savings account and set off alone to visit her sister, Berniece, in Detroit, and Grace Goddard in Chicago (the recent discovery of two postcards dated 28 October 1944 place the visit two months later than is frequently reported). On her arrival in Detroit, she was met by Berniece, her husband Paris, his sister Niobe and Berniece's daughter Mona Rae. They were bowled over by the 18 year old in a cobalt-blue suit and heart-shape brimmed hat.

The visit was a real confidence booster for Norma Jeane, who had never spent any time with her blood family – the last time being the disastrous year or so she had lived with her mother. Both girls only vaguely knew Gladys, and they were able to discuss her and their brother Robert. But the stay was cut short when Jim unexpectedly announced that he would be returning to California on leave. Norma Jeane moved swiftly on to Illinois to visit the Goddards. During the short visit to Chicago and Huntington, she saw Grace's new workplace and reacquainted herself with

Bebe. Norma Jeane spent time with her friends at the Goddard home, 322 Wilson Court, and Maully's South Side Confectionary at 915 8th Street. 'She didn't look like Marilyn Monroe at the time,' recalled Nelson Cohen, who married Bebe in 1950. 'I only met her briefly but she was pleasant enough, perfectly normal.' Another friend, Diane DePree Miller describes Norma Jeane as 'An ordinary looking girl, with light-brown hair. She was very shy and kept to herself.'

In a letter to Grace dated 3 December 1944, Norma Jeane described just how much the trip meant to her and how much she missed her foster mother. The letter also seems to indicate that Norma Jeane was helping her out financially too: 'I shall send you more money a little later,' she wrote. Her generosity towards friends and loved ones – and her financial difficulties – was a recurrent theme throughout her life.

Back home, it was back to work at Radioplane. On the day of her return, she was photographed by an army film unit making a moving picture for army training. Posing for photographer David Conover in her work gear of grey slacks and green blouse with her Radioplane identity card clearly visible, the look on her face said it all – this was far more exciting than inspecting or spraying parachutes. The pictures taken that day changed Norma Jeane from a reasonably content young bride into a woman with ambition, who was excited by life's possibilities. Conover wanted to take more photos, and with the approval of the boss, Mr Whosis, he returned to Radioplane, where she posed for him in a variety of outfits. Conover said she could become a model, that he had contacts; at first she believed he was only flirting. However, after studying the photos and being told that she could earn $5 for an hour's modelling as opposed to working ten hours a day at the factory, she began to see it made sense. But as Jim had just returned to California, she decided to wait until his shore leave was over before making her move.

When Norma Jeane raised the idea of modelling with her husband, he seemed to like it: 'I thought it was easier than working at Radioplane,' he said, though he made it clear that when the war was over he wanted to start a family. At Big Bear Lake for a week's holiday – 'a grand time', as she later described it – there were problems. Jim hated the fact that his wife had started to drink alcohol; she wasn't best pleased when he played blackjack with some college girls, and they had an argument about Jim's wish to have children. Shortly after their return home, Jim rejoined his ship, and Norma Jeane put into action her plan to work as a model.

When she wrote to Grace on 4 June 1945, she mentioned that she hadn't worked at Radioplane since January, though they wanted her back. Work at the factory did nothing but tire her out, she said, and: 'I just don't care about anything when I'm that tired.' By March 1945, according to personnel records, she was no longer in Radioplane's employ. Thanks to David Conover, she met Potter Heuth, who agreed to take some photos of her if she would work 'on spec' – paid if and when he found a buyer for the work – to which she agreed. She soon discovered she was a natural at modelling; it was fun, the photographers seemed to like her, and she liked the work.

Unfortunately her new career did not go down well with Ethel Dougherty. Understandably loyal to her son and a witness to the frequent arguments between him and Norma Jeane, she saw it as a threat to the marriage, especially the fact that her daughter-in-law spent so much time with other men. Another source of friction was Norma Jeane's apparent neglect of her dog. According to Jim Dougherty: 'The last time I saw Muggsie she was tied to a tree and very dirty. She died soon after.'

Not able to stand the tension at the Doughertys, Norma Jeane moved back to Aunt Ana's in West Los Angeles, though that did not really resolve matters. Paul Kanteman remembers a particularly stressful episode:

'Uncle Jim was on leave and called to see if I could go fishing in a couple of days' time. He picked me up the next day, but Aunt Norma couldn't be with us as she was modelling for a magazine cover that day. We had to get our fishing tackle together anyway, and we could kill most of the day doing that without any problem. The next morning Aunt Norma announced she couldn't go with us that day either as they hadn't finished shooting yet. Uncle Jim didn't seem too thrilled as he really wanted to spend more time with her. Up the coast we went, to just south of the Malibu pier. She dropped us off with our tackle and a lunch with the promise to be back no later than mid-afternoon. Well, afternoon came and went, evening came and went and no Aunt Norma. Back in those days Malibu was no more than a beach and a pier – no food, no phones etc. We were in the boonies in a sense; we had been there since before daylight and had only a lunch, which we ate before noon. We were hungry!

It was about eleven that night when we saw the little Ford coupé pull up and stop. We scrambled into the car and off we went. Not a lot was said on our way back to Aunt Ana's home in West Los Angeles. I do remember going up stairs to my room and passing by Aunt Norma's room and heard her crying. I went downstairs and told Uncle Jim what was going on. He immediately went to see what the problem was, as not much had been discussed about the day at that point. She told him she was shooting a cover for a maga-zine depicting the Thanksgiving turkey, the set was an actual barn in the country with a large pile of hay. [Potter Heuth photographed her in a farmer's outfit on a bale of straw, it is possible that this was the photo session.] Before they could begin, she had to remove her wedding rings as they certainly didn't want a married woman posing for this cover shot, but … they became lost in about ten tonnes of hay. The afternoon had been spent trying to find them, but they were, however, found the next day – to everyone's relief.'

Norma Jeane's relationship with Jim got so bad that an argument was almost guaranteed whenever they spent time together. When Lee Bush from the Schwarz Studio photographed her on 18 May 1945, she posed in a bikini; Jim had begged her not to wear something so revealing but the money, she said, would come in useful for a new motor in their car. Another time Jim again mentioned starting a family, and told her in no uncertain terms that she would have to give up modelling, but it was a demand that fell on deaf ears.

When Jim was away (and often when he was not), Norma Jeane's mind was mostly on her career. She approached photographer Paul Parry by walking into his office and asking him if he thought she could make it as a model. There were two other men in the room, and their positive response was plain to see. As it turned out, when Parry used her for a fashion layout, an advertising manager was not impressed and said she'd never amount to much as a fashion model. But, this did not put her off pursuing other options. She heard that William Carroll from the AnscoColor film-processing and printing service in Los Angeles was looking for a model for an advertising counter display. As luck would have it, David Conover and Potter Heuth went into Carroll's shop regularly; one particular day Heuth was armed with slides of Conover's photos of Norma Jeane. 'Those Conover pictures displayed a girl of outstanding charm,' Carroll says in his book, *Norma Jean: Marilyn Monroe 1945*. 'Not totally beautiful but fresh in a most delightful girl-next-door manner. And that was the exact type I wanted to decorate our point-of-purchase counter display for my laboratory services.'

In red sweater and white braces, at a photo session with William Carroll

Carroll took her number from Heuth and rang her later that day. She was 'very calm and sounded serious as she questioned me as to the source of her number and my contacts with Potter and David. At this point in time I'd say she was concerned about my level of professionalism to eliminate potential trouble of working with an amateur photographer who is just trying to meet a pretty girl.' When they finally met for a beach shoot, for which she was on time: 'Norma Jeane brought with her a good selection of personal clothing, all of which had been ironed and was ready to use. Note that this was not 'model' clothing as I have no reason to believe she had any. Just a good clothes-closet selection from which we used almost everything.'

As they drove to the beach, Carroll explained his intentions for the photos, and Norma Jeane suggested informal shots and avoiding bathing suits, so as to not offend the clients in his shop. They stopped at a local beach, where Norma Jeane set about putting on her make-up, while Carroll took informal shots, in which her hair

An early photographic
assignment, 1945, with
William Carroll

seems lighter than usual, perhaps sun bleached. Her natural beauty is apparent, as Carroll recalled:

'She had no professional manner. This is a point I must emphasize by comparing her conduct with the many other models photographed during that period. Norma Jeane was naturally a competent person who constantly demonstrated a strong desire to help me make the best possible use of our time on the beach. We had many laughs and shared ideas easily because her model-based reactions were simply that of a young woman seeking to give the best possible assistance to producing excellent pictures. Keep in mind that at this point she had little professional experience except of her two-week trip with David [Conover], whose pictures proceeded mine by just a few months.'

Although still wearing her wedding ring, Norma Jeane shared some of her marriage woes with Carroll, who even now refuses to discuss what was said:

'We did talk at length, during our lunch break, about personal problems and pleasures. I had recently ploughed through a difficult divorce and (probably) felt that talking with a non-involved neutral person, as Norma Jeane was, could ease my bad memories. Norma Jeane responded rather completely but her very personal comments were hers and should not be made a source of public concern.'

After lunch both Carroll and Norma Jeane were devastated to discover that the film in his camera had stuck. They could risk losing all the pictures they had worked hard to create all morning. An emergency solution would have to be found:

'With a bit of thought I asked if I could borrow her unused slacks to make a temporary changing bag. Norma Jeane rolled the waistband down a few inches and held it tightly closed. I covered her hands and the upper section of the slacks with my jacket, then put my hands and camera inside her slacks and opened the camera body inside this improvised dark room, and rolled the 35mm film back into its metal cassette.'

At the end of the session, Carroll paid $20 for the day's work. When he rang about a month later: 'She told me she had signed with the Blue Book Agency. Her daily rate [set by Blue Book] had jumped to $50 a day; a figure I decided I would not pay so never used Norma Jeane again.'

Emmeline Snively owned the Blue Book Agency, which was based in the grounds of the Ambassador Hotel. On 2 August 1945, when Norma Jeane walked in, Snively noted that: 'She was cute-looking, but she knew nothing about carriage, posture, walking, sitting or posing. She was a California blonde – dark in winter, light in summer.' She also considered Norma Jeane's curly hair unmanageable and knew it would have to be bleached and straightened. 'We wished she could get her hair straightened but she couldn't afford it.' That said, she did see potential in the 'round-faced girl with an astonishing bust which made her size 12 dress look too small'. She asked for a photo and was presented with one of David Conover's shots, which impressed her enough to recommend Norma Jeane attend a $100, three-month long modelling course, which she could pay off with her modelling assignments. Norma Jeane filled out the application form immediately, lying about her age (claiming to be 20 not 19), and noting that her hair was blonde and curly, and her height 5' 6". She mentioned no ambitions to act, but did say she danced a little, and sang.

The Blue Book Model Agency in the Ambassador Hotel grounds, LA

Arriving for her first modelling class, she was friendly to everyone, and Snively gave her lots of attention because she arrived alone (other girls all had their mothers with them). She gobbled up all the advice and instruction, and became skilled at the hand positions, posture and make-up techniques taught by Maria Smith and Mrs Gavin Beardsley. She began studying photos of herself and learnt how to improve her technique; asking the photographers to tell her where she was going wrong. She never repeated a mistake, nor missed a class, leading Snively to believe that with her guts and gumption, she would become a big star.

Nonetheless, Snively did note her clothes were a problem, as she seemed to own just two different outfits; a white dress with a green yoke and a teal-blue tailored suit 'that didn't do a thing for her', Snively said. (Even though she wore the suit for an early agency shoot with Larry Kronquist for an American Airlines booklet.) On 2 September 1945, she did a test shot with eight other girls in the grounds of the Ambassador Hotel. On 5 September, she got her first booking as a hostess in a Holga Steel Files booth at an industrial show, showcasing files and handing out leaflets. She was a hit. The $90 she earned for ten days' work, she gave to Snively to pay for the modelling course, supporting Snively's belief that she was working with 'a fair, honest and very fine girl', for whom she made a point of getting as much work as she possibly could.

Norma Jeane attended audition after audition and built up a good relationship with photographers such as Lazlo Willinger, John Randolph, and Larry Kronquist. 'She was sincerely eager,' Snively recalled. 'She made everyone she talked to feel as if he were the only guy in the world. She did this naturally without design or premeditation.' Her photos, though, were surprisingly difficult to sell, as art directors complained that her nose was too long and her smile cast shadows. According to Snively, 'She smiled too high ... and it made deep lines around her nose. We taught her how to bring her smile down and show her lower teeth.' At Snively's insistence Norma Jeane would specialize in pin-ups because of the way she looked in a bikini.

Snively had many photographer friends who were interested in discovering a new model, and Norma Jeane jumped at this opportunity for 'test shots', even though she was already becoming quite established. As a result she was 'discovered' by an assortment of photographers, but Snively never considered this to be dishonest, since Norma Jeane's style was forever changing.

· · · · ·

Although she didn't gossip about her personal problems, Snively was aware that Norma Jeane's marriage was in trouble, and yet: 'Many of my other girls whose husbands were overseas, dated several nights of the week. But not Norma Jeane.' She would also drive herself home after photo sessions, to avoid any embarrassing episodes. At Christmas 1945, however, Jim came home on shore leave to find his wife about to go on an extended modelling assignment with photographer Andre De Dienes. Understandably perturbed, he urged her to cancel, but she refused, unwilling to jeopardize her career. She was to spend the next few weeks in the company of another man, much to the dismay of her husband.

De Dienes had asked the Blue Book Agency for a girl who might be willing to pose nude. Norma Jeane was assigned to the job and had arrived at his hotel room wearing a pink sweater with her hair tied in a bow. Although she was wearing a wedding ring, De Dienes claims she told him she was in the process of getting a divorce. After posing in a bikini at a nearby beach, De Dienes asked her to go on location with him, and following a meeting with Aunt Ana, she agreed.

From Death Valley, on 15 December, Norma Jeane sent Jim a postcard, telling him how much she missed him. Addressed to 'My Dearest Daddy' and signed 'All My love, Your Baby', it shows no sign of marital disharmony, though makes no mention of the trip. Perhaps Norma Jeane didn't want to rock the boat, or maybe it just wasn't turning out the way she had hoped. Certainly, in the course of it, they had lurched from one disaster to another; accosted by strange men, several flat tyres, a forgotten wallet and a hotel-room theft. So upsetting was the theft that Norma Jeane decided to phone Jim and return home, but De Dienes, who by this point had fallen in love with her, begged her not to and instead to marry him.

Since Norma Jeane was already married, and they barely knew each other, it is hard to know what possessed De Dienes. Marrying someone else certainly seemed to be the last thing on Norma Jeane's mind, but her lack of interest did not discourage De Dienes, and after a disastrous trip to visit her mother (in which Gladys barely acknowledged their presence), he claims that he and Norma Jeane slept together. This was the moment for which he had been waiting, though, apparently, not so Norma Jeane, whom, he admitted, was crying quietly after they had sex. De Dienes says they made love again the next day, before he drove her back to Aunt Ana's. It took several unanswered letters and tense phone calls to convince De Dienes that marriage was out of the question, and the two agreed just to be good friends.

Having fought off De Dienes, Norma Jeane had another fight on her hands that new year. She had long resisted Emmeline Snively's attempts to get her to change her hair, which Snively described as an 'unruly, shapeless, mop'. It was, Snively felt, not her best asset; frizzy hair made wearing hats difficult, and, anyway, blondes were more in demand. Being bottle blonde was a luxury Norma Jeane felt she couldn't afford, until, in February 1946 she was persuaded otherwise. At Frank and Joseph's salon she had her hair straightened and bleached and immediately landed a shampoo advert. It was time, Snively said, for Norma Jeane to be re-discovered, and on 6 March she sent her along to photographer Joseph Jasgur for more test shots. Initially, Jasgur didn't think much of her; hips too broad, clothes too tight, figure imperfect, but he did like her eyes. He took some shots on a street behind Beverly Boulevard and then took her out for dinner. Snively was to say that Jasgur considered Norma Jeane too thin and not sexy; he would always feed her hamburgers when he thought she looked hungry.

A quick succession of modelling jobs followed the re-launch. On 10 March there was another session with Jasgur, this time at the Don Lee Towers, above the Hollywood sign and, on 11 March, she posed for photographer Earl Moran. Two days later, she worked with Richard Miller, a young photographer who was to use her throughout March and April, and on the 18 and 23 March she went with Jasgur to Zuma beach for a shoot alone in the sand and then with the cast of the local theatrical production *The Drunkard*. Jasgur's *The Birth of Marilyn* included a beach-shoot photo of Norma Jeane with six toes, never explained by the five toes she showed in every preceding photograph – perhaps the extra 'toe' in the Jasgur photos was merely a bump in the sand.

The movies beckoned; Norma Jeane was being advised to consider film work, and she mentioned to Emmeline Snively that she might be interested in bit parts. Home on leave, Jim tried to dissuade her but then found himself driving her to a screen test that later turned out to be with 'just a bunch of fresh guys', as Norma

Jeane described it. But the attention from men desperate to make her a star led Snively to introduce her to Helen Ainsworth, a theatrical agent at the National Concert Artists Corporation. As she walked into the office, the string on her hatbox snapped, leaving a trail of hairpins, lipstick, curlers and make-up. Ainsworth's colleague, Harry Lipton, looked up and saw a young girl who looked flushed and confused, like 'a freshly cut piece of strawberry shortcake'.

The interview went well, but she didn't say much; the only thing she did divulge was that she had always dreamed of being an actress. Ainsworth and Lipton agreed that she had possibilities and signed her up, assigning her to Lipton to handle personally. This was the start of Norma Jeane's venture into the movies, and she couldn't have been happier – professionally at least.

She was to become close to Harry Lipton, often calling him at odd hours of the night, just to have someone to talk to, because at home things had got worse. She confided in Lipton that she believed Jim had married her because she had nowhere else to go, describing him as 'a very nice man'. On 9 March, returning after shore leave Jim left a note saying, 'I've gone. After I've finished sailing and can settle on the beach we can give it another try if you like. Don't think there's someone else, there isn't, but, well, I've told you how I feel.' Determined not to give up on the relationship, Jim left hoping against hope that things could be patched up. However, shortly after her first appearance on 26 April on the cover of *Family Circle*, Norma Jeane went to Las Vegas to obtain a divorce. Lipton helped her arrange things, and as he put her on the train he noted that she showed 'neither relief nor joy nor distaste at getting a divorce. Her reaction was that of someone leaving a fairly close acquaintance – not a husband'. On the train she jotted down the reasons she would give for leaving her husband – how he didn't support her, indeed, embarrassed her, ridiculed her, treated her like a child. She also noted the dates she would need to be resident in Las Vegas; 14 May to 10 July.

In Las Vegas, Norma Jeane stayed with Minnie Willett, a relative of Grace Goddard, at 406 South 3rd Street. She was not happy at being there, given her modelling career was going so well, and in a letter to an unknown friend, she lamented: 'Oh what an awful time,' describing how she was in and out of hospital with a mouth infection and the measles. However, her luck changed when she walked out onto Winnie Millette's porch and caught neighbour Bill Pursel's eye.

Bill Pursel at the time
he and Norma Jeane
were dating, late 1940s

'She was a beautiful gal. We were just two young adults going out; we'd go to the movies, the lake, and all over the place. We would find a café or somewhere

PART ONE: 'SPRING' 1926–1952

out of the way and sit opposite each other. She would stare right into my face and it would make me nervous because she was so beautiful. We would often write notes to each other on napkins and pass them to each other while we were dining.'

While they enjoyed each other's company both knew that it could never go further than that. Norma Jeane was engrossed in her work and didn't want to be tied down again after her divorce, and Bill was getting ready for college:

> 'It was a happy and carefree part of her life, and of my life too. She was again free following her divorce, and I had returned from World War II in one piece. We had a great time together, scribbling notes on napkins, going to movies and just enjoying being together. We didn't try to make waves or draw attention.'

Norma Jeane also spent time with Bill's family, having dinner at least twice at their home at 925 South 3rd Street, as Bill's sister Jeanne Chretien recalled:

> 'She was a lovely, lovely girl; a very sweet girl. She could have been the girl-next-door – my mom liked her a lot, and mom was very particular about people! In fact Norma Jeane later wrote to mom, who was very approving of her going out with Bill. She would also speak with her on the phone – she wouldn't speak to just anyone, but she loved Norma Jeane.'

Jeanne and her husband Henry would tease Bill about the relationship: 'What a beauty – how are you getting such a gorgeous doll?' But they saw that 'She was a very down-to-earth person ... very intelligent, smart, sweet and wholesome. She liked poetry and talked a lot about the poet Carl Sandburg.'

On the countless rumours that Norma Jeane travelled back and forth to LA when she was supposed to be resident in Vegas, Bill Pursel says:

> 'I doubt it, because after we met we saw one another nearly every day. She also would call me at the service station where I worked, and, she brought her little Ford in for me to service. I think she stayed the whole six weeks, and I think she stayed at this same home on South 3rd Street.' She was certainly a resident in Las Vegas when Jim Dougherty phoned her. He had received a letter and divorce papers while he was at sea. He didn't respond immediately except to cancel her allotment or allowance. As soon as he reached dry land, he phoned her but was hardly reassured when she answered with a bright, 'Hi, Bill' and then started to scold him for cutting off her allotment. Still in denial, Jim decided to visit his wife when he arrived back in LA.'

Norma Jeane left Vegas left on 18 July. Bill Pursel offered to drive with her some of the way in her Ford coupé:

'We got about 90 miles south of Vegas to Baker. We were driving down Baker Grade when the car started missing … we just made it to a service station in Baker. I realized we had lost the fuel pump and told the mechanic this, as he was busy ogling Norma Jeane. The car was going to take a bit of time to work on, so we walked about a mile up the road to Failings, and Norma Jeane complained it was so hot she could feel the heat coming through her shoes. We stayed for an hour or two before walking all the way back, only to find the mechanic had stripped the car and had parts everywhere … [Eventually] the car was OK but cost $32 to fix and I didn't have much cash left.

As we drove on we reached a checkpoint at Yermo where we were asked whether we had any fruit or veg in the car. Norma Jeane was wearing a white halter and shorts and her hair was pulled back with a ribbon. The male officers at the checkpoint ordered her to get all her suitcases out of the trunk to be searched. She became angry because [that] entailed several suitcases. When we continued our drive she scolded me some, and my response was, 'You are most beautiful when you are angry,' and she was! To cool off we found a park in San Bernardino and soaked our feet in a pond. I then bid her farewell as I had to go back to Vegas by bus.'

Norma Jeane found herself followed home by a gentleman admirer. In a letter to Bill, she wrote: 'He drove like a crazy person, he would drive his car real close to mine and kept saying, "When are we going to get together?" Something new – a highway wolf!' She also thanked Bill for his company and asked him to visit whenever he was in town.

But back in LA, apart from Jim, Norma Jeane had her mother, Gladys, to consider. In July 1945, Gladys had been released from the mental institution on condition that she spend a year adjusting to life outside with her aunt Dora Graham in Oregon; afterwards she was free to do what she wished. However, she became bored of her confinement in Oregon, and before her adjustment year was up, decided to travel to Los Angeles and live with Aunt Ana. Norma Jeane may have shared a room with her before the trip to Vegas, but the ultimate test was living together full time on her return. For sisters Norma Jeane and Berniece, this was a time of great optimism and change but ultimate disappointment. For Norma Jeane, it was also a time of huge change in every aspect of her life.

'THIS IS THE END OF NORMA JEANE'

Coming home from Las Vegas, closer than ever to being a free woman, Norma Jeane must have had mixed feelings about the prospect of living with her mother. This was the first time since childhood that she had had any prolonged contact with Gladys; the relationship was strained to say the least. Bill Pursel had arrived to visit, staying with his aunt in North Hollywood, and his presence must have been welcome. Gladys and he crossed paths briefly on Nebraska Avenue:

> Norma Jeane and I were leaving Aunt Ana's one day around noon when an attractive lady was emerging from an apartment basement below Aunt Ana's home. Norma Jeane introduced me to this lady as her mother; the lady acknowledged the introduction with a smile and then promptly turned and retreated back down the few steps to the basement apartment. I would guess this lady to be in her forties, rather slim, quite attractive, but noticeably shy. Norma Jeane said nothing more, and I didn't ask.

Although Jim Dougherty never mentioned it in either of his memoirs, Bill recalled:

> I did meet Jim Dougherty when he came to Aunt Ana's home to get some keys from Norma Jeane. She was expecting him ... Aunt Ana let him in, and Norma Jeane introduced me to Jim in a polite way — she didn't identify me as anyone special. He acknowledged the meeting with a friendly handshake; he was very polite and I think he said, 'Glad to meet you' ... He was only there a few seconds — it was obviously an arranged quick meeting ... I was just a bystander, but I was impressed with Norma Jeane for introducing us. I noticed no animosity or jealousy on his part, nothing seemed awkward or confrontational ... Norma Jeane ... was also very polite to him. We did not discuss the meeting afterwards

Marilyn outside her
house, a photographic
memento for boyfriend
Bill Pursel

– I felt it was not my business to ask her anything; in fact Norma Jeane never talked about Jim, or her many boyfriends, to me.'

Aside from tying up loose ends with Dougherty, July and August seemed like a fresh start. During her summer in Vegas, Norma Jeane had featured on various magazine covers. It was her appearance in *Laff* that drew her to Howard Hughes's attention; his office expressing interest to Emmeline Snively who made sure the press knew. The result was Norma Jeane's first mention in a gossip column. A call from Twentieth Century Fox followed and a meeting with casting director Ben Lyon; then a screen test on 14 August. In preparation, Bill Pursel recalled: 'Norma Jeane came up with a short script which we practised at my aunt's home in North Hollywood. I don't know if the skit she had was the same one used at the studio or if there was more than one skit, but the script we practised had two parts, one female and one male.'

Even then, as Bill's sister Jeanne recalls: 'Bill said that he knew Norma Jeane's lines long before she did – she didn't learn them very quickly.'

The screen test was an important break: 'Norma Jeane came home … running up the walk and into the house all bubbly. She was smiling and happy because after the black-and-white test they had taken a second test in Technicolor.' The second test was key and led to her first contract, signed on 24 August. There'd been a discussion about her name; Norma Jeane didn't just didn't have star quality, Lyon felt. When he said she reminded him of actress Marilyn Miller, this was the name they went with; Monroe, Norma Jeane's mother's maiden name, was her personal choice. Pursel says:

'She didn't make a big deal about it to me, but she wasn't happy about it. She didn't like Marilyn but the Monroe part she liked OK because it was a family name, or something. The part she was irked about was she wasn't consulted before it was a done deal – I think she wanted the name Jeane kept because she was fond of Jean Harlow. But I continued to call her Norma Jeane.'

That night, Norma Jeane went home and scribbled on the mirror in lipstick: 'This is the end of Norma Jeane.' Marilyn Monroe was born.

* * * * *

Events moved quickly after being signed to Fox. A studio biography was prepared, saying Marilyn was an orphan, discovered when babysitting for a Fox executive. It was pure fantasy, but she went along with it. She would go into Twentieth Century

Fox each day at 8 a.m. for lessons; pantomime and dance three times a week, as well as acting, music and speech. She posed for publicity photos; sometimes took part in crowd scenes – in a parade or at a banquet – but mostly she would hang around the studio and learn fast.

Alan Young, the British-born comic actor, was organizing a few girls to sit on a float in the Hollywood Christmas parade, and Marilyn (then still calling herself Norma Jeane) was one of the four or five girls selected by Ben Lyon to sit on the float. Young remembers:

'After the parade, we went to the Brown Derby for drinks, but I didn't drink, and neither did Norma Jeane, so we decided instead to go and get some cocoa. I asked if she would like to go to a party with me, which was taking place several weeks later, and she said yes. She seemed like a frightened rabbit at first, and I didn't realize she had been raised without parents. I really liked her.'

The couple only went on a couple of dates; the first to a friend's party:

'I went to pick her up from Aunt Ana's house and Ana looked at me with great suspicion, as I was taking out her 'daughter' and was a little older than Norma Jeane, but she let her go anyway. I had seen a photo of a church in Ana's house, and Norma Jeane told me it was the Christian Science church and that she used to go to Sunday School there and loved it. We spoke a lot about it in the car.

On the way to the party we got lost and I realized that I'd have to go home and get directions. Norma Jeane looked at me very suspiciously, and when we pulled up outside the house, she refused to go in with me. I assured her that my parents would be there, so she did go in, and it was all very friendly. Of course my parents thought it was a serious thing because I'd brought a girl home! My mother was a Christian Scientist too, so they both had lots to talk about.'

That date was a success, after which Marilyn appeared in several publicity photos with Young. However, the second date wasn't so successful: 'Well, I thought I'd better kiss her goodnight,' Young recalled, 'because I didn't want her to think I was square. I went to kiss her cheek, and she turned her head so I got her ear instead. I was so embarrassed about it that I never phoned her again.'

That was the end of their short relationship; they didn't meet again for years until:

With actor Alan Young, whom she met after signing with Twentieth Century Fox in 1946

'I was working at the studio and was sitting in make-up, when a blonde girl rushed up and yelled, 'Alan!' She kissed me and asked about my parents and asked me to give her a call. After she had gone, the make-up man asked how long I'd known Marilyn Monroe and I answered, 'About two minutes!' That was the last time I ever saw her.'

In those early days, long before her later success, she'd return home from the studio and practise under her mother's critical eye – a somewhat thankless task as Gladys didn't approve of her daughter's desire to act. Berniece (who visited in late summer 1946) tried to get her to be more positive, but all she'd say was, 'I don't like her

Marilyn's half-sister Berniece Baker Miracle

business'. Later that year, when Berniece returned home, and Gladys moved back to Oregon, it was time for Marilyn to move too. Her divorce had been granted in Las Vegas on 13 September; in defence of her charge of mental cruelty against James Dougherty, she'd said: 'My husband didn't support me, and he objected to my working, criticized me for it, and he also had a bad temper and would fly into rages, and he left me on three different occasions, and he criticized me and embarrassed me in front of my friends, and he didn't try to make a home for me.'

Marilyn found a small apartment at 3539 Kelton Avenue, embracing the chance to live alone for the first time. She started to frequent Schwabs drug store, a café and hang-out for budding actors. She made some new friends, among them screen, vaudeville and stage actress Shelley Winters and reporter Sidney Skolsky (who had an office at Schwabs and remained a staunch and life-long supporter). A young Charles Chaplin Jnr was also part of her circle, someone with whom she may have had a brief, though unsubstantiated, liaison. She also indulged her interest in books – on everything from acting to literature to psychology – frequenting bookshops like Pickwick Books, Martindales Book Store and Marian Hunter's Book Shop.

She continued her trips to the Fox studio but was growing ever disheartened. Head of studio Darryl F. Zanuck seemed in no hurry to use her. None the less, in February 1947 her contract was extended, and to her great relief roles in two films, quickly followed. She had an uncredited part in two scenes in *Scudda Hoo, Scudda Hay*, although one ended up on the cutting-room floor, and only a trained eye could spot her in the other. Of her speaking part as a waitress in *Dangerous Years* she wrote in a letter to her sister: 'for heaven's sake don't blink your eyes, you might miss me'.

On 15 April, Marilyn attended the Annual Ceremony and Presentation of

Honorary Colonels at the Hollywood Legion Stadium, where she received a badge of honour along with seventeen other Studio Starlings. The event didn't do much for her career and is just one example of the work she found herself doing when her only real concern was to become a good actress. With that in mind, she and Shelley Winters started to attend lessons at the Actors Lab, run by Morris Carnovsky and his wife Phoebe Brand at 14355 Laurel Ave. Winters also suggested they attend classes by actor Charles Laughton at his home on Curson Avenue. But, just starting out and not classically trained, Marilyn felt intimidated by her other classmates and the intensity of the classes. She left only after only a few sessions but she did, however, continue attending the Actors Lab.

Marilyn's belief in the Actors Lab was so strong that she tried to persuade Bill Pursel to join. But, Pursel had returned to Las Vegas and the two met that summer when she went to Vegas for a show at the Flamingo Hotel:

> 'Norma Jeane [as he continues to call Marilyn] asked me to meet her there, but when I arrived I wasn't allowed in. The curtains were pulled across the door and when I told the security man that there was a girl in there I was meeting, he said, 'Oh, sure there is'. However, he parted the curtains and I could see some dance girls on stage. Norma Jeane's group was seated right in the centre of the room, flanking a long table just below the stage, and she spotted me and yelled and waved. I was very embarrassed, especially when I entered the showroom and the spotlights went right on me! She had saved me a seat and when I made my way to her, we hugged one another and everyone cheered.'

When the show had finished, Marilyn and Bill went outside to the pool for a quiet moment together. After ten minutes or so one of the men from Marilyn's group came out and demanded she go back in; he was: 'Very aggressive and I confronted him by threatening to throw him in the pool', Bill recalled. Not wanting to cause trouble and for the sake of group solidarity, they complied. Marilyn joined the other starlets while Bill sat at the bar with David Niven and Sonny Tufts, leaving shortly afterwards as he had to get up for work the next day.

The next day, according to Pursel's sister, Jeanne Chretien: 'Bill told me they were trying to boss Norma Jeane around and I was appalled. I said: "That's awful, she's such a sweet girl", to which Bill replied: "No one's going to treat her like a tramp while I'm around." '

· · · · ·

On 20 July, Marilyn appeared, inconsequentially, at the Brentwood Country Club for Fox's Annual Golf Tournament. Another tournament on 17 August, at which she was assigned as caddy to actor John Carroll and his wife, MGM talent scout Lucille Ryman, proved vital. When, subsequently, the Carrolls befriended her, their support couldn't have come at a better time. On 11 June Marilyn's agreement with Twentieth Century Fox had been reconfirmed, but Harry Lipton had the unenviable task of telling her that Fox wanted to drop her, which they did on 25 August. 'Her immediate reaction was the world had crashed around her ears – unhappiness and tears. And then typical of Marilyn she shook her head, set her jaw and said: "It really doesn't matter. After all, it's a case of supply and demand."'

Marilyn had been rehearsing for the Twentieth Century Fox annual show, held on the Fox lot. Despite her departure, she was determined to go through with it, as actress Kathleen Hughes Rubin remembered:

> 'The show was made up 90 per cent from secretaries, mailroom people etc., but there were always a few contract players too. My cousin was in the show and had told me all about Marilyn, saying that she was incredibly talented but had just been dropped. She was sure that if the executives saw the show, they would re-sign her.
>
> Marilyn sang 'I never took a lesson in my life' and wore a sexy dress. I can still remember what it looked like! She sang and danced a little – the song was a double entendre, and she did it wonderfully. Actually it was supposed to have been performed by my cousin, but it was taken from her just days before the show, and given to Marilyn. Fox did these shows every year, sometimes putting on a play and other times a variety show. This year it was a variety show but although Marilyn was wonderful, the executives didn't re-sign her.'

Dropped by Fox, Marilyn's income plummeted, and she often had no money for food or rent. Her finances were complicated by a hire-purchase commitment, taken out when she first signed to Fox, to purchase a record player. It was 'splendiferous', as she recalled and custom made at $1500; it did everything but fry an egg. Harry Lipton had considered that she 'was out of her mind' to take it on, and, according to him, helped out with several payments. When finally she couldn't scrape the money together, someone arrived to repossess it, as she later recalled: 'I was almost heartbroken as I watched him carry it away.' Although she claimed to have learnt from the experience, this wasn't the last time she would find herself in financial difficulties. Friends began to worry that she had no idea about money.

Marilyn's days of unemployment were long and filled with insecurities. Sometimes she just moped around her tiny apartment. Other times she would read and keep herself busy, studying at the Actors Lab, taking singing lessons, involving herself with occasional modelling work and neglecting a social life in favour of her career. Her friendships started to suffer, and Bill Pursel, who, although living in Nevada as a university freshman, remained in close touch via frequent phone calls, remembers at least one occasion when their plans had to be cancelled: 'Marilyn was going to come up to the University of Nevada for a dance, but she was too busy … She was very unhappy about this, but it just wasn't possible with all that she was doing with her career at the time.'

But sometimes work took a back seat; at the racetrack with Shelley Winters, 'people-watching' at Union Station or star-gazing in Hollywood. Johnny Grant, Hollywood's honorary mayor and friend, the man always pictured when actors got their star on Hollywood Boulevard, remembered how:

> 'She used to like to sit in the Roosevelt Hotel lobby, observing people and would occasionally make new friends. She had a mad crush on Clark Gable and would stand in front of his house, hoping to see him come or go. She would also often place her hands and feet in the moulds of other stars at Grauman's Chinese Theatre.'

At this time rumour has it that Marilyn was so strapped for cash that she became a call-girl, fell pregnant and gave the child up for adoption. However, it seems unlikely that the woman who constantly complained of being pestered by 'wolves' would ever sell herself like that. Bill Pursel laughs at both theories:

> 'Wow! … As far as I know this is a bunch of poppycock. I do know there were several women jealous of her after she became Marilyn Monroe. Besides, call-girls earn big money – I saw no evidence of this with her. I would put no credence at all in these rumours … someone's cheap imagination. It sorta makes me angry … She wasn't pregnant when I knew her; she probably had several boyfriends over the years, but when these stories exaggerate the involvement into pregnancy or even intimacy they are way out of bounds. She had too much class to be so careless about who she dated. At least this is where I come from.'

Harry Lipton echoes this sentiment in an article for *Motion Picture* in May 1956, in which he described an incident at a party where a high-powered man offered Marilyn gifts in exchange for favours; turning to Lipton, she demanded they leave and cried on the way home. 'What can I say to men like that, Harry?' she asked, to which he replied: 'You'll learn' – hardly the behaviour of a seasoned call-girl, and a hungry one at that.

Because of her financial difficulties, Marilyn was constantly on the move. While living on Avon Street she was the victim of an attempted break-in, the consequence of which was the arrival of a newspaper photographer. The unwanted press

Avon Street, today, where
Marilyn was disturbed by an
intruder

attention, and the ongoing trauma of the attempted intruder, led her to contact Lucille Ryman and John Carroll, to whose El Palaccio Apartment at 8497 Fountain Avenue she escaped (and from whom she, under the name Journey Evers, had taken a series of loans from September 1947).

'It was just wonderful,' remembered Marilyn in 1952. 'It was the first nice place I'd ever had, and I felt really independent and sure that something good was going to happen to me.' But she still had trouble forgetting the intruder incident and Harry Lipton recalled that she was afraid to live alone (Ryman and Carroll had decamped to their ranch in the Valley). As a result, she would often spend nights at the Ryman-Carroll ranch. Out of it all, though, what had hurt her most was the fact that after the break-in her neighbours had refused to get involved when she had asked them for help. According to Lipton, this revived disturbing memories of her insecure childhood.

Life began to look up professionally, though, when Marilyn landed a part in *Glamour Preferred* at the Bliss Hayden Theater. The play ran from 12 October to 2 November, with Marilyn alternating her part with another actress. It would seem she played Lady Bonnie Towyn (described as 'blonde, smartly dressed, and beautiful in a rather obvious way'), a starlet who tried to steal the lead's husband. Originally performed in New York in 1940, the play wasn't particularly thrilling, but it did give Marilyn a chance to work in the theatre; although terrified, she shone in the part, prompting one of her co-stars to comment that when she walked on stage, no one else got a look in.

By December, Marilyn had moved out of the Carrolls' home and into 4215 Rowland Street, Burbank. However, they were all still very much involved especially as Marilyn had signed an agreement for them to manage her career for three months from 1 December 1947 to 29 February 1948, at $100 a week. In exchange they would take any acting earnings, minus Harry Lipton's 10 per cent. The Carrolls were to introduce Marilyn to people of influence, initially businessman Pat De Cicco then, via De Cicco, 69-year-old Joseph Schenck, a big player at Fox. Schenck found Marilyn dazzling, and she began spending time at his 141 South Carolwood Drive home – little more than a sexual plaything for the ageing mogul, according to some. However, Marilyn always publicly denied this; they were just friends, she said, and his cook served food too good to resist. She later told the distinguished stage and screen director Elia Kazan that Schenck had asked her to marry him, wanting her to be taken care of whatever happened to him.

When interviewed by Ezra Goodman in the mid-1950s, Schenck himself said:

'She used to come here quite often for dinner. I think she liked to eat. We have good food here. No, I never had any romantic thoughts about Marilyn and she never had any such thoughts about me.'

141 South Carolwood Drive, where Marilyn visited ageing movie mogul Joseph Schenck

Although she never asked him for career favours, Schenck persuaded Columbia Pictures boss Harry Cohn to take a look at her screen test. Although widely believed that it was this introduction that got Marilyn her contract at Columbia, in her article on 'The private life of Marilyn Monroe' drama coach Natasha Lytess tells a rather different story. Lytess says Max Arnow from the Columbia talent department had asked her to take a look at Marilyn. He didn't think much of her and wanted a second opinion – and she wasn't sure either: 'The first time I met Marilyn Monroe, I thought to myself, That voice! My ears couldn't take it. Her manner was also almost apologetic and plainly revealed a "I know I'm not good enough, but I'll try" attitude.'

However, something about the girl impressed her enough to want to work with her for a couple of weeks; Marilyn paid for the lessons. When Arnow called to complain that she was 'spending a lot of time with her. Too much. I suggest you drop her,' Natasha instead helped her refine an audition piece from *They Knew What They Wanted*. It was this piece that impressed Columbia enough to sign Marilyn for a six-month, $125-a-week contract on 9 March 1948. Marilyn made it clear to Natasha that for the first time in her life she would have the security to do anything she wanted; work at her acting and not have to worry about rent or food. 'The Columbia contract was different,' Marilyn later wrote. 'I was sure that my big opportunity had come.'

It was a big opportunity clouded by the death of Aunt Ana: 'I was left without anyone to take my hopes and my troubles to. I was miserable,' Marilyn said. Ana had shown her unconditional love and encouraged her through thick and thin. Among other things, Ana left her a book entitled *The Potter*, with a note on the title page that read: 'Marilyn dear, read this book. I don't leave you much except my love. But not even death can diminish that, nor will death ever take me far away from you.'

· · · · ·

Marilyn kicked off at Columbia in a low-budget musical *Ladies of the Chorus*; shooting began on 22 April through to 3 May. She played Peggy Martin opposite Adele Jergens, nine years her senior, playing her mother. Marilyn later admitted to hating the film though it gave her the chance to sing and dance and expand her repertoire. She had assured the producer she could dance but having told Harry Lipton she was worried

Hollywood Studio Club, 1215 Lodi
Place, where she lived in 1948

about her dance skills she began 8 am dance classes that
continued all day till 10 pm.

She also had two songs to perform, 'Every Baby
needs a Da-Da Daddy' and 'Anyone Can See I Love You',
under the guidance of musical supervisor Fred Karger at
Columbia. In his early 30s and recently divorced, Karger
was living with his mother, sister and child and in no
mood for a serious relationship, but this did not stop a
mutual attraction developing. On 3 June 1948, Marilyn
moved into a double room at the Hollywood Studio Club, where she paid $12
for room and board, in a building located at 1215 Lodi Place, in the heart of
Hollywood. It was built in 1926 to help women who worked in the industry.
Karger helped her move into the room she was to share with opera student
Clarice Evans; Marilyn was not overly impressed. It reminded her of the
orphanage with its rules and regulations – no smoking in the lobby, no shorts in
the dining room and no men on the upper floors. She decided to keep herself to

Lobby of the Hollywood Studio
Club, hardly changed since Norma
Jeane's era

herself, with a reputation for never joining in any of the
gossip or small talk. Still, Evans later told biographer
Maurice Zolotow that she went on more dates than any of
the other girls, and received more phone calls too,
despite her on-going affair with Karger.

Marilyn's mind was very much on her career. On 15
August she opened in *Stage Door* at the Bliss-Hayden Theater.
The play by Edna Ferber and George S. Kaufman centres on
young actresses sharing rooms in a boarding house. The
main character Terry is trying to make it in the theatre and
ends up not only with her dream role but also resolved
never to share a bedroom again. Marilyn's part in the play is not known, but its story
must have resonated with her. Perhaps it is no coincidence that she soon took a room
of her own at the Hollywood Studio Club for $16.50 per week.

That September Bill Pursel found himself in Los Angeles again, when he
enrolled to study advertising at Woodbury College:

> *'I suppose it would be somewhat correct to say our relationship had a lot to do with my
> moving to Los Angeles after my freshman year in Reno. However, the University of Nevada
> didn't have the business courses I was after, so moving to a business college like Woodbury,
> was what I wanted. Also, it gave me an opportunity to play baseball and to see Norma Jeane
> more often.'*

Despite her involvement with Fred Karger, Norma Jeane hung out with Pursel, lunching in the Columbia commissary and enjoying each other's company, as Pursel described:

> 'We didn't have a favourite place to go ... just stop on the spur of the moment at a place that looked quiet and secluded. She was rather close mouthed about her personal life; she didn't talk about her foster-home experience, nor her ex-husband Jim Dougherty. She did talk about what happened in her modelling career some or where she had been on certain shoots. But, most of our conversation was quiet and private like, and then there was the notes on restaurant and bar napkins – I sure wish I had those – we wrote back and forth about the kind of house she – we – wanted, the number of children, the type of dog, and all sorts of other stuff including little games back and forth.'

They also attended the popular Palladium dance hall in Hollywood. Marilyn made quite an impression that night, says Pursel: 'As the two of us danced close to the stage, Woody Herman [who was playing that night] was looking at Norma Jeane and almost fell off the stage! She didn't see ... her back was to the stage, but the oohs of the packed crowd got her attention. We laughed about this later.'

Perhaps one of the most interesting things about her friendship with Pursel was the sense of her being relaxed and interested; her times with him enjoyable and carefree:

> 'She would always ask me about my studies at college and about my baseball playing and stuff like that. She never dressed up for me, this is one of the things I liked about her. She was very beautiful with little make-up and her hair pulled back with a ribbon. We played on the Santa Monica beach and romped in the surf with a big beach ball. On one occasion, she had just rubbed some oil on to my back and then asked, 'Are you hungry?' I said I was and gave her $5 to go and get cokes and hot dogs. She came back with her arms full! She was well aware of her attractiveness, but she didn't flirt, and her appearance was always one of class. When we were together she was with me and when she talked to me (sometimes it was just a whisper) she looked me squarely in the eyes.'

With Pursel, Marilyn shared her dreams, and in return he gave her the friendly support she very much needed:

> 'Norma Jeane was determined to become an actress, and she studied hard to make it happen. I kept encouraging her to keep reaching for the stars, which she did, and she made it to the big time even though she tragically crash-landed. It has always bothered

me because she didn't make it to the little white house with the picket fence, three kids and a dog.'

Marilyn needed all the support she could get in her attempt to reach for the stars, because there were times when they seemed especially distant. Although the rushes of *Ladies of the Chorus* had been well received, she attended a meeting at the studio hoping for a new role in a big production only to be told that, though they rated her, they had no work for her. On 8 September, Columbia dropped her. Later, she was able to look back and admit that she hadn't been ready for a career at that time, but that September the news came as a crushing blow.

She went back to modelling, posing for advertising spreads for bikinis and doing the odd cheesecake shot, but it was not enough to make ends meet. When she had signed to Columbia, she had bought $200-worth of clothes on credit: two suits, a black dress, shoes and hosiery. However, with her contract expired, and the clothes shop demanding payment, something had to give and she almost lost her car, on which she relied on to get her to auditions. 'Once again I had to scratch enough together to bail it out.'

Marilyn had finished in *Stage Door* on 12 September and on the 21st was en route to an audition when she was involved in a minor car crash on Sunset Boulevard. Photographer Tom Kelley happened to be driving down Sunset at the time and stopped to help. A tearful Marilyn explained that she was late for her appointment with no money for a cab, so Kelley gave her $5 and his business card. There was another chance encounter that autumn that proved portentous. Marilyn went on a few dates with editor Dan Cahn, whose friend Stanley Rubin had a TV series in development. Rubin had made a successful 30-minute pilot, and by the autumn the American Tobacco Company had commissioned 26 episodes for him to adapt, cast and produce. Rubin had shared his news with Dan Cahn, who told him about the beautiful, talented, young actress he was dating who was in need of a job. Rubin remembers:

> *'Dan asked if she could be used in the show, and I told him to get Marilyn or her agent to call and make an appointment to come in and read. Her agent ... brought her into the office. She looked at the script for twenty or thirty minutes then said she was ready to read. She was pleasant and beautiful; she read for me, I thanked her and she left.'*

Rubin liked Marilyn but was concerned that her inexperience and nervousness might hold up shooting. He'd think about using her another time. When the two finally did work together some six years later on *River of No Return*, she never held his initial rejection of her against him. 'She was gracious enough never to mention the failed audition for the TV series,' chuckled Rubin.

For the moment, though there was nothing new on the horizon, *Ladies of the Chorus* went on release. It received little attention from audiences or critics although one person did take an interest; James Dougherty, as his nephew, Paul Kanteman, reports:

> 'Uncle Jim had just come out of the police academy when her first picture came out and he was walking the night-time beat on Van Nuys Blvd. Just about every time he passed the movie theatre he would go in and watch a bit of the movie and continued to do this for awhile. I would imagine he saw most of her pictures even though he would never tell anyone. We used to talk about these times when travelling to a place where we were going to hunt. He would open up to me but not to anyone else that I am aware of.'

By the end of 1948 any serious romance with Fred Karger had fizzled out. Embittered after his divorce, Marilyn often felt he put her down. The relationship wasn't working, but as Marilyn looked towards the New Year, a new man would enter her life in William Morris Agency vice-president and agent, Johnny Hyde. The moment Hyde laid eyes on Marilyn he was smitten.

The already married Hyde was 53 years old (to Marilyn's 22), a small, slightly built man with a heart condition and one of the most influential players at the agency. The fact that he didn't know where she lived didn't stop him somehow bombarding her with letters, gifts and cards. 'All is forgiven because you say you miss me', he wrote in one letter; addressing her as 'My Precious Girl' on a card while in public she was 'Baby'.

He began to encourage her to continue her acting career and made plans for her to leave Harry Lipton and sign with William Morris, as she later remembered: 'When I first mentioned my acting hopes to Johnny Hyde, he didn't smile. He listened raptly and said: "Of course you can become an actress!" He was the first person who ever took my ambitions seriously and my gratitude for this alone is endless.'

Actually he wasn't, but Marilyn was so grateful to him that she was willing to give him full credit. In return Hyde introduced Marilyn to a great deal of literature and classical music, and taught her how best to manage her time. Usually when out of work, Marilyn would sleep late, enjoy a long breakfast and while away the hours on the phone, but Hyde encouraged her to study and use every spare moment to better herself. As a result, she became more confident, started speaking up for herself and even improved her punctuality. Introducing her to a dramatic script of *The Brothers Karamazov*, he encouraged Marilyn to aim higher and take herself seriously; as a result, he became an inspiration, a father figure, protector and eventually her lover. Johnny Grant remembered him as 'a short little fellow' and how 'he really broke his ass on her behalf. I used to see them together at Ciros quite a bit – she was truly fond of him.'

On 29 February 1949 Marilyn's contract with Ryman-Carroll came to an end. According to Lucille Ryman, Marilyn had become a nuisance, repeatedly calling them at work. 'Under Marilyn's baby-doll, kitten exterior, she is tough and shrewd and calculating,' she claimed in an interview in the mid-1950s. When the relationship soured, Ryman claimed Marilyn had attempted to seduce Carroll and subsequently asked her to divorce him. This may all be true, but if so why did the couple stay on friendly terms with Marilyn, especially Ryman, knowing of her underlying interest?

On 2 March, thanks to Johnny Hyde, Marilyn signed with the William Morris Agency. On the 13th, she left the Hollywood Studio Club and moved into a one-bedroom suite at the Beverly Carlton Hotel, complete with kitchenette and space for her books. Hyde had left his family and moved into 718 North Palm Drive. He installed booths and a dance floor in the dining room, in emulation of Romanoffs, Marilyn's favourite Hollywood restaurant. She spent many nights in the house – more than at the Beverly Carlton – but never moved in. By keeping her hotel room, or having an address courtesy of her drama coach Natasha Lytess, she was assured not only independence but also respectability. But just living part-time with Marilyn was not enough for Hyde. He constantly begged her to marry him, emphasizing that if he were to die, as his wife, she would inherit everything. But, Marilyn would only marry for love, and although she did care, she was still seeing other men.

Hyde was in love with Marilyn, but he wasn't averse to making arrangements for her to see Dr Michael Gurdin, a plastic surgeon who inserted a prosthesis into her jaw to soften her profile. The resulting slight scars are reputedly visible in a photo on page 75 of James Haspiel's *Marilyn: The Ultimate Look at the Legend*. Although the rumour mill churned out nose surgery too, medical notes acquired by Haspiel show this to be untrue.

In April 1949, photographer Philippe Halsman was assigned to write a story for *Life* magazine on the acting merits of eight Hollywood Starlets. The starlets were found by editor Gene Cook, and Halsman photographed them in his room at the Beverly Hills Hotel, asking each girl to act out four basic situations: listening to a good joke, enjoying an invisible, delicious drink, being frightened by a monster, and kissing a fabulous lover. When Marilyn walked into the room Halsman was unimpressed by a painfully shy, rather wooden girl. But when it came to kissing part, his opinion changed. He wanted to encourage her to move to New York to continue her acting career. She didn't go: 'but I was thrilled by his encouragement'.

She might have been tempted because at this time money was extremely tight: she had fallen behind with not only her rent but also payments on her car. But the chance to up her income came via photographer Tom Kelley who'd been asking her to pose nude for him several months. Threatened with the repossession of her car, she called his number and on 27 May arrived at Kelley's studio at 736 North Seward Avenue, to pose nude for a calendar distributed by John Baumgarth. To add a touch of respectability to the proceedings, Marilyn requested that Kelley's partner Natalie Grasko be in attendance. She explained that she had agreed to pose nude because she was flat broke and felt a debt of gratitude to him for his kindness to her, a complete stranger, on the day her car broke down.

'Begin the Beguine' played on the turntable as Marilyn reclined on a red-velvet blanket; she was paid $50 for her efforts. Years later she described the experience as, 'Very simple … And drafty!', and although the photos are tame compared to modern standards, she was so anxious not to be recognized that she signed the release 'Mona Monroe'.

• • • • •

Early in 1949, Hyde found a part for Marilyn in the Marx Brothers comedy *Love Happy*, alongside Groucho in a small but memorable role as a woman who requires detective Groucho's help, because: 'Men keep following me.' The detective rolls his eyes, shrugs and exclaims: 'Really? I can't understand why.'

It was a cameo appearance, but an important role that took her on a publicity tour that summer, starting in New York. The tour was an important step for Marilyn, though: 'I was on screen less than sixty seconds, but I got five weeks work … going on the PA tour, which promoted the film in eight major cities. I felt guilty about appearing on the stage when I had such an insignificant role in the film, but the people in the audiences didn't seem to care.'

Marilyn took with her nothing but winter clothes, believing the East Coast was always cold. The warm clothes came in useful for publicity shots (when she was photographed cooling off with an ice-cream), but she quickly assembled a summer wardrobe. On 21 June, she travelled to Warrensburg, New York, to present keys to the winner of a *Photoplay* competition to win a dream house. A crowd of some 500 local people turned up to watch Marilyn together with actors Don DeFore, Donald Buka and Lon McAllister make the presentation. It was good exposure for a budding actress, and the results appeared in November 1949's *Photoplay*.

Andre De Dienes happened to be in New York at the same time, and he took Marilyn to Long Island for a bathing-costume photo session on the beach.

Publicity-wise, she also did an interview with columnist Earl Wilson that appeared in his column for 27 July 1949. Nicknamed the 'Mmm Girl' by cinema-goers to *Love Happy*, the interview was mostly taken up with discussing this, plus minor details about the film and her early life. Wilson was not overly impressed and dismissive of what he saw of her publicists' speak – something for which he would later apologize.

The tour proved tiring – film-screening and publicity appearances, autograph-signings and constant photos. By Chicago, Marilyn was exhausted, physically and mentally, and had taken to wearing a slave bracelet on her ankle. 'I wore it because I didn't belong to anyone although I longed to.' She had had enough of the loneliness of being on the road and wanted desperately to go home. Bill Pursel received a disturbing phone call from her:

> 'Norma Jeane called from Chicago; she was crying ... threatening to throw acid into her face to put a stop to the constant picture taking of her. She had no privacy, and some of the photographers were rude and demanding, as though she owed them something. I tried to console her, and even though she owed them nothing, I told her it was part of the game. I asked her to immediately contact her agent to intercede and call off the wolves or she was going to fire him immediately.
>
> I told her to tell her agent she was not a piece of meat and even though she understood the photo shoots were important to her career, and she tried to be congenial and co-operative, there comes a time when she deserves some space, and this was the time. I offered to fly to Chicago, but she said it wasn't necessary 'cos she would be home in a few days. She finally stopped crying and settled down.'

Pursel's sister, Jeanne Chretien, remembers: 'When Norma Jeane rang from Chicago, she was very upset ... wanted Bill to go to see her.'

When Marilyn arrived in Los Angeles a few days later, she called Bill and: 'We spent a very quiet evening together, and all was normal. She was starting to have some second thoughts about following a movie career – she wanted to be an actress, not a sex object. We discussed schooling and training, and the difficulty involved and how only a few beautiful girls become stars.'

Pursel later reflected on why she would be so upset with the constant attention:

> 'Norma Jeane was a very attractive female who could draw men like flies. She was constantly being pursued, and she had an engaging personality – she was kind and gentle. So, when beauty and kindness are wrapped in a glamorous package like her, things can be explosive on the outside, but underneath this sparkle there was a profound softness and glow.'

Ex-husband Jim Dougherty, by now happily remarried and working as a policeman, also received a call, as his nephew Paul 'Wes' Kanteman recalls: 'She had become rather disenchanted with the whole Hollywood thing and called uncle and asked if she could come home. He was or could be pretty stubborn and told her no; that she had already made her bed and would have to sleep in it. She was pretty upset and hung up.'

For Jim, this must have been a difficult phone call, but his heart had been broken once, and now remarried, he was not willing or indeed able to react in any other way. Paul Kanteman knows just how much this must have hurt his uncle:

'He really loved that woman, and in my mind did till the day he passed away. I watched him many times and saw the tears come to his eyes. Yes, there was a great love there, and I still believe it was mutual. It was a love that had gotten past both of them, and they had gone in other directions and could do nothing about it.'

5

LEARNING TO FLY

Marilyn and Jim had gone their separate ways for ever, but Marilyn's career wobble was only temporary. Although she had briefly flirted with giving up acting, she was soon back on set – in Twentieth Century Fox's *Ticket to Tomahawk*. The movie, in which she played Clara, a showgirl in a troop, starred Dan Dailey and Anne Baxter, and she was to join Dailey in a rendition of 'Oh, What a Forward Young Man You Are'. Actress Kathleen Hughes Rubin had been up for the part but:

> *'Unfortunately, I couldn't dance and even after spending all day with a dance instructor, I couldn't remember a simple time step …*
>
> *The studio then called for Marilyn because they knew she could dance. Although the film was mostly shot on location, one scene was a dance scene on the Fox lot. I went to see the shoot and thought Marilyn was terrific in it. Between takes Marilyn, Dan Dailey and the others would come and sit in a circle to chat; she was very nice during that time, and I really liked her a lot.'*

Marilyn's wasn't an important role, but it did give a first taste of location work. The local newspapers in Silverton, Colorado, were buzzing, and by mid-August the town's Empire Street had been returned to the early 1900s. The filming, which took place around Silverton, Molas Lake and Rockwood, went on for a month or so, though it is likely that Marilyn did not stay permanently on location, as her part was small.

Shortly after shooting *Ticket to Tomahawk*, Marilyn changed her look, cutting her hair into a shoulder-length bob in a whole new image and sophistication that was missing from the girl-next-door look of long, wavy hair. Johnny Hyde was continuing to escort her around town, showing her off and making sure she rubbed shoulders with influential people. According to A. C. Lyles, who worked at

Paramount Studios, and with whom Marilyn had become friendly around this time:

> 'It was very obvious he was extremely fond of Marilyn and wanted to do everything in his capacity as a highly respected agent to advise Marilyn's career. She was extremely fond of Johnny. Her friends also liked him and were grateful for his friendship with Marilyn. I don't know if he ever asked Marilyn to marry him. We all loved Johnny and I'm sure that included Marilyn.'

Lyles had first met Marilyn when:

> 'I was in St Louis opening a picture for Paramount when I read Erskine Johnson's column, in which he listed some young actors and actresses who[m] he thought had a chance to make good. One was Marilyn Monroe. At that time, I didn't know Marilyn. I sent the column to her care of the Screen Actors Guild. When I returned, there was a message at the studio for me to call her. She came to the studio to have lunch with me and that was the start of our friendship. My first impressions were the same as Erskine's. She was most attractive, a saucy personality, and had all the qualities to be successful given opportunities. After that, we had lunches in the Paramount commissary, went to see movies at Grauman's Chinese Theatre, and sometimes dinners at the Brown Derby.'

Marilyn's first job after her image change came towards the end of 1949 in the John Huston movie *The Asphalt Jungle*. On 28 October, major Hollywood columnist Louella Parsons reported that Marilyn had called her with great excitement to tell her about her part. During the call she lavished thanks on Joseph Schenck, 'who gave me my first job in the movies', Johnny Hyde for signing her and John Huston for accepting her. 'I am just grateful to everyone,' sighed the woman described by Parsons as 'one of the sweetest girls I know'. This was a far cry from the desperately unhappy girl who had phoned Bill Pursel and James Dougherty just a few months earlier; for once she was enjoying her success and making the most of her new-found popularity.

Extremely nervous but determined, Marilyn had rehearsed with Natasha Lytess for three days for the audition with Huston. She performed it seated on the floor, and afterwards begged the director to let her do it again – unnecessarily, as Huston was impressed enough to hire her anyway, for what was the most important part of her career so far. Natasha Lytess was a constant presence on *The Asphalt Jungle* set, even giving up her job at Columbia to give 100 per cent. Marilyn relied on her totally. This was a potential nightmare scenario for Huston, as Marilyn looked to her, not him, for guidance. In one scene, she can be seen glancing off set to check out her performance with her coach. But whatever it was she did, she did it right;

when *The Asphalt Jungle* was released on 23 May 1950, both the film and Marilyn gained favourable reviews.

By this time, Twentieth Century Fox were warming again to Marilyn, and on 5 January 1950 she began work on their production of *The Fireball*. In April she

On the set of *All About Eve* with
co-star Anne Baxter

had a small but pivotal role in *All About Eve* (also Twentieth Century Fox), a vehicle for film legend Bette Davis (with co-stars Anne Baxter, George Sanders and Celeste Holm). It was Marilyn's first appearance with such a stellar cast, doubtless daunting, though she managed to hold her own. On set she made few friends; her constant lateness delaying the shoot. Celeste Holm recalled fellow actor Gregory Ratoff declare: 'That girl will be a big star!, to which Holm retorted: 'Why, because she keeps everyone waiting?' To which Ratoff said: 'No. She has a quality.'

But Zsa Zsa Gabor, George Sander's wife, saw no such thing in her after rumours that Marilyn was having an affair with her husband.

Marilyn probably didn't spend much time worrying about set gossip. She was still so very much in demand. On 17 May, Earl Leaf travelled to North Palm Drive to take her photo in Hyde's garden as she played with her new chihuahua, Josefa. A screen test for a gangster film, *Cold Shoulder*, got her the lead opposite Richard Conte and Victor Mature, though studio boss Darryl Zanuck had the movie shelved. She was attracting journalistic attention from Sheila Graham among others; Louella Parsons even compared her to Lana Turner, a flattering comparison that Marilyn dismissed: 'I think I have a personality all of my own.' But during the summer, when it was reported that Twentieth Century Fox had bought the rights to Anita Loos's *Gentlemen Prefer Blondes*, prophetically, Parsons wrote in her column on 2 September that they should consider Marilyn for the part of Lorelei Lee.

For the moment she was stuck with small roles; in *Right Cross* and *Hometown Story* plus a TV commercial for Royal Triton Gasoline. Her perseverance paid off via frequent mentions in the gossip columns, with Sheila Graham reporting on 12 October that she had been seen at the beach with British light and leading man Peter Lawford. But while publicly attached to Lawford, in private she was still close to Bill Pursel, although by that summer, their relationship had begun to cool. One of their last dates was at a drive-in movie:

'It was a double feature and Norma Jeane had been on a photo shoot at Catalina Island all day. We were as close to being in love that night as we ever were; she laid her head in my lap and went to sleep, and I could feel the warmth and closeness. Later, while we dined (it

was late at night), I looked into her eyes and told her I might be falling in love. She smiled and said, 'That's my line, even though you said it first'. We kissed across the table; the waiter appeared and asked us if we would like to order some dessert, and we laughed.'

Despite their closeness, when Bill graduated from college that summer, they both knew there was no future for them: 'The problem was that neither of us could afford to stand in the way of the other's progress, so we moved apart. I could not be a man and keep chasing her all over the country, and I could not stand in her way in her quest to follow her dream. I think we made the right decision.'

The last time Pursel saw Norma Jeane was on the evening before he left Los Angeles.

'I was packed to go home early the next morning; it was around 7.30 pm, and I called her to say bye. She said she had a couple of pictures for me and could I come by in the morning; I said we are leaving at dawn, could I come by now? She said OK! So, I drove to her apartment, and she answered the door with a smiling 'Hi'. She was in a white terrycloth bathrobe, did not invite me in and said, 'I'll be with you in a minute', then disappeared … leaving me standing in the hall. There were two large suitcases just inside the door, and both had the initials RR on them. Norma Jeane came back to the door and asked me if I had a pen; I didn't; she said hers was about out of ink, but she would try to make it write, and she again disappeared for a few moments …When she reappeared she handed me two large photos; I said thank you, she smiled, and said, 'I hope you like them.' We just stood there looking at each other. Finally I said, 'Goodbye', and she responded 'Bye.' I turned walking away feeling like an intruder, which, I guess I was.'

The friendship had been important to both of them, through some high and low times, but they were never to see each other again:

'It was an exciting time of my life — I was settling down after 22 months of war in Europe, I was getting good grades in college, I was maturing, and I had a gorgeous blonde to squire around, but I knew it wasn't going to last, and it didn't. I knew early on that this interlude in our lives wasn't going to last; Norma Jeane was hell bent to make it in Hollywood, and I just kept encouraging her. I had a long way to go in college, and even though she wanted me to go to Actors Lab and pursue an acting career I had other ideas. I knew I had to let her go, but it was a great (and personal) ride while it lasted. I was saddened, but not surprised, when she crashed a few years after we lost contact with one another. There wouldn't be anything to gain to embellish this connection between Norma Jeane and me — it's best to just say we were close and had fun together.'

Pursel heard from Marilyn once more, years later, when she rang to tell him she had met Joe DiMaggio, but by then Bill was married, and she had become a memory – albeit a fond one.

• • • • •

1309 North Harper: Marilyn's home in 1950 with drama coach Natasha Lytess

Marilyn was on the move again, this time to an apartment on North Harper Drive that she shared with Natasha Lytess, Lytess's daughter and cook. It was an arrangement that suited Marilyn, enabling them to work together more often, but not one that was always appreciated by Lytess (particularly when it came to clearing up after Marilyn's dog). In August 1950, Marilyn had taken a vacation with Lytess to Palm Springs, prior to Lytess starting work at Twentieth Century Fox in early September. The end of the month saw a flurry of activity that included signing a release form for a LeGalion perfume campaign.

But tragedy hit early in November, when Johnny Hyde was admitted to hospital, reportedly, with flu, though in fact as a consequence of his worsening heart condition. The press described Marilyn as 'devotion itself to her agent and best beau', a daily visitor at his bedside. Natasha Lytess saw it differently, saying Marilyn was forever late for visits, and once Hyde had even phoned to ask where Marilyn was and complained of her self-centredness.

Marilyn's behaviour might appear callous, but it simply reflected the truth about her feelings for Hyde, whom she liked, maybe even loved, but with whom she wasn't in love. She knew he longed to marry her, but she just couldn't take that step – yet Hyde refused to let it go. Perhaps turning up late at the hospital and other delaying tactics, such as fussing with her hair and make-up for hours, were Marilyn's way of putting off the inevitable marriage conversation. Her friend and lover, stage and screen director Elia Kazan, summed it up when he wrote to her, '[Johnny] made you his when you really didn't love him – which is a terrible thing to do to anyone. You took shelter under his roof like a hurt animal.' Yet, she told Kazan, the more Hyde begged her to be his wife, the less she loved him; indeed she began avoiding him because of his anxiety over their relationship. And still Hyde's infatuation continued. Once when she turned him down yet again, after an initial retreat, he tried a different tack; couldn't she pretend to be his fiancé? The answer was always no.

Nonetheless, it was thanks to Hyde that she was invited for a screen test at Twentieth Century Fox in December and auditioned for a small role in *As Young As You*

Feel, which she got. That paled into insignificance, though, when on 18 December Hyde died from a major heart attack. Marilyn later told reporter Jim Henaghan that Johnny had once told her that if he were to die, she was to hold him in her arms, and he'd come back to life. She was in the corridor outside his room when she heard of his death and claimed to have run to him and held him for half an hour – hardly a likely scenario, given that Hyde's family had already refused her entry into the room. 'They thought I was awful,' she later said. So awful that they ordered her to stay away from North Palm Drive and from his funeral.

On 19 December, Marilyn went shopping for a funeral outfit at I Magnin; that night she stole into the North Palm Drive house, and, according to Elia Kazan, kept vigil till morning beside Hyde's body. During the funeral at the Forest Lawn Memorial Park later that day Marilyn is said to have become so hysterical that she threw herself on to the coffin; rather far-fetched behaviour that was never reported in any newspaper. In fact a dignified silence was more likely, a quiet goodbye to a man she loved, but to whom she had not been able entirely to give herself. Perhaps Hyde's death made Marilyn realize just how deep her feelings had been for him. It appears that way from what she said later to Jim Heneghan: 'Once I was in love with a man. He was old enough to be my father, and people called me a dumb blonde because they didn't understand, and I knew they didn't understand, and I was afraid to talk about it. And then he died.'

Marilyn received nothing from Hyde's will except some bed linen and a few towels – despite accusations of being a gold digger. Just a day or two after the funeral, Lytess returned from work and found a note on her pillow that read, 'I leave my car and my fur stole to Natasha', and another on Marilyn's bedroom door, 'Don't let Barbara [Lytess's daughter] come in.' Marilyn was lying in bed with her cheeks 'puffed out like an adder'. When she didn't respond, Lytess forced open her mouth and discovered a handful of dissolving pills.

What is important to note is that Marilyn did not swallow any of the pills. If it were a suicide attempt, it was half-hearted and more like a cry for help. Marilyn was in a desperate, depressed state, but the evidence makes it unlikely that she was seriously suicidal. Still, she was grateful to Lytess for caring enough to 'save' her, and on Christmas Day 1950 Marilyn presented her with an antique cameo broach, with an accompanying note that said, 'I just want you to know that I owe you *much* more than my life.'

Another person who was to play a key role in Marilyn's life arrived in LA in early January 1951. Playwright Arthur Miller had come to LA with his friend Elia Kazan to drum up interest in Miller's screenplay, *The Hook*, which Kazan planned to direct. Kazan stayed with producer Charles Feldman, soon aware that Feldman and friends Pat De Cicco and Raoul Hakim enjoyed running around town with a few girls. Mention was made of Johnny Hyde's girl, now free, but, unfortunately, still in mourning, something of which Harmon Jones, director of *As Young As You Feel* was only too well aware. He complained to Kazan that Marilyn spent the day crying and hiding out on the adjacent set. Kazan had been a client of Hyde's and had liked him; so when he met Marilyn, moved by her grief, he invited her to dinner. Initially, she refused, though when she did eventually accept it was the start of a friendship; though Kazan was married, they soon became lovers. He was a good listener, just what Marilyn needed, though when she told him that Natasha Lytess was virtually her only friend, he considered the situation unhealthy and urged her to move out and enjoy life on her own.

Charles Feldman was to host a party in honour of Arthur Miller, to which Kazan, not able to go, asked Miller to take Marilyn. They had already met briefly on the set of *As Young as You Feel*. Miller said he'd pick Marilyn up in his car, which surprised her, as she told Kazan, who wrote: 'Why should you be "used" to going to parties in a taxi? ... For Christ's sake you're so much better than the people who throw the parties!'

At the Feldman party and thereafter Marilyn found she enjoyed being with someone who was interested in her opinions; Miller felt himself drawn to Marilyn, despite his marriage and two children. In the days following the party, Kazan, Miller and Marilyn enjoyed some fun together that included Marilyn disguising herself as a temporary office secretary to wind up MGM boss Harry Cohn (who had signed Marilyn in 1948 and had also asked her to travel to Catalina Island with him to which she said no). Whether Cohn actually realized it was a prank, or, indeed, recognized Marilyn, is unclear.

But it wasn't all fun and games. Marilyn had fallen for Miller and didn't attempt to hide her feelings from Kazan – even when they were making love. But Miller was terrified by his feelings for Marilyn and cut short his trip, returning to his wife before he could have any regrets. The two were to keep in touch, writing letters, sharing book lists, but it would be four years before they were to meet again. Kazan left California shortly thereafter, but not before Marilyn confided that she was pregnant (though later wrote and told him she'd miscarried). There has been speculation about whether Marilyn was ever pregnant: that she had made the whole thing up to put pressure on Kazan; or, that it was a stunt to gain attention and make him feel guilty. But this seems a little harsh; Kazan and Marilyn were sexually active, as Kazan confirmed in his autobiography, so it was possible that she could have been pregnant.

On his return to New York, Kazan wrote to Marilyn saying he would do everything in his power to stay close to her, urging her to learn everything she could about acting. That she spend more time on her own; drop friends such as Pat De Cicco; go to college; speak up for herself: 'Don't take any shit from anyone'. She moved out of Natasha Lytess's apartment, as he'd already suggested, and into 8573 Holloway Drive with Shelley Winters. The two young women were ideally suited and spent hours together playing classical music, listening to Sinatra and talking about men. They also went to the theatre together; on one occasion even taking Natasha Lytess to the Circle Theatre to see Sydney Chaplin rehearse a play directed by his father, Charlie (from where they had to leave abruptly when Lytess was overheard criticizing Chaplin senior).

8573 Holloway Drive: home with friend and fellow actress Shelley Winters

That the time, after Hyde's death then Kazan's departure, was difficult for Marilyn is confirmed by *Wells Fargo* star Dale Robertson, who got to know her well at this time, the point at which they were both at the beginning of their careers. 'We would go to ball games together and she was very pleasant company, but we were never boyfriend and girlfriend because we just weren't attracted to each other.' They enjoyed each other's company, but, even so, Robertson could sense her sadness: 'She had a rough time for a while, and her biggest enemy was herself,' he said, by then more than fifty years later.

It wasn't made any easier when, with Natasha Lytess, Marilyn went on a trip to Hemet to visit her father, hoping that he might acknowledge her now that she had begun to make a name for herself in movies. But she was wrong, as she discovered when she attempted to call him from a payphone several miles from his home. Gifford did not want anything to do with her; he already had family, he said, and, indeed, a wife. Marilyn, already fragile, found his rejection traumatic, leading Winters to introduce her to a $25 an hour psychiatrist, Dr Judd Marmor, in the start of the long and often painful process of psychoanalysis.

· · · · ·

On 8 February 1951, newspaper reports claimed that Marilyn, who had been in virtual retirement since the death of Hyde, was to appear in Fox's *AWAC in his Life*, as Roberta, an ex-WAC. The film was subsequently retitled *Love Nest* to avoid misleading audiences about the extent of her role. William Lundigan and June Haver were to star as landlords in an apartment building full of crazy tenants.

Just before shooting began, Marilyn took some more of Kazan's advice and enrolled at University of California, Los Angeles, for a course in 'Backgrounds of Literature', described as 'Historical, social and cultural aspects of various periods with an introduction to the literature itself'. According to Marilyn's school record, it began on 5 April and was run by a Ms Claire Soule in room 616 of the UCLA Extension's Hill Street building in downtown LA. It meant a 7 pm start every Thursday until the end of class at 9 pm then back home to prepare for the day job. Marilyn enjoyed the course, but less so the stares of her classmates. The attention was hardly surprising. She had, by then, appeared in several high-profile films and even, on 29 March, presented an Academy Award at the Pantages Theater. But while her fellow students knew who she was, Ms Soule was none the wiser. When Marilyn told her she would have to drop out before the class ended on 31 May she replied: 'Why, I thought you were a young girl straight out of the convent.' Years later Marilyn would laugh about it, remembering, 'She was very sincere when she said it.'

On 5 May 1951, Marilyn's relationship with Lytess was put under strain when Lytess wrote to her, c/o William Morris, to explain that her dentist was going to sue for payment of $1000 owed to him for Lytess' dental treatments. He had agreed to be paid in instalments of $200 per week by Marilyn, which Lytess promised to repay at a rate of $25 per week. Thankfully for both actress and coach, Marilyn signed a new, renegotiated contract with Fox on 11 May 1951 and began filming on another tiny part in *Let's Make It Legal*, starring Claudette Colbert and Macdonald Carey. Marilyn was cast as Joyce Mannering, yet another sexy blonde

Being interviewed, early 1950s

with little to do or say, but she certainly made her presence felt. In trouble for being continually late on set she told director Richard Sale to call Joe Schenck if he had a problem with her behaviour. Sale retorted that he would call Darryl Zanuck instead; causing Marilyn to storm off set, only to return shortly thereafter and apologize.

While Twentieth Century Fox was still wondering how exactly to use Marilyn, she was loaned out to RKO for a small part in *Clash by Night*, starring Barbara Stanwyck, Paul Douglas and Robert Ryan. Her friend Sidney Skolsky helped her get the role, which was by far the best she had ever played and which she really made her own. But while her performance was superb, there were still problems on set – mostly not of Marilyn's making. First, director Fritz Lang seemed to dislike her and did not appreciate Natasha Lytess's presence. Second, some of the other members of the star-studded cast did not know how to deal with the media and public attention Marilyn was beginning to receive. Paul Douglas, particularly, seemed to cause more than his share of bad feeling; one of the extras described him as intoxicated on several occasions. He objected to Marilyn's name being above the film titles and even lost it when she referred to him by his first name. Marilyn determined to do her best regardless, and she worked exceptionally hard, as writer Richard Baer, who spent a lot of time on the set of *Clash by Night*, remembered:

> 'Marilyn was always on set on time, she wasn't yet a big star and was very anxious to please. I didn't think she was at all difficult or demanding and she was concerned about what people thought of her. Sometimes other actors gathered around to watch her scenes because they knew she wasn't classically trained and they would laugh and smirk. I thought that was unkind, but she wasn't terribly accomplished and had no real training, which made her easy to ridicule. She was ambitious and determined with her eyes on the goal, and Jerry Wald [the film's producer] knew there was something special about her. I have nothing bad to say about this woman at all.'

A publicity still for 1952's *Clash By Night*

Some of the actors, as Baer confirms, were less than helpful to Marilyn. One rather sad example of this was a scene in which she fell down some stairs – to the great amusement of some of the crew who actually laughed out loud. Fortunately, Marilyn had come to no harm and continued shooting her scene regardless, which required a great deal of guts and emotional backbone. Baer and Marilyn became good friends while on the set, and she relied on him to let her know how her performance came out in the rushes, but he became exasperated when she refused point blank to give him her telephone number or address. She would call him many times to discuss everything from Johnny Hyde to her work on the film, but still she would not cave into his requests for her number. 'I would often say, "My hand is aching and my ear is sore from being on the phone, can't we just do this face to face?" But she would always refuse, somewhat giving the lie to the idea that she gave herself freely to every man she met.'

Much of *Clash by Night* was made in the Californian seaside resort of Monterey, and it attracted its share of visitors, among them Charles H. Page:

> 'We heard that a movie was being filmed on Cannery Row ... [with] Barbara Stanwyck ... So a group of us went down to see her, as I admired her and wanted to get her autograph. I really did not pay much attention to the blonde in blue jeans sitting next to her – at that point I had never heard of Marilyn Monroe. We hung around watching the filming over the weekend; Barbara was not very friendly and would not give us an autograph, claiming that she was 'too busy'. It never occurred to us to ask for the autograph of the blonde, but had we known we were in the presence of someone who would be famous very soon, we would have drooled over her!'

Another eyewitness was Nanciele Finnegan, then 17 years old, who had a front-row seat when the film crew set up camp in her parents' front yard. Several members of her family were involved in the production: her sister filmed sitting on the front porch, petting a rabbit; her brother Paul shown rolling a large tyre down the driveway; and even the family Model T Ford, filmed for the huge sum of $50 per day. The most amusing contractual obligation was Nanciele's, paid not to appear on camera: 'What a disappointment to have a contract to not appear in the film. Still, the money did help to ease the awkwardness involved in having to avoid using the doors or walking by the windows whenever the director yelled, "Action".'

For most of filming, Marilyn's trailer was parked outside the Finnegan home, and this gave Nanciele an almost direct line to Marilyn, with whom she enjoyed speaking: 'I found her very sweet and approachable. Sometimes when waiting for filming to start she'd catch my eye and wink, other times we'd drink Coca-Colas and laugh. It's such a joy to recall the laughs we shared over Coca-Colas.'

The tyre scene involving Finnegan's brother caused a minor distress: '[The tyre] narrowly misses Uncle Vince played by J. Carrol Naish, and in the scene Uncle

With short hair and in a simple white shirt, publicity shot, early 1950s

Vince gets angry and kicks the boy. During one of the takes Naish accidentally did kick Paul and he was so embarrassed and apologetic. As I recall, he gave Paul $5 to go buy candy to soothe the hurt.'

She also remembers being asked by the cast to join them for a catered meal, but while most of the cast were friendly and professional, she wasn't so impressed with Barbara Stanwyck: 'She was aloof and avoided the others – including other cast members as well as her fans. She definitely refused autographs. Marilyn made a point of being available to chat with fans and to sign autographs. I wondered at the time if Barbara was going through some personal crisis to appear so cold to both fans and co-workers.'

Once *Clash by Night* was in the can, Marilyn returned to Fox and auditioned unsuccessfully for a part in *Wait Till the Sun Shines, Nellie*. A test that followed for *Night without Sleep*, for which she worked for days on end with Lytess, was so successful that not even Darryl Zanuck could deny that she was good for the part of Nell, a psychotic babysitter. Marilyn was thrilled by the chance to do something different, and even decided to move back in with Lytess to work on her part day and night. She also took early-morning jogging sessions around the back alleys to keep herself fit and began receiving fan mail – mostly from men proposing marriage. Her increasing popularity was reflected in titles like Miss Cheesecake, Miss Pin-up 1951 and – her personal favourite – 'Miss Flamethrower', while *Stars and Stripes* magazine voted her the GI's favourite pin-up, confirmed by the huge amount of mail she was receiving from GI's every day. Grace Goddard helped to answer all the fan mail; Marilyn even took to including photos at her own expense, as she felt the studio ones were too small. Fame was at last knocking on her door, and she was determined that her new fans would know how much they meant to her.

When she won a Henrietta Award for Best Newcomer, Marilyn bought her first expensive evening gown – red low-cut velvet that clung to her as far as her knees before flaring to the floor. It was designed by Oleg Cassini, and Marilyn loved it. Though it caused a sensation, with many women declaring it offensive and extreme. It was the first time her taste in clothes had subjected her to such harsh criticism, but it would not be the last. When she wore a strapless red-silk taffeta gown to a party shortly afterwards, the press declared it was proof that she was utterly lacking in taste. Marilyn was defiant: 'I'm truly sorry, but I love the dress,' she declared; of the Henrietta Awards dress. 'Frankly I love the gown and wish I had more occasions to wear it.'

She soon realized that no matter what she wore, she couldn't win. One day at the studios an executive berated her for wearing jeans and a T-shirt, declaring: 'An actress should always look her best'. She got her own back, however, when photographer Earl Theisen dressed her in a potato sack, proving that it didn't matter what she wore, she would always look terrific. The fans loved it.

While Marilyn's fans were learning more about her professionally, her private health details were kept hidden and remain shrouded in mystery. She continued to suffer with endometriosis (Lytess recalling occasions where Marilyn would literally stop dead and bend over in agony). Although her medical records are sealed, from cheques written in 1950 and 1951, some idea of her medical problems at the time emerges. On 5 November 1950 and again on the 15th, cheques were made out to a Dr Seligman, each for $40; on 26 October 1951, a cheque for $200 was paid to a Dr A. Gottsman. Finally on 9 November 1951 $50 was paid to an unknown doctor. What these treatments were for is impossible to confirm, but her health was certainly an issue at the time.

Whatever health problems she might have had, they did not stop her working on her acting. On the advice of Lytess and actor Jack Palance, Marilyn began classes with renowned drama teacher, Michael Chekhov. He was her introduction to the acting technique known as 'The Method'. She confided in Chekhov that she was tired of fluffy parts with nothing to do or say; though in public she brushed off her image as a dumb blonde, in private it was driving her to distraction. Chekov told her she kept getting those parts because of the sexual vibrations she gave off, which upset her and strengthened her resolve to be an artist, 'not an erotic freak'.

Chekhov liked Marilyn, but grew ever frustrated with her lateness and absenteeism. After one lateness too many, he suggested they stop the classes. Marilyn was devastated, writing a note to ask him not to give up on her, that she was only too aware of how much she tested his patience. Her pleading worked, and Chekhov allowed her back on the understanding that she would take her lessons more seriously (which she did; so much so that she once arrived at his home a day too early).

By the time *Night without Sleep* began shooting in December 1951, the film had been re-titled *Don't Bother To Knock*; it was to give Marilyn her first starring role. Completely different from anything she had done before, the story concerns the mental disintegration of Marilyn's character Nell, already emotionally disturbed, who finally comes off the rails one night. Marilyn requested Natasha Lytess's vital presence on the set and bombarded Zanuck with begging letters. Zanuck relented, but it led to problems. Lytess felt she had been put on the spot by Marilyn and worried about her job at the studio. She was proved right one day when Marilyn told the director that Lytess was the only person who could help her with a particular scene. The moment it was done, he made a phone call, and Lytess found herself fired. According to Lytess, Marilyn ignored her calls over the next few weeks, leaving her distraught. Finally she decided to advise Marilyn that if she wasn't prepared to help, she would harm herself and rocket them both into the headlines. Faced with emotional blackmail, Marilyn responded, and Zanuck had Lytess reinstated.

Don't Bother to Knock was released to mixed reviews, with audiences confused to see Marilyn in such a dramatic role. Nanciele Finnegan recalls: 'The intense shock I felt when I went to see it. I expected to see the chum I'd come to know, but recognized in the fragile psychotic portrayed there, that Marilyn was an actress.' Nanciele is astute in her observation; even though the film was shocking at the time, and Marilyn's character entirely unlikeable, there was no doubt that she could act.

As the year drew to a close, in late 1951 Marilyn went on a few dates with *They Live by Night* director, Nicholas Ray. She also began a friendship with business manager David March, who was interested in signing her to his company Leslie and Tyson. They talked initially on the phone, but during their subsequent face-to-face conversations Marilyn admitted she was lonely. March recognized her many insecurities and constant need for reassurance, and they would often sit beside the fire and cheer each other up. March made the mistake one day of telling Marilyn that she procrastinated too much. Her explosive response was brief; he was soon forgiven, a fortunate outcome given she'd need all the friends she could get in the year to come. 1952 was to prove a challenge, professionally and personally.

UNSEEN PHOTOGRAPHS

1942–1952

ABOVE AND RIGHT

During her first marriage to James 'Jim' Dougherty, Norma Jeane often spent
time with other women and their children, as these photos suggest, but she
was not keen on starting a family of her own. But when Dougherty was to
leave the Maritime Service Training Station on Catalina Island to see active
service in World War II, Norma Jeane (seen here with a mass of swept-back
naturally wavy brown hair) became scared at the prospect of being alone and
begged him to make her pregnant. Dougherty refused her request, worried
that if he didn't return from the war, she would be left with a child to raise
on her own, something quite rare in the 1940s.

ABOVE

During her marriage to Jim Dougherty, Norma Jeane tried hard to fit into his
lifestyle by supporting his interests. She accompanied him on fishing trips to
Lake Sherwood and on hiking expeditions in the Hollywood Hills. Here she is
seen catching fish on Catalina Island.

ABOVE

Weekends on Catalina Island were quiet and low key, and could involve horse-
riding or fishing or just exploring the island. Here Norma Jeane poses with a
rare hornbill perched on her arm, during a visit to Wrigley Bird Park on
Catalina Island with her husband and friends.

A slightly wary-looking Norma Jeane in sympathetic pose beside the penguin
pool at the bird sanctuary established in 1929 by bird lover William Wrigley Jr
on Catalina Island.

ABOVE

As Mrs Dougherty, Norma Jeane moved to Catalina Island, c. 1943, when husband Jim Dougherty took up a post there as a Physical Instructor at the Maritime Service Training Station. Here looking relaxed and happy, they pose beside the ocean and the docks, Dougherty in his naval uniform, she in shorts.

ABOVE AND RIGHT

On Catalina Island, where these photographs were taken, the Doughertys
enjoyed an idyllic lifestyle: 'We had a very normal life,' Jim Dougherty recalled.
'Norma cooked and cleaned and I was the bread winner.' And part of being
normal meant they also argued, once falling out at a party at Catalina Casino,
because Norma Jeane proved too huge a hit with the servicemen.

LEFT

Norma Jeane at the beach on Catalina Island (fashionably exposing her midriff and wearing bobby sox with her sandals). Seaside trips were not always relaxing, given the huge amount of male attention Norma Jeane attracted.

ABOVE

Norma Jeane, second left, having fun with her Radioplane colleagues at the annual works picnic in July 1944, where she was crowned Queen of the Radioplane picnic, winning a $50 war bond and a mention in the 15 July edition of the Radioplane Static. A popular and trusted member of the team, her managers rated her above average. But working ten hours a day on her feet was exhausting, and she couldn't wait to leave, enabled to do so by her incipient career as a photographer's model.

ABOVE AND RIGHT

When, in 1945, photographer William Carroll was looking for a
model to use in an advertising counter display, he hired Norma
Jeane. The shoot, one of the first she ever did, and for which Marilyn
did her own make up, took place on a local beach, where Marilyn,
playing noughts and crosses in the sand or posed against the rocks,
smiled dazzlingly for the camera in an extraordinary array of
colourful outfits from her own wardrobe. Carroll was to describe her
as 'a girl of outstanding charm … Not totally beautiful but fresh
in a most delightful girl-next-door manner'.

ABOVE

RIGHT AND PAGE 110

Bill Pursel, late 1940s, at the time when he and Norma Jeane were dating. The two met in 1946, while Norma Jeane was in Las Vegas obtaining her divorce from first husband Jim Dougherty, and they remained close for the next four years. Pursel was to say of their time together: 'It was a happy and carefree part of her life, and of my life too.'

These exceptionally rare photos, late 1947–early 1948, were a gift from Norma Jeane to friend and early boyfriend Bill Pursel, during one of his first visits to Los Angeles. Norma Jeane, as Pursel knew Marilyn all her life, stands confidently, hands on hips, outside her home at 4215 Rowland Street, Burbank, and leans against a car, perched jauntily on one leg. These were good times: her modelling career was going well; she was single again and her movie-star dreams were about to come true.

ABOVE

A Scottish theme for The Alan Young Show finds Marilyn in a kilt, playing
the bagpipes, with actor Bill Thompson (right) and British-born comic actor
Alan Young (left), whom she met shortly after signing with Twentieth
Century Fox in 1946 when Young was looking for volunteers to appear on a
float in the Hollywood Christmas Parade. Their meeting led to a few dates
along with this rare photo opportunity. Young was to say of her: 'She seemed
like a frightened rabbit at first, and I didn't realize she had been raised
without parents. I really liked her.'

ABOVE

RIGHT

In April 1950, Marilyn took the small but important role of Miss Caswell in All About Eve, which starred box-office queen Bette Davis. While the prospect of appearing with the legendary Miss Davis must have been daunting, Marilyn, seen here enjoying a conversation with co-star Anne Baxter, more than held her own.

An early 1950s publicity still, showing a relaxed, happy Marilyn. Her career was blossoming, and despite emotional upheavals, for the most part, she was enjoying her rise to stardom, as can be seen in this photo.

PART TWO:
'SUMMER'
1952—1956

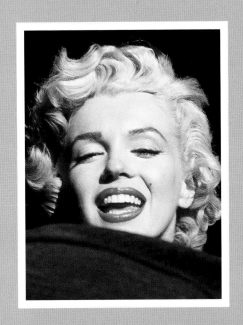

6

THE PAST VERSUS
THE FUTURE

Although Marilyn was to claim 'I have a horror of signing leases,' she didn't
seem able ever to settle in one place. She had been on the move since she'd
left Aunt Ana's in 1947 and was beginning to tire of it. In early 1952 she
took an apartment in West Hollywood at 1121 Hilldale Avenue. Sometimes she
would relish her time alone, filling her home with white flowers, lounging on the
sofa reading books and listening to music while grabbing a bite to eat. Other times
the solitude got to her. She would drive to the beach or spend evenings walking
around the streets, enjoying the anonymity of the night, its still and quiet, or find
solace in writing poetry, something that she did throughout her life.

During 1952, she made small appearances in *We're Not Married* and *O Henry's Full
House*. She also had a part in *Monkey Business* (starring Cary Grant and Ginger Rogers),
in which one of the other members of the cast was Bob Cornthwaite. He had
worked with director Howard Hawks before, and when Hughes asked for him, he
was happy to oblige. Arriving several days into production, Cornthwaite's first
encounter with Marilyn was when John Wayne and Gary Cooper were visiting the
set during a break in production:

> *'Marilyn walked past and everyone was looking. Hawks turned to me and said: 'I think that
> the overdeveloped quality in the little blonde girl is going to be funny.' I thought, My God,
> because she was becoming quite a star and everyone was jumping around for her. But
> Hawks had hired her because he had to, not because he wanted to. He didn't like her abil-
> ities and didn't conceal it.'*

But Marilyn wasn't the only actress Hawks didn't rate:

'[Ginger Rogers] was rehearsing a scene with Grant, and Hawks stopped it. "No, no, no, Virginia," he said — he always called her Virginia, not Ginger — and walked on to the set. He paced up and down in complete silence, while everyone wondered what was wrong — he ruled the roost, and everyone was silent. Rogers was watching him, wondering what she had done wrong, when he said, "Let's do it again and see if we can get it right."'

Meanwhile, Bob began to feel sorry for Marilyn, as it was obvious that some people on the set just didn't understand her:

'She was very likeable and also stubborn, which is what saw her through. Lots of people didn't cotton on to her. She had the strength of a puppy dog that hadn't been indulged and had been abused but would not give up. She was persistent, and that stood her in good stead, but people just had to go along with what she was because she was not going to change — she was stubborn, which was both her strength and her weakness. Working with Marilyn — there was a blankness. She was both aware and divorced from things, and sometimes I would wonder where her mind was at. I had grown a beard for my last role, and Hawks had asked me to keep it on; one day Marilyn and I were waiting for our cue to do a scene, and she stared at me, before finally saying, "It's real, isn't it?" I didn't know what to say to that!'

Beards aside, Marilyn's behaviour on set was a cause of concern. She was continually late, something Cornthwaite saw as a defence mechanism against inexperience: 'She was determined to hold on to her position but was afraid to be there. Marilyn was ambitious and didn't want to spoil her chances of success but knew if she stuck to her guns and made demands, she might get away with it.'

Even though she was regularly late, the cast and crew enjoyed the play between Marilyn, the actors and director Howard Hawks. They enjoyed some humorous moments too, not least when: 'The monkeys fell in love with Cary Grant and would leap across the set to give him cuddles. They hated Marilyn and would pinch her and pull her clothes, and she was flummoxed by it – she had had that behaviour from men, but not from monkeys!'

Talking to Cary Grant on the set of
Monkey Business

On set Marilyn seemed like a lost child, the new girl who couldn't quite fit in or make friends. According to Cornthwaite:

'Ginger Rogers and Cary Grant were both professionals, and there was no overt behaviour towards Marilyn, but they didn't particularly welcome her — she had a different level of

professionalism. But what held it all together was Howard Hawks because he had such
power. He was the producer and although there was meant to be another director, he was
never there – it was always Hawks who directed as well as produced.'

But not even Hawks could completely control Marilyn's behaviour. The stubbornness that was her greatest strength was also her supreme weakness. 'Perhaps she couldn't help her behaviour,' says Cornthwaite. 'She so was disturbed emotionally and psychologically.'

She had physical problems too. Suffering from a persistent stomach ache, she booked an appointment at Cedars of Lebanon Hospital on 1 March 1952. Cornthwaite recalled how:

'She kept saying she had appendicitis and couldn't work … she had to shoot a scene with
Cary Grant in the car, which was set for a particular day. Hawks called Zanuck in advance
and said, 'I don't care if she has appendicitis. She can go to the hospital, and I want her
back on the set on that day and every day.' He had the prestige to do it.'

In 1951 with baseball
legend Gus Zernial

With the operation delayed until the end of production, Marilyn returned to the set with something to distract her from her health problems – a date with baseball legend Joe DiMaggio.

In 1951, Marilyn had done a series of photos with the Chicago White Sox during spring training at Brookside Park in Pasadena, California. One of the players to pose with her was Gus Zernial: 'I was really attracted to her beauty but more than that. She was attractive both inside and out – a beautiful person to talk to, and I also believe she had a lot more to offer than the way she was shown by Hollywood.'

Yankee player Joe DiMaggio saw the photos, liked what he saw of Marilyn and engineered a date via mutual friend David March. On 8 March 1952, March managed to persuade a reluctant Marilyn to accompany him to the Villa Nova Restaurant to meet DiMaggio. She had no idea who he was and wanted to call the whole thing off, worried he would be a big-headed sports star with a large ego and no personality. March accompanied DiMaggio and actress Peggy Rabe to the restaurant for 6.30 pm dinner, but Marilyn did not show up. At 8.15 pm, DiMaggio sat nervously drinking Vermouth and tearing a menu into tiny pieces when she finally made her appearance, wearing a blue suit and white, low-cut blouse. She was happy to find DiMaggio was not the ego-driven individual she had expected but rather quiet and shy. Marilyn drove DiMaggio back to the Knickerbocker Hotel at the end of the evening, but politely refused his request for another date. However, subsequently they drove out to spend an evening by the ocean, and on 17 March Marilyn watched DiMaggio play baseball – for the one and only time.

But DiMaggio came with baggage; he had responsibilities to his ex-wife, actress Dorothy Arnold, and 10-year-old son, Joe DiMaggio Jnr. A relative who knew Arnold well gave her opinion on the feud that developed between her and Marilyn:

Booth at Villa Nova Restaurant, setting for Marilyn and Joe DiMaggio's blind date, 1952

'[Dorothy] was not one to talk about anyone – she was a very caring, down-to-earth person. I only remember her great dislike for Joe and Marilyn as they were taking Joe Junior to bars, which upset Dorothy to no end. She fought constantly about child support. Joe Junior liked Marilyn a lot, but he did not like his father. Joe Senior wanted Joe Junior to play ball as well as he did – the son was always pressured to do better, but he couldn't live up to his father's standards.'

DiMaggio had retired from baseball and had no interest in fame or showbiz. He was attracted to Marilyn as a person; not to the parties and award shows she had to attend (to which she continued to go with friends such as Sidney Skolsky). Despite that, he was anxious to make a success of things; on a visit to the set of *Monkey Business* he allowed photographs to be taken of the two of them together. Cornthwaite remembered how 'Joe DiMaggio would pick her up every night after work, and I would run into him coming into the studio while I was leaving, but we never got to speak to each other.'

Within days of meeting DiMaggio, rumours that Marilyn had once posed naked were impossible to deny when a calendar featuring the nude photos started to appear throughout the country. Marilyn had been forewarned of this by a man in the street who approached her clutching one: 'This ought to be worth quite a bit of money to you. Suppose I showed it around town?' Marilyn refused to be drawn: 'Mister, I'd just adore for you to show it around Hollywood – would you like me to also autograph it for you?'

Her studio went into a frenzy, with executives demanding first she lie, then say nothing. Ultimately, a prepared statement allowed Marilyn to explain her version of events – she'd been broke and needed money for her rent. She played the sympathy card and was not only forgiven but also loved for her honesty and candour. Once it was clear that the photos would not negatively affect her career, she became quite proud of them. Mayor Johnny Grant, who delivered her a calendar, confirms this: 'She … was happy to receive it. She had just gotten out of the shower and the only thing she was wearing was a towel – on her head! When she opened the door, she half way hid behind it, exposing almost the same scene I had just seen on the calendar.'

Tom Kelley later said that Marilyn had some role in the photos' notoriety, since she had given numerous autographed calendars as gifts. Nonetheless, in December 1952, she tried to stop them being used on ashtrays, glasses and cocktail trays: 'I don't know exactly what rights I have, but it seems to me I should have some say in the way my own picture is used.'

• • • • •

With filming on *Monkey Business* done, Marilyn booked herself into the Cedars of Lebanon hospital to have her appendix out, mortified on arrival to discover that she needed to supply the name of her next of kin in case of emergency. As she later told reporter Isabel Moore: 'It was so strange and awful to realize I just didn't have anyone to call on. But of course, I've always been alone and I guess I always will be alone.'

Aware that she wasn't close enough to DiMaggio to mention him as next of kin, it was David March's name she gave. In the hospital that night, she had time to think and scribbled a note to Dr Rabwin, requesting him to avoid large scars and not remove either of her ovaries to ensure she could still have children. The latter was a major concern. Dr Rabwin was anxious enough to have a gynaecologist on hand throughout the operation, which in fact went smoothly.

Still recovering and at a low ebb, from her hospital bed Marilyn heard the news that reporter and Hollywood columnist Erskine Johnson had found Gladys Baker, Marilyn's mother, and she was well and truly alive. Apparently, Marilyn was not the orphan she professed to be. She rallied as best she could, saying that she had never lived with Gladys and had kept quiet about her because of her mother's ill health. While her explanation won public sympathy, the media were not so forgiving.

One person who took the news badly was journalist Jim Henaghan, with whom Marilyn had become friends. From interviews with her, in which she had opened up to him about her childhood – her father had died in a car accident, an event quickly followed by the death of her mother – he had written a piece for his paper, giving ample column inches to the orphan story. He felt shocked and humiliated by what had happened, and his initial reaction was a call to the studio, in which he described Marilyn as a lying blonde who had made a jerk out of him to his editor. They should 'take her hearts and flowers and peddle them some place else in future'.

Marilyn phoned Henaghan to apologize – her excuse was her shame about her sick mother whom she had never got to know. It was too late to stop publication; 'So Far to go Alone' ran in *Redbook*'s June 1952 edition. In a letter of apology to the editor, Marilyn wrote: 'I frankly did not feel wrong in withholding from you the fact that my mother is still alive … since we have never known each other intimately and have never enjoyed the normal relationship of mother and daughter.'

Still in pain from the operation, and obviously thinking about it all, Marilyn opened her heart to reporter Isabel Moore, who'd arrived at the hospital with David March. 'I know how I'd feel if I had children. I'd never want them to feel I didn't love them more than anything else in the world. If I ever have a little girl, I think I'll be a wonderful mother to her, and if I can help it, I'll never be away from her for a minute.'

* * * * *

Marilyn was earning $750 a week at Fox, but by May 1952 her finances were in a parlous state. Fox came up with the idea of pro-rating her salary for fifty weeks with a simultaneous loan of $1700. In early June, Fox representative Tom Pryer arrived with the relevant paperwork. Marilyn refused to sign something she had not requested. For the first but certainly not the last time she would stand up for her rights as an artist, unusual in those days, when no one dared rock the boat where the major studios were concerned. This small but significant step proved Marilyn was no pushover.

On 1 June, Marilyn's twenty-sixth birthday, she was thrilled to learn that she had got the role of Lorelei Lee in the Fox production of *Gentlemen Prefer Blondes*. Shooting was due to begin the following January. Before that she was to star in *Niagara*, as a faithless wife who plots to murder her husband (Joseph Cotten), who turns the tables. Filming was interrupted briefly on 26 June, when Marilyn was called to testify against two men charged with 'unlawfully using the name of Marilyn Monroe for the purpose of selling nude and indecent pictures. These were falsely represented to have been posed by Marilyn Monroe'. Jerry Karpman and Morrie Kapland had mailed hundreds of letters reportedly signed by her, promising 'un-retouched photographs in almost every pose imaginable' and declaring they were up for sale because she was out of a job and needed the money. Marilyn arrived at the court, dressed in a blue skirt and jacket, and open-toed white shoes and took the witness stand as Norma Jeane Dougherty. Her presence was brief but effective; Judge Kenneth L. Holaday found the defendants guilty of five of the nine charges against them.

Court appearance over, Marilyn travelled to Niagara for location shots. Checking into a local hotel,

Long-distance shot on the *Niagara* set, taken by fan and Niagara resident George Bailey

Getting ready to shoot the
bus-station scene in *Niagara*

she met chambermaid Blanch Maj, who shared her memories of the encounter with her niece, Pat Brennan:

'One morning my aunt was cleaning the suite, when Marilyn returned to the hotel. My aunt was admiring her shoes and the fact that her shoe size was so petite, like her own. When Marilyn checked out, she left a very generous gratuity and two pairs of her own new shoes!!!! We were all so excited and most impressed with the fact that we had Marilyn's very own shoes in our family.'

The filming went well, and Marilyn became friendly with the locals employed as extras. Patricia Henderson was around Marilyn's age, and the two women 'hit it off like sisters', according to Henderson's son, Timothy. 'My mother said that she was like a school girl chum at lunch breaks and liked "getting away from Marilyn" even for an hour. She remembered her complexion as being perfect and that she ate a lot.' In the scene where the husband wreaks revenge: 'She was paid $50 for doing two of Marilyn's screams in the final bell-tower scene, which was about what my dad made a week teaching. Mom was used for the screams in order to save Marilyn's voice for the speaking parts.' She was also involved in a scene in which Joseph Cotten chased Jean Peters down the Cave of the Winds. 'There is a treacherous series of wooden stairs directly under the Falls and … my mother slipped and almost went into the rapids! It was so spontaneous and real that they kept the scene in the final cut.'

Despite his aversion to the movie business, Joe DiMaggio occasionally visited; they dined quietly at secluded restaurant Shimshacks and even agreed to be photographed together. When Joe could not be with her, Marilyn spent time eating out with other members of the cast. Joseph Jacob worked at the Red Coach Inn, one of the restaurants they frequented:

'We gave the screen stars some privacy and kept an area of the restaurant closed so they could enjoy some quite time without interruption. As you might guess, people followed Marilyn Monroe everywhere she went, wanting to sit in the seat she was in, wanting the napkin she used, asking what did she order, etc. I had the privilege of serving Marilyn that afternoon, and it was a day I'll not soon forget. I say this because that day I didn't meet Marilyn Monroe, I felt that I met a beautiful, statuesque vision of what God intended a woman to look like. She could have been wearing a potato sack and had curlers in her hair, and it would not dull her beauty, which I found to be both inside and out.

I had the fortune of speaking to Miss Monroe directly that day while the others walked in the lobby and the outdoor patio taking in the view. I found her to be nothing of the glamour queen we portrayed her as, but more the down-to-earth girl we all wish superstars to be. She drank a vodka martini, and although we spoke casual conversation she did ask if I could imagine knowing a thousand people and not having any friends. This chance meeting with Marilyn Monroe showed me that under all of the glitz and glamour beats the heart of one person, one single person, that gets happy, sad, frustrated and lonely. Just like the rest us. Go figure.'

A rare shot taken from above the set of *Niagara* by fan George Bailey

On other days, Marilyn took a tour of the local sights, meeting a variety of people including Robert Slatzer (who was also photographed with her). On 29 August columnist Dorothy Kilgallen commented on their meeting, declaring Slatzer 'a dark horse in the Marilyn Monroe romance derby'. On 18 September, Slatzer stood in for Kilgallen with a short article about his friendship with Marilyn. In it he revealed that they had first met in 1947, both employed by Twentieth Century Fox. They lost their jobs at the same time: 'I didn't see her again until last June in Niagara Falls. I didn't know that Norma Jeane was now Marilyn.' He said he had sent Marilyn a number of books, including a couple by Thomas Wolfe, *You Can't Go Home Again* and *Look Homeward, Angel*.

This would all have been harmless enough if he had left it there. But years after Marilyn's death, Slatzer was to claim a long romance and a secret marriage, annulled on the instructions of Twentieth Century Fox. According to Slatzer, the couple were wed in Mexico on 4 October 1952 and later bribed the judge to burn the marriage certificate. But Marilyn was with Natasha Lytess that day, shopping, as the cheques she wrote show, and nowhere near Mexico. Anyway, her views on marriage were clear. Later that October, in response to rumours that she was secretly married to DiMaggio, she'd said: 'If I wanted to get married now, I would. And if I already were, the studio's wishes would not be important enough to make me keep it secret.'

In August a party was held in Marilyn's honour at the home of American bandleader Ray Anthony and on the 24th she recorded a radio play, *Statement in Full*. On 2 September it was Atlantic City's Stanley Theatre that set the scene for the world première of *Monkey Business*. A mixture of Marilyn's lateness and traffic problems ensured she and her entourage missed the 9 am train; the studio had to charter a plane to get to

Looking relaxed between takes on *Niagara*

Atlantic City at a cost of $800. Staff who travelled with Marilyn felt nervous at the cost, while she sat at the back and slept. Grilled about it later she retorted, 'It didn't set the studio back as much as they let on. They could afford it.'

At a photo session that day with four female members of the Armed Forces, an enterprising photographer stood on a chair and aimed his camera down the front of her low-cut dress. Nobody thought anything more about it until an Army Public Information Officer wanted it banned because it was too revealing. This attracted huge interest in the photo, requiring a statement from Marilyn: 'I am surprised and hurt. People looked at me all day – I thought they were admiring my Grand Marshall's badge.'

In response, Marilyn found herself bombarded with letters from women, enclosing bras and underwear, saying things like: 'You need these more than I do.' Of course, Marilyn's dislike of underwear was legendary: 'Girdles and bras are unnatural. They distort a girl so. So I never wear them!' More seriously, though, she responded to some in which, 'They accuse me of starting the rapes. Rapes went on long before I came.' Reflecting some more, she concluded, 'It's a little dull when [women] don't make remarks isn't it?' Subsequently, she wrote an article entitled 'Am I too daring', in which she thought hard about the comments attributed to her by other women. 'All of my adult life I have preferred to dress for men rather than for women. For this reason, I suppose, I cannot expect other women to appreciate or even like my clothes. But I do, and I was hurt by the accusation that I have no taste in my manner of dress.'

She also expanded on why she had no female friends, reported in *Photoplay* as saying: 'I've never in my life had girls talk – never talked about men, woman to woman … I want women friends … If you had even one girl friend with whom you could discuss all your innermost thoughts I do believe it would be very comforting.'

• • • • •

On 15 September, Marilyn moved to 2393 Castillian Drive, which she leased from Frank Klein Archer. Joe DiMaggio became an almost permanent feature there, inviting friends and family to share meals and evenings together. For the first time in years, Marilyn began to feel as though she had a family and enjoyed learning how to cook steak, toss salad and make spaghetti.

It was not all perfect. Natasha Lytess had disliked DiMaggio intensely from the start, considering him a threat to her role in Marilyn's life and 'a man with a closed, vapid look'. Early on, DiMaggio apparently answered the phone to her, refusing to put her through to Marilyn, suggesting she should contact Marilyn's agent. When she told Marilyn about this shoddy treatment, Lytess claimed that she didn't have the courage to stand up to him; indeed, Marilyn would phone her day and night – sometimes in tears – to complain about how DiMaggio misused her. Certainly on 1 October the couple were reported to have rowed, and DiMaggio had returned to San Francisco. Their separation was short-lived; by Thanksgiving they were dining with friend Bernie Kamber.

Marilyn was busy professionally towards the end of 1952. Following a recording of an episode of the Charlie McCarthy radio show on 18 October, she began preparing for her role in *Gentlemen Prefer Blondes*, attending costume tests on 31 October and moving into the Beverly Hills Hotel to be near the studio. She also began thinking seriously about her future, about which, on 24 November, reporter Aline Mosby ran a story. She quoted Lytess, convinced that Marilyn would one day win an Academy Award: 'I think tragic roles are her forte. There is a strangeness about her… an un-real quality.'

But, Marilyn's view on her life at that time, also reported by Mosby, was rather less upbeat: 'I'm trying to find myself now, to be a good actress and good person. Sometimes I feel strong inside, but I have to reach in and pull it up. You have to be strong inside way deep inside of you. It isn't easy. Nothing's easy, as long as you go on living.'

Part of her plan to become a better person involved a trip to the Goldenberg Galleries on 3 December to bid for a collection of Max Reinhardt notebooks. Her interest in the German theatre producer was fostered by Lytess. She managed to secure the collection of 178 manuscripts containing personal notes on dialogue, action and scenery for $1335. It is widely believed Marilyn bought the notebooks for herself. But she had every intention of donating the collection to a 'worthy' university, as reported in the *Pottstown Mercury* (and others) on 5 December.

The decision about what to do with the notebooks, initially pleasurable eventually became, as Marilyn described it, 'a Jonah to me'. But for the moment it was deferred. By 6 January 1953, Marilyn was involved in production for *Gentlemen Prefer Blondes*, and she had had enough of the whole Reinhardt business and released a statement saying: 'I feel that placement of the books should be the decision of Mr Reinhardt's son, Mr Gottfried Reinhardt. He insists on reimbursing me for the auction price.' What she had wanted was for the collection to be accessible to drama students. Her career was soaring and, in the spirit of becoming a better person, she wanted to give something back.

7

'WHATEVER I AM, I AM THE BLONDE'

Joe DiMaggio had shown up unexpectedly at Marilyn's hotel room on Christmas Eve with a tree and presents in what turned out to be a delightful interlude to the *Gentlemen Prefer Blondes* shoot. Directed by Howard Hawks, Marilyn's co-star was Jane Russell. From the start, the media enjoyed setting up a rivalry between the women, spreading rumours about who was the most demanding, inviting Russell to start a fight for the newspapers. The supposed feud amazed both women, with Russell quick to defend Marilyn as, 'not a girl you can feud with. She is too busy doing the best job she can before the cameras. Her sincerity is impressive and her willingness to listen to and take advice is one of her outstanding qualities.'

Filming had started in the December; the plot revolved around Marilyn's gold-digging blonde Lorelei Lee and Russell's showgirl romantic Dorothy Shaw. It was a musicalized and updated version of the twenties satire, witty and colourful, with its greatest asset the on-screen chemistry between its two female leads. The two got on so well that Russell affectionately nicknamed Marilyn the Round One, while Marilyn defended Russell when she had to do an impersonation of her. 'Why should this bother me?' she asked friends. 'I know Jane wouldn't do anything that would hurt me.'

Make-up artist Allan 'Whitey' Snyder agrees: 'I know the friendship and support of Jane Russell was special to her. She often commented on what fun it was being with Jane. Jane seemed to understand her.'

Russell was earning $150,000 for the entire picture; Marilyn $750 a week, which, she assured the press, was not a problem. What was a problem, though, was the fact that she couldn't get a dressing room and was told – 'Remember, you're not a star'. In the end, she decided to be firm: 'This is *Gentlemen Prefer Blondes*, and I am the blonde. Whatever I am, I am the blonde!' Disarmed by her logic, the studio presented with her own dressing room (which had belonged to Betty Grable).

Blondes boasted a variety of musical numbers, including 'Little Girls from Little Rock' and 'When Love Goes Wrong'. However, the biggest of them all was 'Diamonds Are a Girl's Best Friend', which Marilyn performed with a host of male dancers, one of them the future Oscar-winner (for *West Side Story*) George Chakiris: 'I am so glad that I got to be in the chorus, it was a wonderful thing to be behind Marilyn and Jack Cole!' Chakiris was particularly impressed by Marilyn's dedication to her role: 'I have the loveliest first impression of Marilyn. She was a darling – sweet, quiet and hard-working, and dedicated above and beyond the call of duty. She cared at a level that went beyond what we usually see.'

The shoot for 'Diamonds' went smoothly: Marilyn arrived on time and thoroughly prepared. Wearing no make-up she rehearsed as though her life depended on it, 'concentrated and dedicated to her role,' according to Chakiris. 'It took three days to shoot the scene and at 9 pm on the last day choreographer Jack Cole was keen to return to New York and almost 'left without saying goodbye, and when Marilyn found out he'd gone, she ran off the stage to try and find him and thank him'.

A constant presence on set was Natasha Lytess, this time a problem for Howard Hawks and Jack Cole, as Chakiris recalls:

> *'One day Lytess was on the set when Jack Cole was facing Marilyn, talking to her; but behind him and unknown to him was Lytess. I think Cole must have been giving direction to Marilyn, but there was Lytess, shaking her head to Marilyn, in response to what Cole was saying. Jack had no idea what was going on. I think this showed a real sweetness in Marilyn, as she was being courteous to both Lytess and Cole – she was in the middle of the situation, being polite to both.'*

A reporter on set during the scene in which Russell and Marilyn read through the ship's passenger list recalls Lytess looking as though she were 'quietly having a stroke', as she concentrated on Marilyn's performance. The scene was shot three times, after which she dragged Marilyn away to lecture her on technique.

Another person anxious to get the best from Marilyn was vocal coach Hal Schaefer, assigned to help with Russell's and Marilyn's singing. Schaefer had a fine reputation, and Marilyn respected him. He laid down clear ground rules: 'The first thing I told her was that she better not be late or I wouldn't teach her, so she showed up on time after that.' In that first lesson Schaefer advised Marilyn to buy *Ella Fitzgerald sings George Gershwin*. 'Marilyn had a problem with singing in tune, but everything else she did was wonderful. I told her to listen to this album because never had there been a singer more in tune than Ella.'

Although Marilyn didn't open up to many people on set, she did confide to

Marilyn's dressing room at Fox, once belonging to screen siren Betty Grable

Schaefer that she believed one day she might make a good actress. Unfortunately, she had no such confidence in her ability to sing or dance. 'The essence of singing is confidence because you don't have any other instrument – no trumpet, violin, etc … singing is not rocket science; it isn't such a profound thing. I gave Marilyn help with her confidence and enjoyment of singing – I didn't want her to feel that she had to prove herself.'

Actor Elliott Reid played Ernie Malone in the film and remembered Marilyn as 'lovely looking, beautiful and charming. She was quiet and shy, but we didn't really get to know each other during the shoot because as soon as the scene was done Marilyn would go to her dressing room to work with Lytess.' Like the others, though, he knew only too well that:

> 'She was often late – sometimes ten minutes or so, but not extreme; her lateness was well known, and it was just how she was. She was charming and everyone understood her lateness, and nobody got mad. There were no problems during the making of the film because she was so sweet; she was never aggressive – she just wanted to do her best.'

Jane Russell was sympathetic to the anxiety behind Marilyn's chronic lateness and made a point picking her up from her dressing room to walk with her to the set each day. This helped with her punctuality, but she still shook visibly between takes, as George Chakiris observed: 'Marilyn was sitting on the round sofa used during the song, and I noticed the muscles in her back quivering from nerves.'

She may have been terrified but she was determined to do her best and took to writing little notes to herself on her script such as 'Know the lines, go over it intelligently'. She wanted to focus on what was going on inside, as Chakiris remembered. 'Marilyn would do the take, and if it was not right, the director would shout, "Cut". She would not go to her dressing room or a mirror; instead she would go back to her starting position and just wait for it all to start again. I never saw her look in a mirror.'

* * * * *

In February rumours circulated that *Niagara* was not doing well at the box office. Meanwhile, Marilyn attended a *Photoplay* awards dinner, dressed in the gold gown briefly glimpsed in *Gentlemen Prefer Blondes*. When she got up to receive her award, the audience yelled and shouted, and Jerry Lewis stood on a table to whistle. Marilyn, lapping up the attention, gave it her all, and the result was electrifying. But one person not impressed was actress Joan Crawford, who commented a few days later at the end of an interview with columnist Bob Thomas in answer to his alleged question, 'Don't you think that dress Marilyn Monroe wore at the awards dinner was disgusting?' She replied, off the record, 'It was like a burlesque show. Someone should make her see the light; she should be told that the public likes provocative feminine personalities but it also likes to know that underneath it all the actresses are ladies.'

Her comments reached Marilyn on 3 March when Thomas published them in his column. Marilyn had been on a high after appearing on the Martin and Lewis show on 24 February, performing the skit 'So Who Needs Friends', before collecting another award – Redbook's Best Young Box Office Personality. But she was devastated by Crawford's remarks, couldn't credit them and didn't know what to say when asked for her response. When Louella Parsons spoke to her, she noticed that Marilyn sounded as though she were suffering from a bad cold (from so much crying). 'I don't believe Miss Crawford said those things about me,' Marilyn said, before reflecting that perhaps Crawford had spoken impulsively, without thinking.

But Crawford told Parsons, 'I wish I could say I didn't say those things but I did say them! I was not misquoted! But believe me, in the future I will think twice before I talk so openly.' She started receiving scathing letters from Marilyn's fans, and through Parsons released a statement apologizing but 'for this thing to go on and on, as though someone has been murdered, is ridiculous'.

Marilyn too began receiving letters, albeit more positive ones, as GIs bombarded her with support; even Betty Grable, co-star on her next picture, How To Marry a Millionaire, took her to lunch, advising her 'just keep on plugging'. Eventually, Marilyn just drew a line under the whole sorry business: 'I'm beginning to look at it as a blessing in disguise. If it had never been printed, I might never have realized how many friends I have, even ones I have never met.'

But the Crawford episode wasn't the only challenge she faced at that time: she was concerned about her mother, who had reportedly married a man she'd met in Portland, a Colonel Ely – possibly bigamously on his part, though Gladys refused to talk about any of it. When he died Gladys had returned to California, living first with Grace Goddard then the Bolenders. Mrs Bolender, who had never seen any of Marilyn's movies, later recalled:

'I talked to Norma Jeane on the phone when her mother was staying with me between times in hospitals … "Norma Jeane why don't you come to see me?" She said, "I always thought because I'm in the movies you might not like me anymore." I said, "Because you're in the movies don't make any difference, you come to see me," but she didn't.'

Courtyard of Marilyn's home at 882 Doheny Drive

Eventually, on 9 February 1953, Gladys was dispatched to Rockhaven Sanitarium and, on 1 March, Marilyn sent a cheque to Grace Goddard for $851.04 to cover her expenses.

Like her mother, Marilyn had been leading a peripatetic existence, albeit within the boundaries of Los Angeles. On 18 March, she moved into a three-roomed apartment on Doheny Drive. It was comfortably furnished, with thick carpets, a white and beige colour scheme, her piano and, of course, her book collection. It was the first home into which she was fully to settle as an adult, and where she remained for almost all of 1953 (to return in 1961). Her new friend Jane Russell had helped her decorate along with interior designer Thomas Lane.

Another new friend at this time was actor and author John Gilmore, whom she met at neighbour John Hodiak's party:

'Marilyn told me she'd dreamed of waltzing through movies as another Jean Harlow. Even then she didn't know she'd someday eclipse Harlow and emerge from a kind of imposed, personal cocoon as the most beautiful and important movie star in the world. Marilyn was shadowed and strange; diffident yet vivacious, determined while fearful. She was intense and funny at the same time, and was very, very far from being 'dumb'. I remember my conversation with her verbatim; how she looked, what she wore and how she smelled; what her hand felt like and how the aroma of her lingered on my hand after shaking hers. From that time on, Marilyn and I ran separately in and out and backwards and forwards through the Hollywood milieu ad nauseam, her career skyrocketing. We caught up again, encountering the same people, the same spots [clubs] on the Strip – Mocambo, Ciro's etc.'

Amid all this Marilyn started work on her next film, How to Marry a Millionaire, working with Betty Grable, who had extended the hand of friendship during the Joan Crawford débâcle. She was to play opposite her and Lauren Bacall, in a film in which three girls rent an expensive New York apartment and set out to trap a millionaire. The filming followed a familiar pattern: the press tried to create a feud among the stars (they failed); and Natasha Lytess's direction caused friction on set. Marilyn was continually late and leading love interest David Wayne was to describe his experience on set as 'one of the worst times I've ever had in my life'. But someone who was happy was Jim Gough:

'My Father, James A. Gough, did some work as an SCE Electrical Engineer at Twentieth Century Fox studios, and supervised electrical installation and lighting. At the beginning of the fifties, Dad would often work on Saturdays, and I was allowed to tag along and watch the films being produced, and I was able to wander around in the buildings! Dad was well liked by the studio workers and by the stars alike.

One day, in 1953, I saw a beautiful blonde named Marilyn Monroe. This woman stood out from the other stars with her incredible charm, her poise and her happiness. She had such a natural beauty, so feminine and gracious, even when she wasn't in full screen make-up and in costumes. She had a beautiful face and a great figure.

As a young man, I was blown away by her beauty. Thanks to Dad, I was introduced to her and to Betty Grable during the filming of How to Marry a Millionaire. Meeting these two fabulous women was a teenager's dream come true, and it changed my life. Marilyn and Betty were not only beautiful but also very kind and down to earth – without an ounce of pretension. One day, they invited me to have lunch in the Commissary. They were both made up and in costume with dressing gowns over their costumes to protect them. My entrance into the restaurant, between these two women, was the answer to a young man's prayers! During the meal, we chatted about school matters, friendships and, most of all, about pets. Marilyn loved dogs especially.

After the filming of How to Marry a Millionaire, I occasionally met Marilyn, who always seemed to remember me.'

Marilyn herself was memorable – and increasingly in demand, signing a new agency contract with the Famous Artists Agency that April. At the beginning of the month, on the 7th, she'd attended a birthday party with Betty Grable in honour of columnist Walter Winchell. But, a week later she was in hospital for her ongoing endometriosis. Afterwards, she rested at home on Doheny Drive, reading and talking to friends.

Grace Goddard was still a big part of her life, especially since Gladys had been re-institutionalized, and the two women would speak on the telephone every day. As Bebe Goddard recalls: 'It used to drive me crazy! ... she confided every minute of her night and day to Grace. Totally. Everything. And Grace would sympathize and advise, and, believe me, Marilyn never took her for granted.' However, although Grace was more than happy to listen to Marilyn's woes, she had her own problems, including a dependency on alcohol and a heart condition, for which she was taking phenobarbital. That May, Marilyn invited her to rest with her at home.

But any peace was shattered when, during a short break with Marilyn, Joe DiMaggio received news that his brother Mike had been killed in a fishing accident. A devastated DiMaggio went straight to San Francisco, while Marilyn returned to Los Angeles and spent her birthday quietly with Grace, Bebe, and Bebe's brother Fritz. She then travelled up to San Francisco to be with DiMaggio and his family to offer her support. She made a good impression on the family, and it is said that it was during this period that DiMaggio came to realize how much he was in love with Marilyn. For her part, Marilyn confessed to friends that she knew at that time that she really did want to marry him.

· · · · ·

On 26 June, Marilyn received the recognition she had craved since a child when she placed her hand and foot prints in the cement outside Grauman's Chinese Theatre. Alongside Jane Russell, she stood exactly where she had often admired the prints years earlier: 'I did have a funny feeling when I finally put my foot down into that wet cement. I sure knew what it really meant to me – anything's possible, almost.' Two days later, she walked to the theatre in the middle of the night to see how her footprints looked. 'It was like hearing all the applause in the world,' friend Sidney Skolsky later observed.

Marilyn had started work on *River of No Return*, a lightweight Western, with which she was not impressed but liked the songs. She played a saloon singer, opposite Robert Mitchum, an old workmate of first husband James Dougherty. From the beginning, Marilyn got along well with producer Stanley Rubin; the two had a common enemy in director Otto Preminger, as Rubin remembers. 'The problems between Otto and I began when I told him he wasn't my choice for director – he was the studio's choice … Otto had something in him that made him capable of bullying, and he bullied Marilyn, but never Bob Mitchum because he knew he wouldn't get away with it.'

In fairness to Preminger, while he was a tough director, he did have reason to be upset with Marilyn – Natasha Lytess. Rubin recalls:

'When the take was finished, Marilyn looked past Otto to Natasha, who was standing a few feet behind the director. It was not a good arrangement – Otto was a very proud man and didn't like Natasha being on set. The problem went all the way to the head of the studio – Darryl F. Zanuck – and for a while Natasha was banned from the set, but then Marilyn went to Zanuck herself and Natasha came back.'

When the cast and crew went to Canada on location the problems intensified during filming on a raft. Marilyn and Mitchum almost hit rocks and required rescuing; then Marilyn slipped and fell into the water, as make-up artist Allan 'Whitey' Snyder remembers. 'We had a raft tied to the shore and Marilyn and Robert Mitchum were supposed to push it off. The river bed had a rocky bottom, and when she took two or three steps, she twisted her ankle and fell down.'

From then on Marilyn went around the set on crutches with a bandaged foot, though there is a theory that Marilyn over played her injury to take revenge on Preminger. Stanley Rubin thinks not: 'She did sprain her ankle badly. She had to hobble around, and they shot around her for a few days and also shot scenes where she didn't have to move. I find it very hard to believe it was fake. She did trip on the raft – either getting on or getting off – she did fall.'

The ankle incident did have its compensations; the arrival of Joe DiMaggio, who hurried to her side as soon as he heard the news, and some time off. This she spent relaxing beside the hotel pool, where nine-year-old Nancy Thome was on vacation with her parents at the Banff Hotel:

'One afternoon I was swimming in the indoor pool, and my father was taking pictures of me ... Then a woman walked in on crutches; she sat down near the side of the pool and I saw the cast on her broken leg. As a child I didn't understand what was going on, but people were taking pictures of her, and my dad told me to swim over to her so he could get a picture. She heard my father tell me to swim to her, so she called me over; I was shy and embarrassed and I didn't know who this stranger was. I swam over, and she leaned over and told me to take her hand — she was going to help me out of the pool. I was a rather chubby child and was dead weight, and almost pulled her into the pool on top of me. She let go, and I swam away.'

On the *River of No Return* set with fan Win Rosette

Sometime during that summer of 1953, Marilyn was introduced to Milton Greene, a photographer from New York who had travelled to Los Angeles on business. Marilyn knew his photos and was impressed, but when they met she exclaimed, 'Why you're nothing but a boy!' to which Greene replied, 'Well, you're nothing but a girl!' He took a series of photos; when he returned to New York Marilyn kept in touch not just with him but also with his new wife, Amy, whom she met that October. Whether Marilyn and Greene had met before 1953 is the source of some controversy. Donald Spoto cites a telegram from Marilyn to Greene, dated 14 September 1949, as evidence that they had not only met but even had an affair. However, Greene's wife, whose impartiality is assured by the fact that she was not married to Greene in 1949, dismissed any earlier meeting as 'preposterous'.

Autumn 1953 was a strange period. Professionally Marilyn was happy with her television début on the Jack Benny show on 13 September, followed by a charity benefit for St Jude's children's hospital at the Hollywood Bowl. Privately, though, she was devastated by Grace Goddard's death, suddenly, on 28 September. While Bebe

Goddard was 'horribly sad and devastated … Marilyn was 50,000 times as much.' The most distressing thing was that Grace appeared to have taken an overdose of pheno-barbital. 'She did have a whole box of pills like nothing you've ever seen before. And, in those days they were much easier to get.' If Marilyn knew this – and it is not clear that she did – it must have been extremely upsetting. She had believed her mother was the one with emotional problems, and she had leant on Grace for support instead; to discover that Grace had taken her own life must have been truly disturbing.

'I believe that Marilyn loved Grace more than anybody in the world,' Bebe recalled. 'Grace had been a second mother from the time she was born and had been such a fair person, and as much a mother, or more so, than Gladys … Grace was the single most constant factor throughout Marilyn's life.' It has been suggested that Marilyn refused to attend Grace's funeral, something Bebe denies: 'Marilyn absolutely was at Grace's funeral.'

She was also at the premiere of How to Marry a Millionaire: the show must go on. On 4 November, though, she had more gynaecological surgery, and with that, Grace's death and a heavy work schedule, she was quite literally exhausted. As she told reporter Rita Garrison Malloy: 'I'm so tired. I've been working seven days a week at the studio. My doctor Elliot Corday says I'm anaemic. He's giving me iron and vitamin shots, but they don't seem to help.' Dr Corday also prescribed an iron-rich diet including raw ground liver (which she spiked with lime and Worcestershire sauce to mask the taste), but she still felt awful.

Fox announced she was to star in The Girl in Pink Tights, but Marilyn wanted to see the script first, something not done in the 1950s, when actors were just cogs in the machine. Zanuck refused, and she found herself threatened with suspension from the studio. She dug her heels in further on discovering that her co-star, Frank Sinatra, would be paid $5000 a week (to her $1500). She stood firm; when an executive told her, 'I've been in this business a long time, and I know what's good for you,' she retorted, 'I've been in this business a very short time, but I know better what's good for me more than you do.'

'They throw me from one picture into another,' she complained in December. 'I don't travel, see things, meet people and know them under normal circumstances … Directors think all I have to do is wiggle a little, not act.' When she did not turn up for filming on 15 December, the studio was incensed. At Doheny Drive, where they sent staff to persuade her to change her mind, they were met by a furious DiMaggio. Reluctant to get involved, he was none the less adamant that she would not be taken advantage of; if she made millions for the studio, she surely had a right to share some of it. Marilyn voted with her feet and flew to San Francisco on 23 December for privacy and rest in the DiMaggio family home on Beach Street.

8

MRS DiMAGGIO

Marilyn was in a state of near collapse when she reached San Francisco. DiMaggio's sister Marie took charge, ordering bed rest. She quickly warmed to her new houseguest: 'She's plain and honest and warm and shy,' she told reporter Alice Hoffman in 1954, 'just like Joe. They were made for each other. I know it sounds corny but it's true.' Marie still lived in the family home, cooking and cleaning, looking after DiMaggio hand and foot.

Marilyn settled into DiMaggio's world easily and joined in pursuits that he enjoyed such as fishing with his brother Tom, who considered Marilyn the 'tops'. She got into the general running of the Beach Street house and enjoyed simple pleasures such as washing DiMaggio's car, preparing breakfast for everyone, including making coffee (although she drank tea and milk). 'She's really very handy in the kitchen,' remarked Marie DiMaggio. 'I knew she was a good girl the first time Joe brought her up. Right away she was helping with the dishes.'

On New Year's Eve, Marilyn and DiMaggio dined out at the famed DiMaggio's restaurant, run by family members Tom and Dom and DiMaggio's closest friend, Reno Barsocchini. When they returned to Beach Street, Joe asked Marilyn to marry him, and she agreed. They decided to keep their wedding plans quiet, apart from telling a few friends and relatives. Marilyn went shopping for an outfit with Marie at Joseph Magnin's, where she was mobbed by fans for her autograph and left with a $149.50 ermine-collared suit.

By this time Fox had relented and sent Marilyn the script for *Pink Tights*, but far from persuading her to do the film, the script only reinforced her sense that the part of a teacher turned saloon dancer was not for her. On 4 January she was suspended without pay; newcomer Sheree North would be her replacement on *Pink Tights*. The rumour mills went into overdrive about Marilyn's whereabouts, deciding she had run away to marry DiMaggio – reporting them seen tying the knot in Mexico, Hawaii and the High Sierras. And, even in New Orleans with Rock Hudson, claiming a wedding booked at the Hotel El Rancho in Vegas, cancelled at the last minute. A Fox spokesman denied everything except that she had 'promised to notify us if she decided to get married', adding, 'She's mad at the studio and wants a raise.'

Natasha Lytess was out of the loop entirely and admitted on 4 January that she hadn't heard from Marilyn. Though by then their relationship had started to deteriorate, some say a consequence of a feud with DiMaggio. But things had never been entirely right between them, Marilyn often complaining that Lytess was too possessive. Lytess commenting to the press, in 1953 stated: 'She is not a natural actress. She has to learn to have a free voice and a free body to act. Luckily, Marilyn has a wonderful instinct for the right timing. I think she will eventually be a good actress.' For Marilyn, at heart a private person, such remarks hardly poured oil on troubled waters.

But even private people get drawn into more public projects. Towards the end of 1953, Marilyn had begun work on her autobiography with talk-show host Joe Franklin, deciding what detail she wanted to reveal about her life and selecting photos. Two weeks into it, her studio called a halt because 'she was under contract to work on another book', remembered Franklin, who went on to complete the biography, the first, which he dedicated to Marilyn.

The book Marilyn was under contract to write was to be ghost-written by respected author Ben Hecht, and work started in the new year, on 2 January. Hecht travelled to San Francisco, with secretary Nanette Herbuveaux to spend four days interviewing Marilyn. She was co-operative and agreed to both magazine and book publication, and promised to ask her lawyer, Loyd Wright, to draw up a contract that split the book rights 50 per cent with a 15 per cent share of magazine rights to her.

The interviews held some surprises for Hecht, not least that she had twice tried to commit suicide: 'There was too much pain in living,' she told him. She also claimed that when she had been revived after the second attempt, she felt angry about being forced to live, 'but now I'm glad it happened the way it did. I'm glad I'm alive. I hope to stay glad for a long time.'

While it is known that Marilyn had attempted (or pretended) suicide after Hyde's death, when the other attempt was made is not known, though Marilyn gave a clue when she told Hecht that both occurred after men had abandoned her. Marilyn emerges from these interviews as somewhat sad and unfulfilled, especially when she confided, 'I've never liked sex. I don't think I ever will. It seems just the opposite of love.' Although she didn't admit to Hecht that she had never been able to achieve orgasm, this has been widely rumoured since, which, if true, makes for an ironic and tragic twist. The world's most famous sex symbol never found any fulfilment in sex.

Hecht returned to Los Angeles to write with an advance from publishers Doubleday of $5000 and *Ladies Home Journal* considering serialization. But within days, Hecht received word from Loyd Wright that Marilyn had changed her mind about the book though she was still happy to go ahead with magazine publication. Hecht felt dismayed but continued work nonetheless and awaited further contact from Marilyn.

But Marilyn had other things on her mind; she and DiMaggio had decided to get married so that they would be together when DiMaggio travelled to Japan on a baseball-coaching trip that February. DiMaggio's old friend Judge Charles Peery was happy to arrange the licence and suggested they should marry during the lunch hour when it would be quieter. Despite Natasha Lytess detailing over the phone to Marilyn her grievances about DiMaggio, declaring him a punishment in her life, Marilyn wasn't persuaded. At 12.30 pm on 14 January 1954, she called Fox to say she was about to be wed. She felt a loyalty towards them, a duty – despite being suspended – to let them know. Unfortunately, her sense of propriety wasn't matched by the studio, which quickly spread the word.

By the time Marilyn, DiMaggio and their witnesses arrived at the San Francisco City Hall, at least 500 people were present. They 'were amazed when we walked into the City Hall and saw that mob of people', DiMaggio said subsequently. Due to a slight mix-up with the licence and subsequent delay, there was time to fire questions at Marilyn and DiMaggio as they stood outside about how many children they would have, would she give up her career, were they excited? Marilyn retorted, 'What difference does it make? The studio has suspended me.' Once deputy county clerk David Dunn appeared with the licences, Judge Peery threw everyone out of his chambers to begin the ceremony at precisely 1.46 pm.

As they emerged from the courtroom, they found themselves wedged in by hundreds of reporters and fans, forcing them to take the lift to the basement, accompanied by a disconsolate fan: 'This is a fine thing – dodging your loyal fans like this,' to which DiMaggio is reported to have snapped back, 'Don't tell me what to do.' Once outside, they sped off in DiMaggio's blue Cadillac, Marilyn responding to a question about when they had decided to get married with the enigmatic, 'We've been thinking about it for a long time, but we were not too sure until we walked into the door here now.'

Driving away after marriage to Joe DiMaggio, 14 January 1954

In order to put the press off their scent, Marilyn and DiMaggio headed to Monterey, registered at the Mission Inn Hotel then left for Paso Robles. They ate at the Hot Springs Hotel and checked into the Clifton Motel, where manager Ernest Sharp promised not to reveal their presence. He remained true to his word, but a rumour spread from staff at the Hot Springs Hotel that Marilyn was going back to Los Angeles to work.

This would have been welcome news for Fox if they had not instead headed to a mountain hideaway in Idyllwild, close to Palm Springs, where Loyd Wright loaned them his house.

With Joe DiMaggio on
a 1954 trip to Japan

On 16 January, Fox reinstated Marilyn requesting that she return on 20 January. When that day came and went without her, another letter was sent, demanding she report to *Pink Tights* producer Sol Siegel's office at noon on 25 January, reminding her that the part in the film was within the terms of the contract she had signed on 11 April 1951. It is highly unlikely that Marilyn made it to Mr Siegel's office, but after her honeymoon, she did go to Los Angeles for a meeting with her business manager. By this time presents of silverware, linen and so on had begun to arrive from friends, family and fans, but, as Marilyn later told Sidney Skolsky, 'I didn't get a present from anybody at the studio or from any player.'

On the evening of 28 January, after a vaccination so she could travel with DiMaggio to Japan, Marilyn broke her thumb: 'I just bumped it against the door,' she claimed. This could be true, although over the years DiMaggio has been blamed with claims that he was violent towards her from early in their marriage. Certainly, a relative of DiMaggio's first wife, Dorothy Arnold, believed this: 'Joe was extremely possessive of Dorothy; also Marilyn. He once broke Marilyn's finger on their trip to Japan.'

A relaxed Marilyn
during the trip to Japan
in 1954

In Tokyo, the newly weds were greeted by thousands of fans and reporters; so much so that they had to leave via the baggage door. A stampede followed as fans climbed on top of their car before they swept away to the Imperial Hotel, along with companions Frank 'Lefty' O'Doul (DiMaggio's friend and a baseball expert) and his wife. When they reached the hotel it was riotous chaos as people fell into the hotel pond, tried to break down the doors and scaled the walls. Police dragged fans back to get Marilyn and DiMaggio into the hotel, where they held a press conference in the Treasure Room. This was the first time Marilyn had been mobbed like this, and she was scared.

Once the fans and the media had calmed down there were tranquil visits to places like Kawana, a fishing village, where photographs were taken with the local people. When DiMaggio headed off with Lefty O'Doul to fulfil their coaching commitments, Mrs O'Doul kept Marilyn company, visiting GIs in the Tokyo Army Hospital. There was a last-minute plan, too, for Marilyn to entertain the troops in Korea, something for which, 'I didn't bring the right clothes.' Nonetheless, on 16 February she began her tour, accompanied by the band Anything Goes, of which member Don Obermeyer, remembers:

'We were on the road for about three months ... we returned to Japan, landing in Tokyo ... Since I was the show manager, I was introduced to Marilyn Monroe and Joe, and was told that our group was going back to Korea, after a week's rehearsal in Osaka, Japan.

My first impression of Marilyn and Joe was very pleasant. They were both very friendly. At the rehearsal, Marilyn was so very co-operative. She had never seen an upright mike, as she was used to boom mikes in Hollywood. It was pretty funny, but we got her trained in on the PA system. She was so easy to get along with!! MM never really mentioned her private life, but on the way from Osaka to Korea, she excused herself from the brass in the front of the plane and sat down with each one in the show group and asked about where we lived, before going into service and about our lives growing up! She was very personable and [it was] a surprising move on her part. We all appreciated her interest in us.'

Touching heads with Don Obermeyer of Anything Goes, the Korean tour band

By the time Marilyn began the first show in Korea, it was snowing, but even so she appeared in a purple evening gown and later claimed that she didn't even notice. 'In fact,' she said, 'it melted away almost before it touched my skin. That was the happiest time – when the thousands of soldiers all yelled my name over and over.' She performed several songs, including 'Diamonds are a Girl's Best Friend' and 'Kiss Me Again', and joked and chatted in between with the GIs. One of them was Don Loraine:

'I was a young marine in Korea. Marilyn came out dressed in a heavy parka. She started to sing; suddenly stopped and said, "This is not what you came to see" and took off the parka. She was dressed in a low-cut purple cocktail dress. She was so beautiful, we all went wild, and I might add it was colder than hell that day. She brought a lot of joy to a group of combat weary marines, and I for one will never forget her.'

Another marine, R. J. Vannucci, recalls their determination to see the show:

'We made the trip down to see the USO show, which included Marilyn's appearance. We were posted ten [to] fifteen miles [away] and had to find our own way to the show. We started walking, but soon hitched a ride on a passing truck. We found our way back the same way. I remember that it was a very cold day, typical for Korea in the winter.'

Marilyn created quite a stir, says Don Obermeyer:

'Marilyn did not appear to be nervous before or after each perform-ance, except a few times she messed up some of the lyrics, but recov-ered! She was always greeted by a wildly energetic bunch of GIs, and, time permitting, she would stand in front of the stage, talk to them and let them take snapshots. At the end of each day of performances, she was swept off to the Officers Club. From the very first day on tour, she insisted that her 'bunch of guys' would go with her!'

Greeting the troops in Korea
with open arms

Exhausted from appearing before 100,000 servicemen in just four days, Marilyn found time on the last day to give a heart-felt speech, declaring that she had never felt like a movie star before her trip to Korea. She added: 'Now I'm flying back to the most important thing in my life – Joe. And I want to start a family. A family comes before a career.'

On her return to Japan, Marilyn is reported to have excitedly told DiMaggio, 'You never heard such cheering,' to which he replied, 'Yes, I have.' His put-down would have hit home harder because she was unwell, having contracted not just a bronchial condition but pneumonia in the freezing conditions. Back in the US, the tour – and the honeymoon – had ended; she was back to reality.

Almost as soon as they arrived back in San Francisco, DiMaggio left for work in New York. On 28 February, at the very precise time of 11.38 pm (which appears on the letter), Marilyn sat down to write to her new husband, pouring out her heart, saying how much she missed his love and cuddles, felt so sad and wanted to be near him. She apologized for always being late; promised to try a million times harder and shared her hopes that he would be proud of her as a wife and mother of his children. The letter is evidence of problems even early on in the marriage. In an effort to find answers to

Marilyn sang 'Diamonds are a Girl's Best Friend' for the troops

them, Marilyn continued seeing therapists and consulted psychic Kenny Kingston:

Waving to the crowds, dressed for the job, Korea, 1954

'I had my large house high atop Pacific Heights in San Francisco when film great Clifton Webb telephoned me and made an appointment for a 'Mrs DiMaggio' to come for a private psychic reading. The DiMaggio name is fairly common in San Francisco, so I thought nothing out of the ordinary about it. We set a time for the appointment — which I recall vividly as being 9 pm Clients are rarely late for appointments, thus when Mrs DiMaggio had not arrived by 9.15 pm, my Philippine houseboy Modesto asked if he should extinguish the lights outdoors. (The fog was rolling in heavily.) I instructed him to leave the lights on, though I told him he could retire for the evening, and I would take care of it. Shortly thereafter, the doorbell chimed. When I opened the door, there she stood — in a black coat with a white ermine collar and a kerchief on her head. Instantly I recognized the 'Goddess of Love'. She was breathless.

I invited her into the library and asked her if she'd like a glass of water. I also asked her why she was breathless, and with a smile I was to remember for ever, she replied, "I got out of the cab five blocks from your home." I asked her why and she said, "The story broke in this morning's paper that I was seeking psychiatric help, and I didn't want your reputation spoiled." So you see, this was the loving type of a girl that Marilyn Monroe was … It was a friendship that began that night and would last until Marilyn's final days.'

· · · · ·

On 8 March, Marilyn won a Photoplay award for her performance in Blondes and officially signed with the Famous Artists Agency, although, in reality, associates Charles Feldman and Hugh French had been looking after her for some time. They agreed that Pink Tights was unsuitable and began negotiations with Fox, who agreed Marilyn could appear instead in a supporting role in the musical There's No Business Like Show Business. Not thrilled at that prospect, she had the offer of the role of 'The girl' in Billy Wilder's The Seven Year Itch to look forward to. It came with the promise of a new contract in August 1954 that would guarantee a $100,000 bonus. In order for Marilyn to begin work on There's No Business Like Show Business she and DiMaggio had to relocate in Los Angeles, staying first at the Beverly Hills Hotel before moving into 508 North Palm Drive in Beverly Hills with the help of DiMaggio's friend Vic Masi, to whom they became close, often hiding out with him and his family from the ever intrusive media.

On 9 April, Marilyn met up again with Ben Hecht, who had completed some

70 pages of her memoir. According to Hecht, she laughed and cried and was thrilled with the results, promising to go through it and come back to him with her amendments. When they met again, she had edited a dozen pages and promised to do more, but by 19 May he had heard nothing and Hecht wrote to Loyd Wright to ask why. There'd been a provisional sale to *Collier's* magazine, with the proviso that Marilyn should agree the text. But it all came to naught when an unapproved piece appeared in London's *The Empire News*. Sadly for Hecht, he was unfairly credited with its appearance; it turned out his agent Jacques Chambrun had sold it for £1000 without permission, humiliating Hecht and forcing everyone to drop the project. Twenty years later, in 1974, an edited version appeared that was reprinted in 2000 and 2007.

The book fiasco wasn't the only one in Marilyn's life that spring; on 21 May she crashed into the car of PE instructor Bart Antinora, who sued her, only later settling out of court for $500. Maybe Marilyn had been distracted by her new role in *There's No Business Like Show Business*; the shoot had begun on 2 May and the film was the life and times of a family of vaudevillians that starred Ethel Merman. Marilyn played supporting character Vicky, dating Tim Donahue, played by Donald O'Connor.

George Chakiris was involved in *Business*, on a version of 'Heat Wave':

'The choreographer for all dance numbers was Robert Alton, but Marilyn had worked with Jack Cole previously and wanted him for 'Heat Wave'. Alton created the number for Marilyn, using a girl in her place, along with dancers – one of which was me. We worked on it, and when it was finished Marilyn came in quietly and sweetly on her own and sat down and watched. At the end she thanked Alton and left, but she still wanted Cole, so he came in and choreographed the number. She was absolutely right to want Cole; he was right for the number and had a totally different style to Alton. Cole was brilliant with musically gifted women, and Marilyn was gifted in those areas. She wasn't a professional dancer, but she knew how to move.'

Marilyn rehearsed a great deal for the musical numbers, and at the end of one particularly hectic day the cast held a small impromptu party to celebrate getting through it, as Chakiris recalls:

'No one was dressed up, everyone – including Marilyn – was in casual clothes and no make-up. My dance partner, Druscilla, wanted to ask Marilyn to kiss me, but I absolutely didn't want her to do it. Druscilla went over though, and Marilyn turned round, looked in my direction and said, 'But I don't know him'. I thought this was very sweet and meaningful, because she knew it was inappropriate to kiss me. I wasn't disappointed because I was shy and didn't want Druscilla to do it in the first place!'

Marilyn did a lot of work on the songs; Hal Schaefer was her vocal coach once again. He was a sensitive and quiet man, and Marilyn and he had much in common, especially their desire to get the best out of Marilyn's performance. But as shooting progressed, Marilyn found herself reverting to her old habit of turning up late (citing anaemia and bronchial problems), as George Chakiris bears witness. 'She was a wonderfully talented artist, but during the filming of "Lazy", she kept Mitzi [Gaynor] and Donald [O'Connor] waiting until 3 pm Her lateness was never malicious – she was a truly kind human being. But nobody likes to be kept waiting, which is why certain actors have said things about her.'

Disturbingly, when she did turn up, it was with bruises evident on her arms. 'I bite myself in my sleep,' she joked, though no one thought it funny. Rumours of problems at home were not quelled when DiMaggio was said to have told Fox he would not tolerate any invasion of their privacy. His absence from the set was marked, though he did visit during the filming of 'Heat Wave', which, with Marilyn's sexy and revealing costume, wasn't the best time to arrive, given his reputation. He refused to be photographed with Marilyn, all in all creating a sense that all was not well (fans ringing the doorbell at home didn't help either, something that Marilyn admitted bothered DiMaggio no end).

What went on behind closed doors at North Palm Drive will perhaps for ever remain a mystery, though there are clues in a letter from Marilyn to DiMaggio after an argument. In it she admitted she was wrong to say the things she did; she said them because she was hurt; urged him never to be angry with 'his baby', then went on to apologize, signing off 'your wife, (for life), Mrs J P DiMaggio'. They tried to quash rumours of discord via comments to the media. DiMaggio saying that while he didn't interfere in Marilyn's work, he was interested in it. 'It's entirely possible for two people to have careers and live a happily married life. It's going on around us every day.'

Marilyn said: 'Marriage has given me roots. Joe is so strong and vital, so stable and understanding. With him beside me I have nothing to fear.' Friends joined the denials, with Marilyn's hairdresser Gladys Whitten declaring that she had never seen her more bubbly and effervescent, and Sidney Skolsky writing about Marilyn's life as a housewife, declaring DiMaggio had invited him to drop in any time.

When things had started unravelling at home, Marilyn had begun to see Hal Schaefer as more than her vocal coach. But her wish to make a go of it with DiMaggio made her cool things with Schaefer, who, quite shockingly, responded by trying to commit suicide. 'I did it because I didn't see any way out,' he remembered. 'I thought my career was finished, and my relationship with Marilyn was over. I thought there was no solution.' Marilyn raced to his hospital bed to lend her support, which did not help matters at home when it all hit the headlines.

On 30 August, when Marilyn and Ethel Merman filled in for columnist Drew Pearson in the Footlight Reflections column, she gave a glimpse into her private life. 'I work hard and study hard and have little time even for my husband. But I do divorce my private life from my career as an actress and that is why you never see Joe and me posing together around Hollywood.'

· · · · ·

There was even less time for DiMaggio when, with filming for *Business* over, Marilyn flew to New York on 9 September with an entourage that included Natasha Lytess to work on *The Seven Year Itch*. On her arrival at Idyllwild Airport, to a reporter's: 'No Joe?' she replied: 'Isn't that a shame?' and nervously giggled. When asked about why DiMaggio was spending time away from home, playing poker with friends, she denied he was, adding that it was hard enough to get him out of the house – he much preferred pottering around, taking a swim in the pool and lounging in the armchair.

Marilyn's role in *The Seven Year Itch* – the story of Richard, a man who has an affair, largely in his imagination, with the girl in an upstairs apartment while his wife is away – was to be a landmark in her career. Co-star Tom Ewell, who had originated the role of Richard on Broadway, had beaten Walter Matthau to the film role. An exterior scene involved Marilyn waving out of an apartment window. One person lucky enough to witness this was Joe Coudert, assigned to take photos of Marilyn inside the apartment:

'I … had to take a break to reload my camera. When I returned, I was all alone with Ms Monroe! I asked her if I could continue photographing her, she said, 'Yes' and I shot several rolls of film. She was very friendly and talkative. The girl next door, though a little over used, is an appropriate description, and she was a real professional with the camera. She was highly relaxed posing, and she knew exactly how to make my camera fall in love with her, over and over.

She asked me a lot of questions about my wife and my photography – she seemed genuinely interested in learning more about my family. She also talked a lot about the events surrounding the filming and her concerns about the New York crowds that followed her every move.

All told, I would say I had the privilege of spending two [to] three hours with her. She actually asked me to stay longer and shoot some more pictures because she was nervous about the fans and the press stationed outside her windows. She was very anxious; her fans would go to great lengths to touch her as she passed. It was impossible for her to accommodate them all, and she was concerned about being mobbed.'

The famous scene in which the skirt of Marilyn's dress billows skywards as she stands over a subway grating was shot in the early hours of 15 September in front of a crowd of thousands. Unfortunately, Joe DiMaggio had arrived just in time to witness the sight of a crowd ogling his wife's shapely legs and underwear. Back at their hotel, Marilyn and DiMaggio had a huge argument that some claim turned violent. Hotel guests later claimed to have heard the fearsome row, and Amy Greene later claimed that when she and Milton met up with the DiMaggios for dinner shortly after, she saw bruises on Marilyn's back. Whatever happened that night caused irretrievable damage, and by the time they left New York on 16 September, the marriage was over.

The day after her arrival in LA, Marilyn called in sick at the studio; her doctor confined her to bed with flu. DiMaggio returned to San Francisco, where he told his friend Reno Barsocchini he would be travelling back to Los Angeles to see Marilyn, before heading East for the World Series. 'I'm sure everything was OK,' Barsocchini said, when asked about signs that the marriage was in trouble.

But things were obviously not OK. She had decided that while she still loved DiMaggio, divorce was the only option, and when she phoned lawyer Jerry Giesler, she struck him as someone still in love with the person she wanted to leave. Giesler tried to help her to determine what to do for the best, but Marilyn was adamant – she wanted a divorce, with no request for alimony or property.

Hal Schaefer was privy to Marilyn's very personal thoughts:

'DiMaggio had got physical with her, and although she didn't have a great deal of self-esteem, she did finally have enough and picked up and left. She was very serious about divorcing him, which is why she hired Jerry Giesler – she wanted to get away from Joe. Marilyn was a super-sensitive woman and had a real artistic thirst to grow; she loved the arts, but Joe was into none of these things. Marilyn didn't want any part of him – she was hurt and emotionally fragile and turned to me [for support].'

DiMaggio was living on the ground floor of North Palm Drive, while Marilyn spent her time upstairs. When Jerry Giesler arrived on 4 October, he found DiMaggio in the living room and, after talking to him for some time, served him with divorce papers.

At 2.45 pm, Giesler and Fox publicity chief Harry Brand gave a statement to the press. The charges were mental cruelty; neither Joe or Marilyn would comment. Relations were still friendly; the divorce had nothing to do with the skirt-blowing scene, and to cover all options, 'She is not pregnant'.

The next day DiMaggio left, declaring that he would not return; Marilyn departed shortly thereafter, leaning on the arm of her lawyer with friend Sidney Skolsky close by. Although she tried to speak to the press, she was too upset to do

1327 North Vista
Street: home of vocal
coach Hal Schaefer
during his friendship
with Marilyn

so. She was to move into an apartment at 8338 Delongpre Avenue and continue her friendship with Schaefer, visiting him at apartment 203 on 1327 North Vista. The relationship quickly developed: 'We became lovers and were going to get married,' said Schaefer. 'She wanted to convert to Judaism because I was a Jew. She was still legally married to DiMaggio but had already moved out and had started divorce proceedings.'

Whether or not Marilyn was truthful with Schaefer about her feelings, DiMaggio was concerned enough to hire private detectives from the City Detectives and Guard Service to follow them and surveillance began on 20 October. Schaefer recalls: 'It was a sick and hostile situation because of DiMaggio. He hired private detectives and bugged Marilyn's car, my car and my apartment. We were followed everywhere and it was very scary. Marilyn was terrified.'

When she appeared at Santa Monica Court House on 27 October, Marilyn did not mention the on-going surveillance. Instead, she leant on the arm of her business manager Inez Melson and told how her dream of marital bliss had turned into a nightmare of 'coldness' and 'indifference'. 'My husband would get into moods where he wouldn't speak to me for days … If I tried to coax him to talk to me, he wouldn't answer at all, or he would say, "Leave me alone, stop nagging me!"' Tearfully, she explained that she had offered to give up her film career, 'But his treatment of me made me ill and I was under the care of a physician quite a bit of the time.' Despite Skolksy's claims of being invited to drop by anytime, Marilyn said DiMaggio refused visitors to North Palm Drive.

Inez Melson also took the stand. She'd witnessed DiMaggio pushing Marilyn away; he'd admitted to her that he was indeed cold, and he regretted his actions. Ultimately, Marilyn was awarded a divorce and left court declaring that while she was glad it was over, she and DiMaggio would stay friends, though, 'I still don't know anything about baseball.'

But, for DiMaggio, it was a friendship that was verging on the obsessive that came to a head on 5 November when, with his friend Frank Sinatra and the private detectives he'd hired, he stormed an apartment in which he expected to find Marilyn and Schaefer *in flagrante delicto*. Apart from the fact that this was illegal and ludicrous, they had broken into the wrong apartment and succeeded in frightening to death the woman who lived there.

Frank Sinatra later claimed that he had stayed in the car, smoking, and when the case went to court in March 1957, Joe DiMaggio backed him up (though he wasn't in court himself). But detective Phil Irwin insisted that Sinatra was an active participant. Active or not, the raid shook the entire apartment block. At the time, Marilyn and Schaefer denied being in the building, but some fifty years later, Schaefer came clean:

Site of the Wrong Door Raid, 754 Kilkea Drive, Los Angeles

'The apartment belonged to an ex-student of mine who had become a friend. She knew about Marilyn and I, and when she went out of town, she gave me the key … so that we could use it. It was just Marilyn and me in the apartment when the raid took place, and Marilyn was terrified. I don't believe I'd be around today if they'd found me in the apartment. They almost wrecked the building — rammed the door down of the wrong apartment and the woman ended up suing. Marilyn and I managed to get out the back door.'

The very next day, on 6 November, Marilyn had to make a quick recovery for a party in her honour at Romanoff's restaurant. The stars that night included Marilyn's childhood idol, Clark Gable, and she fulfilled a fantasy by dancing in his arms. 'I turned the colour of my red chiffon dress.' Several weeks later, on 21 November, Monroe and Gable were reported, with no grain of truth, as 'Hollywood's Newest Romance'.

Her marriage over, Marilyn was full of plans for the future. She'd been sent the script for *How to be very, very popular*, she knew it wasn't for her. Instead she decided to move to New York and set up her own production company with photographer Milton Greene. But, before she could put any of her plans into action, she had to give priority to a gynaecological operation, for which she went into hospital on 8 November. In spite of everything, DiMaggio sat beside her hospital bed for hours, prompting the press to promote their reconciliation. But Marilyn nipped any such ideas in the bud: 'Joe and I are just friendly, that's all. There's nothing to it.'

Looking glamorous at the 1954 *Photoplay* magazine awards

On leaving hospital, Marilyn sought privacy at the home of old friend Anne Karger. Before she left for New York, however, she had a few loose ends to tie up, including breaking the news of her departure to Hal Schaefer. 'She went to New York to begin her new life, and that was the last time I ever saw her.'

9

NEW YORK,
NEW MARILYN

The move to the East Coast must have been a strange time. Recently divorced, she was living with a family she did not know well in Weston, Connecticut – with photographer Milton Greene and his family in their farmhouse. She found herself in an environment and climate very different from the one she'd known all her life in California. Virtually no one knew where Marilyn had gone. Fox insisted that she was still resident in California; while the press perpetuated rumours of affairs with the likes of Frank Sinatra and Clark Gable.

Marilyn had no intention of enlightening them. She had transferred all her business affairs to New York, dropped Inez Melson as her business manager (although she continued to handle all affairs related to Gladys Baker), fired Charles Feldman as her agent and neglected to contact Natasha Lytess. With Milton Greene, she had started to discuss their new venture, Marilyn Monroe Productions, for which she planned to produce films and television, plus a book to showcase Milton's photos of her. On 3 January Marilyn attended a meeting with the board of directors for Marilyn Monroe Productions that included Milton Greene, his accountant Joe Carr and lawyer Frank Delaney.

On 7 January the 'new Marilyn Monroe', a whole new person, Marilyn the serious actress, a world away from the studios and Hollywood, appeared at Delaney's home. She announced her plans to the press (including her dream of acting the female lead in Dostoevsky's *The Brothers Karamazov*). She also made the surprise announcement that she believed she was no longer under contract to Fox (Delaney had found holes in the agreement and told her she was a free agent). This was news to her studio, and when she arrived at Fox in LA on 9 January for retakes on *The Seven Year Itch*, they were in no mood to discuss it (though Fox said they would use 'very legal means' to enforce the agreement). Marilyn admitted, despite Delaney's continued insistence otherwise, that she was still under contract but hoped that they could reach an understanding. A media frenzy ensued; she could end up a has-been, according to the newspapers. So-called friends declared her 'stubborn and impatient'; even Natasha Lytess got in on the act by commenting: 'Nobody's indispensable'.

But Marilyn did not seem to care about any of it. She moved into the Gladstone Hotel, New York, on 19 January and became a regular theatre-goer, often going backstage to meet the actors. She made new acquaintances, mostly among older women, such as Dame Edith Sitwell and columnist Elsa Maxwell. Maxwell described Marilyn as 'the most exciting girl in all the world', like a child 'who was trying to appear sophisticated and grown-up'. She also began acting lessons with Constance Collier in early 1955, and shortly thereafter, encouraged by Broadway producer Cheryl Crawford, with Lee and Paula Strasberg, who ran The Actors Studio. The studio's technique, 'The Method', derived from the teachings of Constantin Stanislavski, co-founder, co-director and leading actor of the Moscow Art Theatre, and was deemed radical with its requirement that the actors immerse themselves in their characters.

Marilyn began taking private lessons with Lee Strasberg, which she enjoyed. According to what she told *Photoplay* she was also an observer at the studio, though one day she might audition for membership. She was concerned about her place among the other students> 'I guess I'm not a lot older than they are, but I feel like it,' and found herself the object of curiosity, although reports of a hostile reception were perhaps exaggerated. Fellow student Stefan Gierasch was witness to Marilyn's early days at the school:

> '*I was surprised to see someone like Marilyn in the studio. We were like a club, but we tried to welcome her; I don't believe we were unkind to her at all. Strasberg was her mentor, and he and Paula were always around her. After class the students would sometimes dine together for lunch; Lee and Paula would escort Marilyn, and she would be quite giggly. She was quite retiring and quiet, but that depended on circumstances. She sat at the back, blended into the crowd, and didn't draw any attention to herself. She came to be more relaxed in the restaurant as time went on, and she was always tended to by Paula.*'

Another student, Mark Weston remembered Marilyn being known as 'the Golden Girl':

> '*Before Marilyn arrived in Lee's private class, he asked us all to treat her like just another student. My introduction to Marilyn was abrupt and painful; she would attend class and just take up space … wear mink coats in the summer and different-coloured shoes on each foot. Well, I had arrived late to class while a scene was in progress. My usual seat was on*

*the middle aisle three rows behind where Lee sat. I groped myself across the aisle and acci-
dentally stepped on the Golden Girl's open toed high-heeled shoes. I sat and watched the
scene being performed. I eyed the Golden Girl then turned away ... on my third viewing
of her I realized it was Marilyn! ...*

> *My first impression and sympathy towards Marilyn, who sat next to me, was when
something humorous happened on the stage all would laugh, including Marilyn. However,
instead of an instantaneous laugh she would look at someone then laugh, stop and repeat
the action again and again. My feelings were that the studio had created a robot. She was
aware of her every response.'*

While she seemed unapproachable at first, Marilyn longed to make friends and later
said that the greatest thrill came one morning when 'a couple of [the other students]
... waved and said casually, "Hi Marilyn". It was a simple thing, but it meant they
had accepted me. I was one of them.' Eventually she had studio classes five times a
week and found the lessons challenging, as often her mind was elsewhere, and that
made it difficult to concentrate.

Although she had left Hollywood, her fan mail at Fox hit 8000 – the highest
of any star in the studio's history – proof, if any were needed, that she had really

Mixing with fans, caught on
camera by Bement resident
Albert Wimer

arrived. Away from her lessons, Marilyn was happy to
take part in charity and publicity functions, such as
working as an usherette at the première of *East of Eden*
and riding on a pink elephant at a benefit in Madison
Square Garden. On 8 April she appeared on Edward R.
Murrow's TV show, *Person to Person*, and was interviewed
shortly afterwards by Dave Garroway for his radio
show. She followed this with an interview by Peer J.
Oppenheimer, who was then editor-in-chief of *Family
Weekly* (a Sunday supplement that became *USA
Weekend*). Oppenheimer first met Marilyn in 1955:

> 'I took her out to dinner for a story in Family Weekly. I found her totally helpless in
the presence of a man ... although I had a slight suspicion that maybe it was partly an
act. Nevertheless, she gave a great interview. While there were hundreds of people I interviewed for Family Weekly, and later for a television series I created and produced for
NBC, the two hours with her were the most memorable I spent with a star.'

One thing Marilyn wouldn't have discussed was her decision to undergo psycho-
analysis with Milton Greene's ex-therapist, Margaret Hohenberg. She declared Freud

her hero, but due to the psychoanalytic technique of continually going back over childhood problems and situations, the therapy sessions were not easy. One friend who disliked both the psychoanalytic journey and the Strasbergs was Arthur Miller. Although still married, he began to spend time with Marilyn in her apartment at the Waldorf Towers, where she had moved in April 1955.

Keen to downplay any hint of romance with Miller, Marilyn probably didn't discourage talk of other liaisons. Stefan Gierasch one day 'followed her up Broadway while she was walking with Eli Wallach. She had grease on her face and was dressed down, but everyone still recognized her. Everyone always wondered if she was dating Eli, but they never knew for sure.' The rumours reached the newspapers and finally Eli's wife, Anne Jackson, who was assured that her husband was merely a decoy for real-life boyfriend, Arthur Miller, after which the four became friends.

Another person friend made in 1955 was Norman Rosten, an acquaintance of Miller who had first met Marilyn through photographer Sam Shaw.

The friendship with the Rosten family was life-long, though Marilyn could be demanding, for example calling in the middle of the night giving bulletins on the health of her pregnant cat and asking if anyone wanted to meet up for coffee. Norman would accompany Marilyn to the theatre, and she'd visit their Long Island home at weekends, helping to cook, playing badminton and walking in the woods with the cat. Once she and Norman almost drowned as they waded further and further out to sea to avoid fans during a dip in the ocean. The friendship extended to the Rostens' daughter Patricia, too, who was thrilled one day when Marilyn 'plunked me down at her vanity mirror and said that, since I was so intrigued by the art of make-up, she would show me how to do the job right'.

Attempting incognito in headscarf and fur coat, New York City

Marilyn seemed to have an affinity with younger people. Apart from Patricia, she became close to Lee Strasberg's daughter Susan, and Sam Shaw's daughters Meta and Edith were friends too. Edith, with whom Marilyn shared a birthday, even accompanied her to the circus in joint celebration. During the outing Marilyn was spotted by a fan but managed to escape with Edith to get some candyfloss. 'As we went down the escalator,' says Edith, 'Marilyn turned to me and said in a quite soft voice, "When you talk to me, don't call me by my name. Say "Hey, you. Hey, there, or haystack." She laughed. I thought she was so funny, and I will always remember those words.'

• • • • •

Signing autographs en
route to the theatre
with Joe DiMaggio

Despite having moved across country to start again, Marilyn kept in touch with Joe DiMaggio, who was ever hopeful of winning her back. He kept a journal during 1955, in which he wrote notes to himself to stop being jealous and try to be patient. He knew his behaviour had made Marilyn unhappy and determined to make it up to her he spoke to her on the telephone, sent her letters and telegrams, and they met occasionally when he was in New York. Marilyn had even found time to travel to Boston with him in late January, and he accompanied her to the première of *The Seven Year Itch* in June. His hopes were raised, but asked if they'd reconcile, he could only reply, 'I couldn't answer that question if I wanted to or even if I had the answer. Marilyn is the only person who can do that.' To a similar question, Marilyn said, 'No, let's just call it a visit.'

In early August 1955, when Arthur Miller left New York for Cape Cod with his family and the cast and crew of *A View from the Bridge*, Marilyn had her own plans. She told reporters she was 'going to Bement to see the lovely men with the beards; they are so powerful and masterful' (certainly not tricked into going as some sources claim). In Bement she was to take part in the town's Centennial celebrations, and photographer Eve Arnold, would record proceedings. Marilyn made a big impression on the people of Bement, among them Carl and Jeannine Kaufman, who were lucky enough to get Marilyn's autograph, and shared their joy with their daughter, Karla Jones:

> '*My father and mother [had been to the bank and] were caught up in a traffic jam, which of course was Marilyn making her way to Bement. My mom asked my dad to please go up to her car and ask Marilyn for her autograph, but the only paper in the car was the bank-deposit slip. So off he went! Her car was stopped, and other people were there meeting Marilyn and getting autographs too. My Dad asked her for her autograph, she took his paper and signed it, and they talked about how hot the day was. When they told us their story of Marilyn it always made my mom and dad smile.*'

Meeting 100-year-old Clara, during
a centennial trip to Bement, 1955

As well as giving a speech on her idol Lincoln, Marilyn visited a local nursing home, where she met its oldest resident, 100-year-old Clara. Albert Wimer, whose mother was proprietor, got to meet her: 'Marilyn was a very beautiful lady. She had an injured ankle and was hobbling around – walking with a noticeable limp – but seemed happy to be there; enjoyed being there.'

But what she really enjoyed were the three performances of Arthur Miller's *A View from the Bridge* that she saw back in New York. The press picked up on her new-found interest, but after a performance on 29 September she made sure she was seen at El Morocco with composer Harold Arlen. Rumour of a romance with Marlon Brando was just that; by the October, Miller's marriage had imploded. As he moved out and into a hotel, Marilyn's divorce absolute from DiMaggio came through. In her new apartment at 2 Sutton Place, she and Miller spent many evenings together.

2 Sutton Place, New York: home before marriage to Arthur Miller

It was a year for intense relationships. Of the seven teenage fans who would wait each day, six became known as The Monroe Six, while the seventh, James Haspiel, enjoyed a close friendship with Marilyn that lasted her lifetime. Haspiel was so close to her that they would share taxis, drink coffee and generally hang out; the photos he took of her and of her day-to-day life were later compiled into a book, *Marilyn: The Ultimate Look at the Legend*. Peter Mangone was another fan who spent much of winter 1955 outside Marilyn's hotel; she agreed to let him film her out shopping. In today's 'stalker' society, relationships such as this would be rare, but, in 1955, Marilyn welcomed the attention (although she was known to wear disguises occasionally to obtain some respite).

Disguises apart, sometimes she just wasn't recognized as she went around town on her days off. She could be unconcerned about her physical appearance, relaxed about wearing no make-up and sloppy clothes. Her hairdresser at the time, Julius Caruso, complained that after hours fixing her hair, she would mess it up the moment he'd finished. But when Norma Jeane felt like 'being Marilyn', it was all hands on deck, as make-up artist George Masters found out when he was assigned to work on her face and hair later in her life. Describing her as 'the biggest egomaniac I ever worked with', Masters complained that it took her up to eight hours to get ready for a night out; he would spend the first couple of hours trying to get her out of bed or away from sipping champagne and listening to Sinatra. If she were in a bad mood, she would splash water on her face so that he would be forced to start again, or jump into the bath and completely ruin his work. Always 'the blonde', she even became upset when someone mistook the fair-haired Masters for her brother and asked him to dye his hair black. Masters resisted her wishes, eventually dying her hair a shade lighter than his to try and keep the peace.

Smiling and glamorous, with fans, 1955

Marilyn without make-up,
photographed by Milton Greene
in 1955

On 31 December 1955, it looked like time to be Marilyn again when the year-long feud with the studio was resolved. Fox announced Marilyn would receive a new contract: four movies over the next seven years; director approval and the opportunity to take film, TV and stage work outside the studio. At a time when the studio system was very much in force, the contract was remarkable and paved the way for other actors and actresses to gain some flexibility and independence. Marilyn claimed it as a compromise on her part too: 'I do not have story approval, but I do have director approval. That's important. I have certain directors I'll work for, and I trust in them and will do about anything they say. I know they won't let me do a bad story.'

· · · · ·

Marilyn had been finding the regular Marilyn Monroe Productions meetings challenging, as witnessed by a friend who saw her getting 'pretty bored' after a while. 'It's hard to keep her attention after an hour, even on matters that concern her vitally. She sort of stops listening and stops absorbing.' However, on 9 February 1956, at a press conference with Laurence Olivier held at the Plaza Hotel, the announcement of their joint project, *The Prince and the Showgirl*, made those boring meetings seem worth while. It was to be the first film made under MMP, to be filmed in England and financed by Warner Brothers. The relationship began on a positive note – with Marilyn impressing Olivier so much that he feared he would fall in love with her. Olivier had played opposite his wife Vivien Leigh in the stage version of the play, but Marilyn had reservations when it was announced that he intended to direct and star in the film.

By February, Marilyn had invested in a play by Norman Rosten entitled *Mr Johnson*, starring Earle Hyman, who recalls: 'She probably lost the money, because the play was not a success financially – it only ran six weeks. But it was a success for me because I was able to join the Actors Studio because of my performance.' The first time Marilyn saw Hyman in class, she greeted him warmly, and he found her 'Extraordinarily beautiful in a way that was never fully captured on screen. She was an extraordinary actress. She sat at the back, wearing black slacks and a mink coat, and exuded an incredible light. Even if it wasn't Marilyn, people would have still wondered who she was.'

When Hyman performed his first scene at the studio he was nervous, and when he'd finished, Lee Strasberg asked for comments. Hyman recalls:

'People were quite nice about it but then Eli Wallach said, 'I don't think Earl's work was clear.' There was a silence and a pause, and everyone turned to Marilyn who had raised her hand for the first time ever. She said, 'Well, I don't know, Lee, but it seems to me that life is sometimes unclear.' I thought she was extremely brave to stand up and say that and I never forgot it.'

By mid-February, Marilyn had built up enough confidence to perform a scene from Eugene O'Neill's *Anna Christie* with Maureen Stapleton. Stefan Gierasch remembered how word spread: 'Everybody piled in … the studio was full and everyone enjoyed it. After she had done the scene, the students realized she was talented and were in awe of her in a way.' Indeed after she had finished, the audience broke into spontaneous applause, for the first time in the studio's history.

Mark Weston was there too: 'At the end of the scene Lee asked, as always, for comments. I said, "Lee, I couldn't hear a single word from Marilyn." Lee responded, "But you felt her sensitivity!" That was so true. Once, while watching acting exercises in the darkened theatre, I noticed Marilyn doing a "sunshine" exercise next to me. Oh, my, it was so sensual.'

She certainly had something, and the world was paying attention, including legendary photographer Cecil Beaton. Shortly after the scene at the Actors Studio, Marilyn visited friend Elsa Maxwell who found her in excited mood as she had just found out he was going to take her portrait. But, even to Maxwell, at this point, she denied a serious relationship with Arthur Miller, saying that she was happy to have

him as a friend but had no other plans. What plans she did have concerned her work. On 25 February, she returned to Los Angeles to star in *Bus Stop*, a Fox film about a cafe singer who dreams of fame in Hollywood but finds love in an unsophisticated cowboy. As she left for LA she said: 'My real home now is in New York.'

In front of the lens of high-society photographer Cecil Beaton

However, the welcome she received in LA was not quite what she expected. While the media were thrilled to have her back, Judge Charles J. Griffith was not so enthralled. On 21 November 1954, she had been charged with three traffic violations: driving without a licence; driving too slowly; and driving after her licence had expired. By 29 February 1956, the charge of failing to appear had been added. Fining her $56, the judge said: 'Laws are made for all of us … Whether our name happens to be Miss Monroe or not … You may have the idea that this is good publicity … I've received many letters and it would seem that your so-called public doesn't think it's such good publicity.'

Beverly Glen Boulevard home, LA,
where Marilyn lived while working
on Bus Stop, 1956

Marilyn's reply, 'I'm very sorry for the trouble I have caused, but I was out of California, studying acting in New York,' elicited the response, 'Well, this kind of acting won't bring you an Oscar … in the future I would much rather pay to go and see you perform than have you pay to come and see me.'

Court case over, Marilyn got back to business with a press party at the Beverly Glen home she was sharing with the Greenes. She happily answered questions, except about Natasha Lytess, saying only: 'She was a great help to me,' adding, 'whatever road leads to growth, you take.' When Lytess visited the house and asked to see Marilyn, her request was turned down.

Later Lytess remarked how: 'She's surrounded by these people, who don't let her do anything by herself. They're afraid to lose her. She never goes anywhere alone, they're stuck to her like glue.'

Bus Stop was the first movie in which Marilyn had appeared since her training at the Actors Studio; the improvement in her performance was huge. No so, unfortunately, her behaviour on set. A friend offered this explanation of her timekeeping: 'When she is late, she feels guilty, and since she has always felt guilty she feels comfortable that way. It is easier for Marilyn to take guilt then responsibility.' Nor had the lessons helped her confidence; Paula Strasberg's constant presence irritated director Joshua Logan. There were all sorts of flare-ups on set. Marilyn demanded a young press rep assigned to her be replaced. Logan felt the brunt of her anger when she disapproved of him cutting a scene and co-star Don Murray reacted badly when he was cut by sequins stitched to Marilyn's costume. Yet, off set, Marilyn could be charming, playing catch with co-star Eileen Heckart's sons and signing autographs for fans. From this rollercoaster set-up, Marilyn found herself having to be hospitalized for a few days with an acute bronchial infection.

On location in Phoenix and Idaho, it was others who proved disruptive. A police escort jumped red lights and overused their sirens while fans caused chaos as they did whatever they could to get a better view of Marilyn. The press complained they had not been able to interview Marilyn or take any good photos. One who tried felt the rough edge of Marilyn's tongue, 'Don't shoot pictures while I'm making up! Are you crazy or something?' Milton Greene got stick for the lack of media access to Marilyn, after which photo opportunities were arranged, although the media intrusion was relentless, and by the end of May, Marilyn was worn down and miserable. At weekends she had been visiting Miller in Reno, to where he had moved during the course of his divorce. She stayed with him in Los Angeles, at the Chateau

Marmont, but that was only temporary respite. In any case, the fact that Miller did not think particularly well of either the Greenes or the Strasbergs tapped into Marilyn's own growing reservations about them following various disagreements.

But Miller had more on his mind than his dislike of Marilyn's friends; the House of UnAmerican Activities Committee had called him before them on 21 June after he had applied for a passport to travel overseas. Standing before HUAC, they demanded he name the other people who had been at meetings of a communist-tainted organization he had attended in 1947. When Miller refused to do so, he was declared in contempt of Congress.

After his court appearance, asked by the media why he had applied for a passport, he replied: 'I have a production which is in the talking stage in England, and I will be there with the woman who will then be my wife.' It was a proposal that he had not made directly to Marilyn, but one that thrilled her nonetheless.

Their secret now out, Marilyn and Miller could be openly joyful. Visits to family and friends followed. They visited Miller's parents, Isadore and Augusta and friends, the Untermeyers, for whom Marilyn, wearing a simple black shirt, black and white trousers and no make-up, cooked borscht and ham with cloves and apricot one summer Sunday. Untermeyer wrote later of how they had acted as though it were their first date and seemed very much in love. On the day of their marriage, after lunch with Miller's cousin, the car behind them crashed into a tree en route to a press conference. Of the other guests two passengers were injured including Princess Mara Scherbatoff, chief of the New York bureau of *Paris Match*. Princess Mara died hours later. There was nothing to be done other than attend the scheduled press conference, where Marilyn clung to Miller for support and stuttered during her answers to questions.

When the press dispersed, they left for White Plains, New York, where at 7.30 pm they were married in a courthouse ceremony. In fact they were married twice; the second time two days later, on 1 July, in a Jewish ceremony at the home of Miller's agent, Kay Brown. (Surprising everyone, Marilyn had received a short instruction to enable her to convert to the Miller family's Judaism, though the religion never played much part in her life.) On 6 July, Miller was issued with a temporary passport that allowed him to accompany his new wife to England, where they hoped to enjoy a quiet, working honeymoon. How wrong they were.

UNSEEN PHOTOGRAPHS

1952–1956

ABOVE

With Cary Grant on the set of Monkey Business *(1952). During the shoot, the chimpanzees adored Grant but regularly tugged at Marilyn's clothes and pinched her.*

A location shot from 1952, during filming of Niagara, in which she played
Rose Loomis, a faithless wife who plots to murder her husband (Joseph Cotton),
who turns the tables.

ABOVE

Niagara location shot (as witnessed by the destination Niagara Falls, indicated
on the bus), featuring Marilyn in a tailored suit surrounded by the film crew.

LEFT AND ABOVE

On location for Niagara, Marilyn became friendly with local people employed as extras, one of whom, Patricia Henderson, spent time with her during lunch breaks, when she remembered that Marilyn not only had a healthy appetite but also 'enjoyed getting away from Marilyn', if only for an hour.

ABOVE

Amid the paraphernalia of location shooting, Marilyn
looks elegant in a short jacket with wide lapels and deep
cuffs, a calf-length skirt with a slit, a little boxy handbag
and strappy heels. When filming was over, and Marilyn left
town, she also left behind two pairs of her new shoes plus
a generous gratuity, for her chambermaid, Blanch Maj.
'We were all so excited and most impressed with the fact
that we had Marilyn's very own shoes in our family,'
remembered Blanch's niece, Pat Brennan.

RIGHT

On the set of River of No Return in 1953. Marilyn
found the shoot physically exhausting, but that did not
prevent her from welcoming fans such as Win Rosette,
pictured here, who had driven out on location to meet her.

ABOVE

On 14 January 1954, Marilyn and Joe DiMaggio married in San Francisco: the media dubbed the event the Marriage of the Century. Marilyn is here being driven away in DiMaggio's blue Cadillac after the ceremony, having replied somewhat enigmatically to a question about when they had made the decision to wed, 'We've been thinking about it for a long time, but we were not too sure until we walked into the door here now.'

RIGHT

A headscarfed, relaxed candid shot, cigarette in hand, taken during a trip to Japan in 1954, where Marilyn had gone to be with Joe DiMaggio on a baseball-coaching trip. When the opportunity arose to travel to Korea to entertain the troops, Marilyn had jumped at the chance, despite initial worries that she had nothing to wear.

PART TWO: 'SUMMER' 1952-1956

Marilyn and Joe DiMaggio arriving in Japan. They made a glamorous and explosive couple, but the enthusiasm of the Japanese fans scared Marilyn at first as they surrounded her car, rioted at the hotel and even tried to scale the hotel walls: 'These people, they're mad!' she said. When eventually the hysteria stopped, the couple were able to see a little of Japan, going on trips, including one to a Japanese fishing village.

Marilyn on tour in Korea, February 1954, to entertain the troops. She can be seen chatting and joking before she performed from a repertoire that included 'Diamonds are a Girl's Best Friend'.

PART TWO: 'SUMMER' 1952-1956

LEFT, ABOVE AND PAGE 172

On tour in Korea. Although the photos show a bright blue day, it snowed for much
of the time, but, even so, she abandoned her thick coat for a low-cut beaded evening
gown and later claimed that she didn't even notice the snow: 'It melted away almost
before it touched my skin. That was the happiest time – when the thousands of
soldiers all yelled my name over and over.' Unfortunately the winter conditions were
so fierce that on her return to the USA, Marilyn was diagnosed as suffering from
bronchial pneumonia.

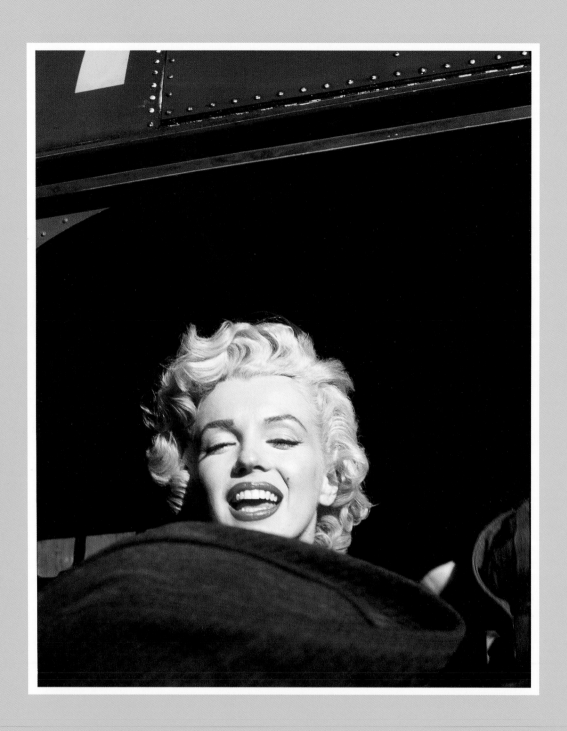

PART TWO: 'SUMMER' 1952-1956

ABOVE

Despite an exhausting schedule in Korea that included appearing before 100,000 servicemen in just four days, Marilyn found time on the last day to give a heart-felt speech, declaring that she had never felt like a movie star until then. She was in exuberant mood, wearing a fashionable military-inspired outfit as she stands at the top of an aircraft steps and even taking a ride in a tank. But the bubble of her exuberance burst when DiMaggio responded to her excited, 'Joe, you never heard such cheering,' with the rather brutal, 'Yes, I have.'

ABOVE

Touring in Korea, 1954, Marilyn with an unidentified colonel. In the words of marine Don Loraine, who attended one of her shows, 'She brought a lot of joy to a group of combat weary marines,' many of whom walked several miles in freezing conditions, there and back, just to see her.

RIGHT

Looking particularly glamorous at the Photoplay Magazine awards in March 1954, where Marilyn received Most Popular Actress of 1953. Husband Joe DiMaggio did not enjoy these occasions, so Marilyn would often attend with friends and be picked up afterwards by DiMaggio.

RIGHT

In New York during 1955, Marilyn was sometimes spotted on outings to the theatre with ex-husband Joe DiMaggio. Here he is seen emerging from a door behind Marilyn, as she signs autographs. At the time, DiMaggio was hoping for a reconciliation but when asked about it, he could only respond, 'I couldn't answer that question if I wanted to, or even if I had the answer. Marilyn is the only person who can do that.' His hopes must have been dashed when, in his hearing, Marilyn responded to a similar question by saying, 'No, let's just call it a visit.'

Behind Marilyn the sex symbol, there was always Norma Jeane, a woman of great natural beauty, seen here in a swimming pool, wearing no make-up and cradling a puppy. The photograph was taken by photographer and friend turned business partner Milton Greene in 1955, a time of great change for Marilyn – her marriage to Joe DiMaggio had ended, and she had fled LA for a new life on the East Coast – but her future looked bright, and life was good.

AUG • 55

ABOVE AND RIGHT

In early August 1955, while living in New York. Marilyn, here a vision of
blondeness, told reporters she was taking a trip to the Illinois prairie town of Bement
'to see the lovely men with the beards; they are so powerful and masterful'. She had
been invited to take part in the town's centennial celebrations, which included her
judging a beard-growing competition and making a speech on the subject of her
idol, Abraham Lincoln. Photographer Eve Arnold recorded it all for posterity.

AUG · 55

LEFT, ABOVE AND PAGE 182

Marilyn always enjoyed meeting her fans and did not shirk from doing so during
her visit to Bement, seen here on walkabout, posing for fans and signing autographs.
She even signed an autograph on a bank deposit slip for Carl and Jeannine Kaufman
(who had just been to the bank and were stuck in traffic behind Marilyn's car on
their way home). 'When they told us their story of Marilyn it always made my
mom and dad smile,' remembered their daughter, Karla Jones.

· AUG · 55

RIGHT

At a visit to Bement nursing home, Marilyn meets its oldest
resident, a 100-year-old woman known only as Clara. The
son of the home's proprietor Albert Wimer took this photo
and remembered Marilyn as 'a very beautiful lady. She had
an injured ankle and was hobbling around — walking with a
noticeable limp — but seemed happy to be there.'

ABOVE

During 1955, after Marilyn had moved to New York, she built up a unique relationship with her fans, particularly seven eager teenagers who would await her each day outside her hotel. Six of them were so well established they became known as The Monroe Six, while another fan, James Haspiel, enjoyed a close friendship with Marilyn all her life. Here, looking particularly glamorous, she is seen smiling for a fan's camera as other fans group behind her, autograph books at the ready.

ABOVE

With fashion and high-society photographer Cecil Beaton in 1956. Marilyn
expressed her delight at working with the legendary photographer to friend and
columnist Elsa Maxwell, to whom Marilyn was 'the most exciting girl in all the
world', like a child 'who was trying to appear sophisticated and grown-up'.

PART THREE:
'AUTUMN'
1956—1960

10

SIR LAURENCE
AND THE SHOWGIRL

In spring 1956, preparations had started for Marilyn's arrival in England, with Laurence Olivier and Terence Rattigan working on the script of *The Prince and the Showgirl* and auditioning the supporting cast. When actress Vera Day walked into the office of Laurence Olivier Productions she was 20 years old and had been in show business for about a year. Olivier looked at her and exclaimed: 'Oh dear, she's so like Marilyn.' While Day was naturally flattered by the comparison, Olivier feared the worst, knowing that Marilyn would not appreciate another blonde on set. And so it was that when Day was hired, she found herself in a brunette wig for her role as Betty.

The media had already started whipping up a storm. On 25 April Ascot farm-house owners Mr and Mrs Cotes-Preedy were reportedly to rent their home, Tibbs Farm, to the Millers. There were confirmatory reports on 26 April and 14 May, and even some interior shots and interviews with Mrs Cotes-Preedy. But the over exposure made the Ascot farmhouse unsuitable (though not for Amy and Milton Greene who rented it instead). Much to the surprise of Mrs Cotes-Preedy who had continued with her interviews and TV appearances, she only heard of the change of plan from her cook, hours before Marilyn's supposed arrival. A Park Lane apartment was considered more suitable, but when owner Michael Ferszt somehow leaked this to the press, that plan was ditched. Eventually, the Millers were to rent Parkside House, a large Surrey mansion in Englefield Green. For the four months of their visit, owners Lord Moore and his wife, Joan Carr, decamped to London, leaving behind housekeeper Elizabeth 'Dolly' Stiles, gardener Bernard Stiles, butler Franz Gettliner and his wife, the cook. Other members of staff would include a chauffeur and a detective to oversee security. They were all briefed to expect long hours and practise discretion.

The house itself had new locks installed on the gates. The room intended for Marilyn and Miller was repainted in white while externally, roof tiles were replaced. Security was tight, starting at London Airport, with a meeting of airport officials, the Ministry of Civil Aviation and Marilyn's publicity team. Airport officials changed their mind about no extra security, after hearing what had happened at Idyllwild Airport on 13 July, when the Millers' plane to London had been delayed due to a stampede of fans and reporters.

On the morning of 14 July, some 150 members of the British press gathered behind the newly erected security barriers, complaining about the rain. At around 10.40 am, one hour later than scheduled, the plane touched down. Marilyn was nowhere to be seen as passengers started to make their way down the steps, though a bouquet of flowers was carried on to the aircraft and a knitwear company delivered a sweater. When she eventually appeared, Marilyn was carrying the flowers and wearing the same jersey dress, dark glasses and raincoat (slung casually over her shoulders) that she'd worn when she left New York. Arthur Miller was close by.

Airport staff could be seen balancing on the wings of the plane to get a better view and take photos, and although security was tight, there were a few fans able to greet her personally, including Frank Williams:

> 'My job [at London Airport] was to dig holes, tunnels and whatever was needed. We were told that Marilyn would be arriving one day with her new husband, Arthur Miller and in no uncertain terms [our boss] wanted no nonsense when she arrived – no whistles, no cat-calls etc. Marilyn and her husband arrived right next to the foundations we were digging – probably only 50 yards away from where the aircraft came to rest. She walked straight up to the foundations trench and she said, 'Hello, boys', and we said, 'Welcome to England, Marilyn'. She was quite stunning and from four feet down in the trench, we had a very, very good view of her.'

Once inside the terminal building, there were more photographs, this time of Mr and Mrs Miller with Laurence Olivier and Vivien Leigh (with whom Marilyn chatted about Leigh's pregnancy). Marilyn's 27 pieces of luggage had to be assembled before she attended a press conference, at which she surprised everyone by refusing to speak into a microphone. She found it too impersonal. But as a result many of those present were not able to hear a word she said and began clambering over chairs and tables in an undignified stampede to get closer. Eventually, Marilyn was encouraged to stand on a platform behind a snack counter, where she took questions from the press directed to her via Olivier, who relayed her reply. The questions ranged from 'What are your plans whilst in England?' to the mischievous 'What do

With Lady Olivier – Vivien Leigh – at the time of *The Prince and The Showgirl*

you think of Diana Dors?' and daft 'Can I have a lemonade, please, Marilyn?' in a reference to her position behind the counter. After declaring that the thing she most wanted to see in London was 'the little fellow with the bow and arrow in Piccadilly Circus', the press conference was wound up.

When the Millers and the Oliviers arrived at Parkside House, the whole thing happened all over again. Marilyn did reveal that she had expected a cottage rather than the grandeur of Parkside House, a place that never did live up to her fantasy of a cosy English country retreat. The following morning, she dozed in bed until around noon when Olivier arrived with photographs of *The Prince and the Showgirl* set as well as the costume she would wear in the film. Afterwards she left for a press conference at the Savoy Hotel, stopping to chat first to the local people waiting outside her new home. Among the small talk, she was intrigued to know if anyone there was from Scotland, declaring with pride: 'Monroe is pure Scots, you know.' She arrived extremely late at the Savoy, met once again by large crowds with only a linked human chain of police to protect her.

Questions put to her and Olivier were largely similar to those she'd been asked the day before. If there were any related to *The Prince and the Showgirl*, they didn't make it into the media coverage the next day. There was much more interest in Marilyn's personal life – and what she was wearing; a tight-fitting black dress with a window of net that showed off her midriff. Pictures of her in the dress were beamed nationwide, its style copied and on sale in the shops just weeks later. When asked to describe it, Marilyn hesitated, somewhat disingenuously dismissing it as 'a simple black dress', but adding, quick wittedly, to reporter

A lighter moment during the England trip: laughing with Arthur Miller and Hedda Rosten

Donald Zec, that although the dress wasn't her idea, it was her midriff, in reference to her exposed flesh, bare under the netting.

Marilyn responded mostly in good spirit. However, she was understandably curt when one journalist asked for her definition of an intellectual, saying, 'I guess you could look it up in a dictionary.' Another asked if she believed in the idea of the Seven Year Itch, to which she exclaimed: 'Do you know, I never understood the point of that film.'

Olivier's part in the proceedings was as a conduit for Marilyn's questions, much as the day before. As for Miller, there to support his wife, press reports claimed that the only time he seemed to smile was when they left the room. His chance to speak came when asked how he saw his wife, to which he had replied: 'With two eyes.'

The questions continued for the next hour or so, and just before they ended, the *Daily Sketch* presented Marilyn with a bicycle. (This was presumably, in response to her remark the day before that she would like to relax after filming by taking cycle rides, if she could borrow a bike.) She was thrilled with her gift, which sported a gift-tag that read 'To Marilyn Love From The Daily Sketch'. While Miller looked on in amusement, she exclaimed: 'There are so many things I must do first. It'll be two or three days before you see me riding round the lanes.'

At a Savoy Hotel press conference, 16 July 1956

Yet another press conference had been scheduled for the next day, 16 July, after which Marilyn headed off to Claridge's in Mayfair to meet Miller for lunch. Eating salmon, turkey and fruit, Mr and Mrs Miller looked every inch the newly weds, and restaurant staff spotted them kissing between courses. However, it was Miller's casual dress of grey sports coat, dark trousers and white shoes that ruffled most feathers and gained its share of column inches the next day. After lunch, it was back to Surrey, for what they no doubt hoped would be a restful evening in the privacy of their new home.

At around 8 pm that night, however, a group of some 80 students from neighbouring Shoreditch Teacher Training College, a men's college that specialized in training PE teachers, set off on the two-mile hike to the Miller house. The intention was to sing under her bedroom window; some had trumpets and other musical instruments. College Principal, Ted Marshall, tried to nip the idea in the bud. But as most of his students were demob happy after their exams, he failed; indeed one young man even borrowed his car to make the journey. As they neared Parkside House, they started chanting, 'We want Marilyn', before lifting the front gates from their hinges and proceeding inside the grounds to sing the 23rd Psalm. While it soon became clear that Marilyn had no intention of coming out, the police had reacted otherwise, as former student Allan R, Pemberton remembered:

'It was dark, and I had fled into long, wet grass. I got soaking wet, and I recall clearly seeing the searching lights being scanned over the area where I was hiding. I'm not sure how long I remained in hiding, but when I thought it safe, I returned to the college, where quite a few of the group had already returned. Quite a few hadn't, I remember [and] there were *many stories of 'escapes', but no one saw Marilyn, and we never knew whether she was aware of our escapade.'*

Marilyn was, indeed, aware of everything, as described by Arthur Miller in his auto-biography, *Timebends: A Life*. He and Marilyn watched it all from an upstairs window, but for security reasons, they didn't get involved. And, although threatened with all sorts of sanctions by their principal, housekeeper Dolly Stiles remembered students continued to turn up from time to time at Parkside and shout for Marilyn.

The following day, 17 July, after what must have been a disturbed night, the Millers accompanied Laurence Olivier to the Lyric Theatre in London's West End, where Vivien Leigh was performing in Noel Coward's *South Sea Bubble*. The play had opened on 25 April to its share of critical acclaim, but that night it was Marilyn who stole the show. Shortly before the performance was due to start, she, Miller and Olivier took their seats in row J. In a flesh-coloured, skin-tight dress and a raincoat almost identical to the one she'd worn on her arrival from New York, Marilyn's impact was immediate, her presence unmissable. By the time the performance had ended, a huge crowd had gathered around the theatre, but with Marilyn's chauffeur parked at the stage door, and Olivier's car at the front, fans had no idea where to wait, resulting in crowds at both exits. Finally, at 10.50 pm, after van loads of police had arrived, Marilyn and her companions made their escape via the front doors. They were taken straight to Olivier's London home at Lowndes Place, Westminster, where they spent a few hours before leaving at 2 am.

Rehearsals for *The Prince and the Showgirl* began on the next day, 18 July (and ran until 3 August). Before Marilyn had arrived in England, *Bus Stop* director, Joshua Logan, wrote to Olivier, advising him on how best to work with her. Unfortunately, although Olivier replied to Logan on 26 June to say that his comments had been 'carefully noted', it would seem that Marilyn's way of working still came as a shock to him. From day one of rehearsals, the two did not get along.

Olivier's initial and perhaps greatest mistake was to introduce Marilyn in what she took to be a patronizing manner. Generally polite, nonetheless he made a big speech to the cast, entreating patience with Marilyn, whose methods, they might find, were different from their own. His comments tapped into Marilyn's enormous inse-curity and made her suspicious of Olivier and on her guard from that moment on.

* * * * *

In England, Marilyn's life was a constant source of speculation in the newspapers; there were rumours that she would be holidaying in Paris and Scotland, visiting the local cricket ground and attending at least one wedding, all of which were false. This did not, however, stop the public willing them to be true, as the major excitement caused when 'Marilyn' showed up in Shakespeare Country shows very well.

During one of the several press conferences just after the Millers' arrival, Arthur Miller had expressed his desire to visit Stratford upon Avon. Imagine the fans' excitement then, when on 18 July, a chauffeur-driven car pulled up outside Shakespeare's birthplace cottage, and a woman remarkably like Marilyn stepped out.

Brenda Porter, who was standing in the crowd of people who swarmed round the woman that day, remembered:

> 'I was 19 years old at the time and was employed as a clerk in our local railway goods offices. My boss came in from calls in the town and said, "There is quite a big crowd in Hemley Street, and there is a rumour that Marilyn Monroe is in town, but the police do not know if it is true or not." Of course I was very excited so I asked my boss if I could go to see what was happening.
>
> There were quite a few people in the crowd [and] we all stood and waited for quite a while when a chauffeur-driven car drew up outside Shakespeare's house. A lady got out of the car, and the crowd tried to cross the road to see her. There was no one with her [and] she took video pictures of Shakespeare's birthplace, but very quickly got back into the car. People in the crowd said it was not Marilyn. I can't honestly say if it was either.'

With no security and, of course, no husband, the chance of her being Marilyn was remote. Indeed the chauffeur, when pressed, named her as a Mrs Horace Dodge, from Windsor, but would say no more. This may have been the first time that a 'fake Marilyn' would make news during the England trip, but it certainly wasn't the last. In October, another impersonator made headlines, this time by making appointments with five of London's top dressmakers and declining to show up, as well as booking singer Tommy Steele for a fake party. The press went wild, but the hoaxer was never found.

The first week in England had been a busy one, both for Marilyn and for the media that reported anything remotely Monroe-related. There was the dance teacher who taught wannabes how to walk like their idol and the three friends who went on a tour of Pinewood Studios in the hope of seeing Marilyn, only to be disappointed. There was also a proposed visit from Dame Edith Sitwell and *The Times* piece of 20 July that reported German communist magazine *Junge Welt* as giving Marilyn the thumbs-up for daring to become a serious actress and for marrying Arthur Miller. Certainly for the first week of Marilyn's visit she could do no wrong.

Wearing dark glasses during a day off, shopping in London's Regent Street

The change in mood from delight to impatience was connected with Marilyn and Miller's desire for privacy. Whereas she had made herself initially available to the media, once the press conferences were over, Marilyn almost completely dropped from public view. The British press were quick to comment on this. When she and Miller decided to spend the weekend of 21–22 July quietly at Parkside House, some members of the press assumed she was playing hard to get. Not only that, she had changed her phone number to discourage unwanted calls, and when one press request for an interview was refused, Marilyn's apparent aloofness was compared unfavourably with the friendly ways of English actress Diana Dors. Highly personal, spiteful stories started appearing in the papers, such as allegations that the honeymooning Millers slept in separate bedrooms (something that housekeeper Dolly Stiles confirms as untrue). There was even an article in the *News Chronicle* that described Marilyn as dowdy, with her spare tyre and crumpled clothes.

During the aforementioned weekend, Oscar-winning cinematographer Jack Cardiff visited Marilyn to discuss his involvement with *The Prince and the Showgirl*. She knew all about his work and was excited to meet him, and Cardiff later wrote that on meeting her, he was convinced he had just seen an angel. While Marilyn couldn't be described as an angel to work with, Cardiff always thought of her as a warm and lovely person, and was one of the few cast and crew to socialize with her off set. He gave her books to read, visited an art gallery with her and even accompanied her to a private screening of *Bus Stop* at the Fox offices in Soho Square.

That same July weekend, the Weybridge Division of the Surrey Constabulary worked shifts around the clock. There was also a personal bodyguard in the shape of PC Hunt. Nonetheless, on the Sunday, fans were spotted in the grounds of Parkside House. Every day dozens of admirers crowded around the front entrance, including Mr G. Pearson, 14 years old in 1956, who spent most of his school holidays outside Parkside's gates. He was thrilled when Marilyn waved to him on two separate occasions. But he was also involved in an incident that showed security was lacking, as Mr Pearson explains:

> 'I was outside the gates with my friend, when a couple of reporters approached us, and asked if we would like to earn a large, silver coin. We stated the obvious "Yes", but what did we have to do ...? One of the reporters handed me an envelope and said, "Go in and give this letter to Marilyn."
>
> The envelope just had 'Miss M. Monroe' written on it. I remember we had to jump over the gates (about four to five foot high), as they were locked, and walked up to the house ... we rang the bell, the door was opened by a maid, and I said, "Would you give this letter to Marilyn, please?" She then shut the door, and we waited.

Shortly after the door opened again, and we were confronted by Arthur Miller. He enquired as to how we got in, and who the letter was from. I answered that we had jumped over the gates and that a man had given us the letter. He then told us to go back the way we had came — his actual wording I cannot remember — but it was loud, abrasive, and in words that I had heard adults use before.

We hastily retreated down the drive, and I do recall being photographed as we hurdled the white gates. The reporters then took details of what had happened and gave us half a crown each. As far as I am aware, a short report of the incident appeared in a national paper.'

Another breach of security occurred when two journalists gained roof access, and one of them even dangled upside down to take a photograph of Marilyn in her bedroom. Thankfully the pair were spotted before any harm was done; no photos appeared in the press.

On Tuesday 24 July, Terence Rattigan hosted a party for the Millers at his Little Court in Sunningdale, Berkshire. It was a lavish affair that required the hiring of 20 chauffeurs, waiters, a porter, chef and candelabra for the occasion. The drinks bill was to total £103 and included 42 bottles of champagne, seven bottles of Gordon's gin and two bottles of sherry. Outside, the garden was adorned by fairy lights to enhance the atmosphere of romance and enchantment. Among the 100 guests were Alec Guinness, Dame Margot Fonteyn, John Gielgud, Richard Wattis and Douglas Fairbanks Jnr but the person everyone had come to see was, of course, Marilyn Monroe. Everyone, that is, except PC Packham, who had been asked to stand at the gate of Rattigan's house, to check invitations and prevent gatecrashers.

Unfortunately for PC Packham, he hadn't been told Marilyn Monroe was on the guest list, so when her car pulled up, he treated its passengers like any other party hopefuls and asked to see the invitation. Newspapers delighted the next day in describing how PC Packham had never heard of Marilyn Monroe and hadn't recognized her. However, his version of events is somewhat different:

'The peace was shattered when what was clearly a VIP limo, travelling from the Sunningdale direction, swung into the drive to stop abruptly at my feet. Some lunatic immediately leapt from the nearside front passenger seat and, actually brandishing an empty wine glass in my face, told me aggressively to get out of the way. It was, to say the least, an unusual greeting; neither did his arrival inspire confidence regarding the other occupants of the car. I relieved him of the wine glass and was desirous of knowing what precisely he was up to.

"It's Marilyn, you fool," he hissed, "get out of the way."

Of course! In a blinding flash of the absolute obvious the penny dropped. Everyone in England must surely have known that Marilyn was in town. The tabloids were full of it.

I looked in at the open door of the limo. It was, of course, Marilyn and, had any further proof been necessary, she was accompanied by her then husband, Arthur Miller. I told the driver to carry on, closed the door, and they sped away without the little dogsbody, or whatever he was. He was last seen hoofing it up the long drive to the house, muttering as he went dire imprecations on all coppers.

Press cars that had tailed the limo down the A30 had by then been bumped up on to the grass verges at the side of the main road, their occupants coming hot-foot to join the fray. They were a trifle late, for their real quarry had by then sped off, but they were not too late to weave their usual fairy tales. The tabloids' following day's accounts were founded principally on the story of one of 'yer ole tyme rural bobbies' who spoke with a rich West Country accent, called men 'Zur' and didn't know Marilyn. Any semblance of accuracy in their reports was purely coincidental.'

A publicity shot for *The Prince and The Showgirl*, wearing a favourite sparkly dress and fur stole

An exaggerated version of the night's events soon reached PC Packham's boss, Sergeant Gay, who was informed, incorrectly, that his constable had been threatened with a broken wine glass. In any case, Terence Rattigan was to send a letter to Sergeant Gay, in which he thanked him for his handling of a difficult situation and enclosed a £10 cheque for him to donate to a charity of his choice.

Thankfully for everyone who had come to see her, Marilyn finally made her entrance, in a dress similar to the one she would wear in *The Prince and the Showgirl*. Looking happy and relaxed, the Millers made an impact as they danced cheek to cheek during George and Ira Gershwin's, 'Embraceable you'. Sir John Gielgud was there:

'Marilyn wore an Edwardian dress – she had, I think, worn it to wear in the tests for the film – and she held court in a tent in the garden, where everyone queued up to shake her hand. As I was speaking to her, a rather formidable-looking lady in black suddenly appeared at Marilyn's side and introduced herself as Louella Parsons. Arthur Miller kept at a discreet distance. I had no opportunity of talking further with Marilyn, but remember how graceful she looked, dancing with Terry Rattigan as I took my departure.'

Marilyn was delighted at such a splendid party given in her honour and wrote a poetic letter on Parkside House stationery, thanking her host and commenting on that memorable Charleston to which Gielgud refers.

⋆ ⋆ ⋆ ⋆ ⋆

For the first two and a half weeks of filming, which began on 7 August, Marilyn reported for work every day, and, during those first weeks, although she was never more than an hour late, she was never on time. But, by the time the film wrapped in mid-November, she had arrived punctually on just three of her 53 days on set. Yet, despite this, she doesn't deserve many of the stories that have been written about her being late, such as keeping everyone else on set waiting until late afternoon while she went cycling with Miller. A document dated 9 January 1957 detailed Marilyn's time of arrival each day; the evidence is that she was continually late, but mostly less than an hour so – at her worst, on 30 October, she arrived at 12.35 pm after a 10.30 am call.

There were other issues. Marilyn had difficulty remembering her lines and this infuriated some of her co-stars. Jean Kent, who played Maisie Springfield, remembered Marilyn seemed most concerned with the bustline of her dress, while Esmond Knight, who played Colonel Hoffman, described Marilyn, vehemently, as 'an absolute cretin'.

Furthermore, Marilyn's Method acting clashed with Olivier's classically trained approach. When he reportedly told her to 'be sexy', it put her on edge. She had no idea what Olivier meant, and despite reassurances from her friends, she never recovered her hope that he would treat her as a serious actress rather than as the sexy Hollywood star stereotype that she was trying to shake off. From that moment on, she referred to him as 'Mister Sir'. Her distrust of her director made her reliance on acting coach Paula Strasberg even more apparent and alienated her from the other actors on set. Whenever Olivier cried 'Cut', Marilyn was ushered away to discuss the scene and to rest. On one occasion when Olivier was in mid-sentence, Marilyn turned to her drama coach audibly to ask what he meant. So enraged by Strasberg, Olivier had her removed from the set but his satisfaction was short-lived when Marilyn stormed off to her dressing room, refusing to return until Strasberg was reinstated.

British-born novelist and screenwriter Wolf Mankowitz – author of *The Bespoke Overcoat*, *Expresso Bongo* and *Casino Royale* – remembered a visit to the set during a hiatus in shooting. The reason: 'Because the relationship between Olivier and Marilyn was very, very bad. He couldn't stand her at all and found her acting – her way of setting about acting – and Mrs Strasberg's presence, absolutely unbearable.'

Many of the actors who worked on *The Prince and the Showgirl* have died, but of the few who remain the influence of Paula Strasberg on set is memorable. Marilyn was the greatest woman living; more popular than Jesus. Marilyn endured this kind of flattery, but generally her colleagues found it amusing, even irritating, and as a result most of them didn't attempt to befriend Marilyn, finding her inaccessible and remote. One member of the cast, Daphne Anderson, who played Fanny, remembered how hard it was to speak to Marilyn because she appeared so reserved and spent so much time with Strasberg. Vera Day recalled a dearth of amusing incidents on set with Marilyn always encircled by her group or keeping herself to herself. It was behaviour like this that led many of the other actors and crew to consider her as aloof; it won her no points in the popularity stakes.

But Paula Strasberg wasn't the only extraneous person on set: Marilyn constantly telephoned Lee Strasberg (running up a bill that was still being discussed months after she'd returned home). Vivien Leigh popped in occasionally and even watched the rushes, and Arthur Miller visited on a regular basis, giving Marilyn a perfect excuse to stop everything and walk off set.

For the sake of everyone working on the film, Laurence Olivier ordered a closed set and banned all press. Despite this, however, one eager fan dressed as a window cleaner and climbed on to the roof to get a glimpse of Marilyn in her dressing room. He failed, but several others succeeded, such as the *Daily Mail* reporter who bumped into her in the corridor. His colleague Edwin Sampson took the photo opportunity, and although his camera was confiscated, it did lead Laurence Olivier to release two photographs as an act of peacemaking. Even so, several months on, reporter Marcus Milne spent several hours in the studio pretending to be an extra before being removed by one of the third assistant directors.

Restricting press access, both at home and at work, just made them even more determined to dig the dirt for whatever they could to make a story. When the Oliviers' sent her a large bouquet of flowers, they even chastised her for not sending a thank-you letter, an accusation that was both unfair and untrue. Olivier kept her note of thanks in his personal files until his death in 1989. Fewer than ever journalists were concerned with reporting on Marilyn's grace and kindness. In August 1956 they were more concerned with the fact that the Parkside butler had been riding the bicycle presented to Marilyn at the Savoy press conference. When she was seen out cycling, on 12 August, journalists were so pleased to see 'that girl' on 'that bike' that they failed to notice it wasn't even the bike in question. One person who saw a biking Marilyn was Englefield Green resident Gerald Searle. As he cycled home towards Egham one evening. Searle noticed particularly how happy they looked together and that they were unaccompanied, with no bodyguards or entourage in tow.

However, not everyone recalled Marilyn's bike trips with such warmth. Joyce Jackson was strolling through Windsor Park with her husband, their toddler and 12-year-old nephew, when the Millers cycled up behind them. According to Mrs Jackson, her nephew was trailing a long stick behind him, which made Miller angry, concerned that his wife could somehow be knocked off her bicycle by the stick.

Unconvinced, Mrs Jackson aired her views that they shouldn't be riding in the park, to which Miller allegedly said: 'But this is Marilyn Monroe, and I am her husband.' Mrs Jackson was highly unimpressed by her 'Marilyn encounter'.

Back in the studio, shooting continued until 22 August, when Marilyn was struck down with a mystery illness and not able to work. Newspapers reported that she was suffering from a stomach complaint, which led to rumours that she could be pregnant. The pregnancy theory haunted the remainder of her stay, unresolved to this day. But a miscarriage during the making of *The Prince and the Showgirl* seems unlikely. Marilyn was open about subsequent miscarriages, and the official announcement of a lost baby would have won her a great deal of sympathy, both on and off the set. But none came; indeed Amy Greene and the Strasbergs' daughter Susan both denied it. Arthur Miller made no mention of it in his autobiography and declined to comment when asked about it some fifty years later.

Furthermore, aside from the third assistant director, Colin Clark – son of Lord Kenneth Clark and brother of the conservative politician Alan Clark, who wrote about his experiences in *The Prince, the Showgirl and Me* – no one on set seems to have known about the alleged pregnancy. There is no record or mention of a miscarriage in any of Olivier's production files; the first Daphne Anderson heard of it was when she read Colin Clark's book. Marilyn's housekeeper was not aware of any miscarriage, either, something that she of all people, living so closely with the Millers, could hardly neglect to notice.

What seems more likely is that Marilyn was suffering from endometriosis, given that her time off work occurred around much the same time each month. Susan Strasberg remembered Marilyn requiring special pills to get her through a particularly bad menstrual attack, while Esmond Knight later wrote that Marilyn didn't come to the set one day because of menstrual problems.

Adding to the pressure of the health speculations was the discovery that the Millers' Parkside cook and butler had been trying to sell their stories to the press, a huge shock to everyone involved. On 24 August it was announced that they had been relieved of their duties. There had been no meetings to discuss confidentiality; in those days it was just expected that the staff would not talk, and, generally, they did not. Furthermore, although PC Hunt was in charge of Marilyn's safekeeping, he had little to do with staffing arrangements, which led to gaps in security. Thankfully for Marilyn, housekeeper Dolly Stiles fiercely guarded her confidentiality, and when she too was approached to sell her story, she refused.

As if all this weren't enough, two weeks into production Marilyn apparently found a notebook that Miller had left open on a table at Parkside. In it, he had written his thoughts on the on-set problems between Olivier and Marilyn, describing how disappointed and ashamed he felt of her. Marilyn read it in disbelief and poured her heart out to the Strasbergs, who were concerned that Miller could write such things about his new wife. Although they tried to console her, Marilyn was convinced the notebook had been left open on purpose and took it to mean that her husband was now siding with Olivier. The incident could not have come at a worse time, and she took no comfort that it might have been written in the heat of the moment. Things were made worse when the crew found out, and although unsure of the exact details, they were fully aware that Marilyn was distraught.

So now Marilyn felt betrayed on all sides: her husband had been disloyal; Olivier was becoming ever more condescending; the press was turning against her; and even peace-keeping Milton Greene experienced Marilyn's wrath, accused of being on Olivier's side. Because Marilyn had begun to consider MMP partner Milton Greene untrustworthy, Arthur Miller got drawn into the business side of Marilyn Monroe Productions. Marilyn accepted his help until he tried to get her back on set, at which point she considered he was taking sides and subsequently began to resent his involvement. Her problems with Greene were exacerbated when Marilyn believed he was buying English antique furniture and charging it to MMP, creating more mistrust between the business partners and increasing the tension with Miller.

Marilyn saw her only allies as the Strasbergs and Hedda Rosten, Norman Rosten's wife, who was acting as secretary to Marilyn. But, even that didn't last long. Lee was to return to New York before too long, and Hedda returned shortly thereafter, deciding not to risk the friendship in a situation that was quickly reaching boiling point. Marilyn took her mind off her problems with a shopping trip to Regent's Street, but even this proved stressful when hundreds of fans crowded round her, and the police had to be called.

The idea of working in a strange country with people she didn't know was made worse on 26 August when Arthur Miller returned to the States to see his children. Still stung by his perceived betrayed, Marilyn went with him to the airport, where they sat quietly in the back of their car, saying their goodbyes. The following day, on 27 August, she was back on set; on 31 August, however, she was again unavailable for work, and shooting had to be rearranged to allow for her absence. Reports surfaced that she was suffering from gastritis and various doctors were called. For the next week Marilyn remained at home, during which time Dolly Stiles recalled her spending time alone in her bedroom or pottering in the garden. On 4 September, Arthur Miller cut short his trip to the States and returned to England.

Although Olivier had problems of his own, when Vivien Leigh miscarried their baby, on the surface at least he took Marilyn's absences calmly. In a letter to his friend Radie Harris, he said they had been able to fill the time with scenes with which Marilyn was not involved. However, the full price of her absence was revealed when it was estimated later that she had cost the film some £38,305. It could have been finished three weeks earlier if she had been on set and on time.

The stress of the England trip was certainly taking its toll on Marily; she was drinking more heavily and was increasingly reliant on sleeping pills. She became hysterical when the pills didn't work or wore off. Her New York analyst was flown in to help, and she received treatment from Anna Freud, daughter of her hero, Sigmund. Still, during quieter moments Marilyn continued to share her dreams with her husband, detailing her plans to study history and literature. She was determined to have a quieter, calmer life in New York.

· · · · ·

On 7 September, although she was unavailable for work, Marilyn attended a production of *The Caucasian Chalk Circle* at the Palace Theatre on London's Shaftesbury Avenue. Once again the event made it into the newspapers, especially the rumour that Marilyn visited the theatre manager, Harry W. Briden during the interval, in order to discuss acting. However, if this were so, he didn't mention it in his desk diary, revealing, instead, how the Millers arrived late and the press crashed their way in behind them in their excitement.

Another theatre trip came two days later, when the Millers visited the Comedy Theatre in the West End to publicize the upcoming *A View from the Bridge*. The play had been refused a public performance licence by the Lord Chamberlain because it included references to homosexuality. However, the New Watergate Theatre Club – a membership-based organization dedicated to presenting banned plays – had agreed to present the drama at the Comedy Theatre. Marilyn sat on stage with actor Anthony Quayle, while Arthur Miller introduced his play to the audience. However, the press seemed to forget that the event was really nothing to do with Marilyn, and some newspapers severely chastised her the next morning for not making a speech herself. The *Daily Sketch*, happy to present her with a bicycle a few months earlier, gave her a thoroughly bad review, calling her appearance a 'strictly dumb blonde role' and criticizing the fact that she had giggled in Arthur Miller's ear and even sucked her thumb.

Come Monday morning, Marilyn was back on the set and seemed ready for work. However, the difficulties surrounding the shoot never really eased. Marilyn caused her share of conflict, especially when she had a row with a crew member who accidentally walked in on her while changing. Some of the cast complained that she didn't bother to say good morning or good night and there was trouble too when *Bus Stop* director, Joshua Logan, visited the set. Marilyn refused to let him into her dressing room. Still angry that a scene had been cut from the film, no amount of apologies would calm Marilyn, and Logan eventually left. Vera Day recalled another episode when Olivier was setting up camera angles and politely told Marilyn that he couldn't see her in the position in which she was standing, to which she retorted: 'Oh, well, if you can't see me I will go home,' and swept off, leaving cast and crew dumbfounded.

In spite of that, and possibly even unbeknown to her, Marilyn still had her allies on the set. Dame Sybil Thorndyke, who was cast as Olivier's mother-in-law, never gave up praising her, often telling Olivier off if she thought he'd been too hard on her. She once told him that Marilyn was the only one of them who really knew how to act in front of a camera, and according to her son, John Casson, she was very fond of Marilyn and had detected sadness in her. Vera Day also cared about her co-star, saying that she was 'Difficult, yes. But there was only one Marilyn, and she jolly well deserved to be difficult … She was sensationally beautiful [and] I know she irritated nearly everyone but she was surrounded by a lot of "po-faced actors" who gave her a hard time.'

With Laurence Olivier,
as a young Alan
Whicker (behind)
takes notes

During this difficult time, Marilyn took a great deal of comfort from her fans and the people local to where she lived at Englefield Green. Several admirers reported being invited into her home for tea, while one fan was lucky enough to be the Parkside House paperboy at the time of Marilyn's stay. Bryan Godfree recalled how excited he was when Marilyn found time to say hello to him from her bedroom window as he delivered the papers. Englefield Green resident Margaret Gillon recalled another touching story. Marilyn would be driven home from Pinewood the same way every evening, and if she were in the garden, Mrs Gillon would always wave as she went past. Marilyn sent a signed photo to thank her for the gesture. Another signed photo was given to Beryl Belmont, daughter of housekeeper Dolly Stiles. She recalled meeting Marilyn during a visit with her mother, when she jokingly asked if she could take the ten-year-old back home to America. In September, Marilyn was also happy to participate in a local charity event, by donating a self-portrait of 'Myself Exercising'. The yellow watercolour was signed Marilyn Monroe Miller and later purchased by Terence Rattigan at auction.

These happy, albeit rare moments were precious to Marilyn and helped keep her spirits up. Another person who helped raise her morale, however, wasn't a member of the general public but comedy actor Norman Wisdom. Wisdom had acted in *Trouble in Store* and starred in numerous low-budget comedies for the Rank Organisation. He was working at Pinewood at the time:

'I was making my film A Stitch in Time, and on several occasions she came in to watch my work. In fact, she quite unintentionally ruined a couple of takes. Obviously, of course, once the director has said "Action", everyone must remain silent, no matter how funny the situation might be, but Marilyn just could not help laughing, and on two occasions she was politely escorted off the set. The nicest thing that happened was that we passed each other in the long hallway one lunchtime. It was crowded, but she still caught hold of me, kissed and hugged me, and walked away laughing. Everybody in the hall could not believe it, and I remember my director, Bob Asher, shouting out, "You lucky little swine" — I agreed with him.'

On 28 September Marilyn was not available for work, but her mood must have lifted when she received a letter from TV channel ABC offering her a part in *The Brothers Karamazov*. At any other time this would have been her dream job, but it was not to be. With personal and professional strains at breaking point, the last thing Marilyn needed was yet another project, and the offer was turned down. During her time in England, she was presented with various opportunities by the BBC to further her dreams of becoming a serious artist. She was invited to participate in a production of Aristophanes's comedy *Lysistrata*. Her input was also requested for a tribute to NBC, in which she was asked to talk about how radio and television should be used for the education of children. Both she and Miller were asked to take part in an interview for a series entitled *At Home and Abroad*, as well as a discussion on 'Man's Role in Society' for the *London Forum* series. Unfortunately, none of these projects came to anything, and the only reply the BBC received was from agency MCA, stating that Marilyn would be unavailable for any engagements during the making of *The Prince and the Showgirl*.

On 11 October, unavailable for work all day, Marilyn nonetheless accompanied Arthur Miller to the opening of Miller's play *A View from the Bridge* at the Comedy Theatre. To show a united front, the Millers left for the theatre from the Oliviers' home and caused a near riot when they arrived with Marilyn wearing a scarlet satin gown and wrap from designer De Rachelle. The gown was tightly fitted and extremely low-cut, and photographers wasted no time climbing into the theatre balcony to take photos that looked directly down the front of her dress. Sitting in seat 16, three rows from the front, Marilyn appeared relaxed and happy, with her husband on one side and Lord and Lady Olivier on the other. Any tensions from the set of *The Prince and the Showgirl* were well hidden, and during the evening Marilyn even found time to converse with members of the audience seated behind her.

After the production had ended, the Millers took a bow on stage, and then met members of the cast and crew backstage. Author of *The Outsider*, Colin Wilson remembered driving past the Comedy Theatre and seeing a huge crowd gathered around the stage door. Realizing what was going on, he and his companion gate-crashed the after-show party and met Marilyn in Anthony Quayle's dressing room. Wilson found her to be very attractive and charming, while his companion was amused to see her quite shamelessly standing in front of the mirror, desperately trying to heave up her low-cut gown.

The next day filming continued, with Marilyn present, but tensions were still high, particularly behind the scenes. Marilyn's expenses were now causing concern, and on 17 October, Cecil Tennant, managing director of Laurence Olivier Productions, sent a letter to Milton Greene, requesting a complete breakdown of her expenditure. However, there was no response to this and subsequent letters, until after 12 August 1957 when a final demand had to be written. On 4 September, there was another letter from Tennant, saying they could not accept charges for Sidney Guilaroff (Marilyn's private hairdresser), Paula Strasberg as coach, Hedda Rosten as secretary or one of Marilyn's lawyers, Irving Stein. But while none of this added to harmony on set, it wasn't all doom and gloom. There were lighter moments: Elizabeth Arden's assistant paid a visit to pamper Marilyn, Olivier and Greene with manicures and pedicures and hairdresser Gordon Bond taught Marilyn rhyming slang in her dressing room. Then there was the time when Marilyn's shoulder strap broke and she laughingly called out: 'Is there a man on the set?'

Thankfully, the bulk of the work had been completed by this time and Paula Strasberg returned to the States in October, much to Olivier's joy. Marilyn shocked everyone by becoming more co-operative and working better with her leading man, but this soon changed when it was claimed Strasberg was not able to return due to a visa problem. Marilyn hit the roof, though Strasberg did return, much to the dismay of almost everyone – especially when her costs later showed up on Marilyn's expense report.

The week beginning 22 October was an eventful one for Marilyn. On the Monday she arrived some 85 minutes late, then kept everyone waiting for a record-breaking two hours and 55 minutes. On the Tuesday and Wednesday she called in sick, yet taking delivery of clothes and shoes from Paris House, Anello & Davide and De Rachelle. On Thursday and Friday Marilyn was on set, filming an exhausting ball-room scene. Finally, on the Saturday she met up with Dame Edith Sitwell (having turned down an invitation from Dame Margot Fonteyn to attend the Bolshoi Theatre Ballet). The meeting with Dame Edith was daunting, but nothing compared to the one that would take place on the following Monday evening, when the Queen of Hollywood met the Queen of England.

On 29 October 1956, hairdresser Gordon Bond attended Parkside House to ready Marilyn for her trip to the Empire Theatre, Leicester Square, for the Royal

Command Performance. It was to be a glittering night, full of celebrities and royalty, at which she wanted to look her best. Bond created a regal-looking hairstyle, complete with a 'bun', and although at least one reporter complained that it was the untidiest he had ever seen Marilyn's hair, she looked stunning and confident, despite having turned down a rehearsal the day before.

She arrived at the Empire Theatre with her husband, wearing a gold-lamé gown, with topaz strap, and gold cape. Her outfit included white gloves worn past her elbows, and she carried a gold handbag while expertly negotiating clogs with two-inch platform soles. The film screened that evening was *The Battle of the River Plate*, and afterwards Marilyn was presented to both the Queen and Princess Margaret. Although she was anxious about where she should stand and what she should say, everything went well, and Marilyn performed an expert curtsy. In footage of the event, Her Majesty can be seen admiring Marilyn's revealing outfit, before the pair talked for a minute or two about being neighbours (Windsor was just minutes from Englefield Green), while Marilyn claimed that although she was leaving England in a matter of weeks, she was doing so reluctantly. When the Queen moved on to other stars in the line-up, Marilyn talked to Princess Margaret about the possibility of her attending a performance of *A View from the Bridge*. Much was made of this in the newspapers the next day, as it was considered highly controversial for a royal to see a banned play, but Princess Margaret did attend a performance shortly afterwards.

As she emerged from the theatre, Marilyn declared that the evening had been one of the nicest things that had ever happened to her, adding that she hadn't been at all nervous and had found the Queen to be warm-hearted and sweet. She joked with reporters about her curtsy, giving them an impromptu replay to prove she could do it correctly. Unfortunately, by the next day, Marilyn had lost the glow of the night's success and instead was highly agitated and angry on set. Complaining to Gordon Bond, she revealed the source of her anger as another blonde – Brigitte Bardot – who had been at the Royal Command Performance too. Upset that she had upstaged her, Marilyn was heard to call the French starlet 'that silly little girl' and ask: 'Who does she think she is?' Her fury was unfounded, however, as a look at the morning's newspapers would have shown her that although Bardot was mentioned, the bulk of articles were dedicated to Marilyn.

By this point production of *The Prince and the Showgirl* was almost at an end. Marilyn was given four official days off in early November, and she had only two more days' work on set that month. Eager to end filming as soon as possible, she managed to get to make her 6.45 am call on both days, although she did keep everyone waiting for two hours 20 minutes on the first day. Still, despite the hold-ups and lateness, the film finally wrapped for Marilyn on 16 November, 11 days after it was scheduled to end. Before leaving the set, she found herself apologizing to the cast and crew for her behaviour, claiming poor health as the reason and begging them to forgive her. This proved to be a worthwhile thing to do; although some members of cast and crew would never hold Marilyn in high regard, others proved more forgiving and would always speak well of her.

Although Marilyn's part in the film may have been complete, she did not leave England immediately. Miller had recently spent several days away from his wife, meeting distinguished French leading actress Simone Signoret and her husband, the actor–singer Yves Montand, in Paris. Now that he was back, the couple spent a quiet few days together at Parkside House. On 18 November, during a last public appearance in England, the Millers attended an intellectual discussion at the Royal Court Theatre. The event was supposed to be dedicated to the state of British drama but quickly transformed into a war of words between authors Colin Wilson and Wolf Mankowitz. The two writers had opposing views on most subjects, leaving the other

Attending a debate at the Royal Court Theatre, London, November 1956

members of the discussion panel, Arthur Miller, Kenneth Tynan and Benn Levy, lost for words. Sitting on the fourth row and dressed demurely in a black suit, Mrs Miller looked tired but calm, as the discussion took place on stage. Mankowitz remembered the ripple of excitement when Marilyn entered the building, as once again there were rumours that she was pregnant. He recalled there was a lot of fuss about finding her a seat, and how people were 'running around as if she were about to have a baby on the spot'.

Having been brought into discuss great British drama, Mankowitz was disappointed to discover that Marilyn's presence destroyed the point of the occasion. The audience were far more interested in trying to see her and Arthur Miller seemed so preoccupied that he could hardly concentrate. Still, Mankowitz managed to say a few words to Marilyn at the end of the discussion, although he remembered she wasn't too communicative – something he put down to the rumoured pregnancy. Colin Wilson also remembered meeting Marilyn in the backstage of the theatre, after the discussion had ended. By this time the crowds outside had become huge, so Wilson found himself helping the Millers make their escape by the back door and recalled Marilyn grabbing his hand in the rush.

On 20 November 1956, in Englefield Green, Marilyn said goodbye to her staff, bid farewell to the baby fish she'd befriended in the Parkside aquarium and climbed into her car for the last time. She surprised everyone by arriving at the airport on time, and a scheduled press conference was held at 6.15 pm, but contrary to the huge excitement that erupted when Marilyn arrived, her departure was reported in unflattering terms. There were comments about her untidy hair; snide observations about the lack of autograph hunters at the airport and absurd remarks about her intellect, with one newspaper commenting that she mentioned Charles Dickens 'as if she read books every day'.

Leaving London, November 1956, with a pipe-smoking Miller

Before Marilyn climbed the steps of her plane, she told reporters how reluctant she was to leave, how she had enjoyed meeting the Queen and took pleasure in attending the opening of Miller's play. She even tried to dampen talk of a rift between herself and Olivier; there had been difficulties on set, but no more than usual. Olivier returned the compliment by declaring Marilyn a wonderful girl; he was delighted with the film, and he'd do it all over again if he had to. Whether this were true is another matter, since when he later travelled to New York to show the film to head of Warner Brothers Jack Warner, he made it clear that the event was private; Marilyn did not receive an invitation. Perhaps it is best left to her to sum up her experiences of the England trip, in a remark she made years later: 'It seemed to be raining the whole time. Or maybe it was me.'

With Arthur Miller, 1956,
waving farewell to fans at
London Airport

11

MRS MILLER

During the first six months of married life Marilyn's new husband attributed his weight gain to 'her [Marilyn's] cooking and [his] general contentment'. After a brief honeymoon in Jamaica, the Millers were back in New York with the lease on an apartment at 444 East 57th Street, while their newly acquired farmhouse in Roxbury was being modernized. It was time for some normal life.

444 East 57th Street, New York: home with Arthur Miller was on the 13th floor

Marilyn began redecorating, painting most rooms white; she hung a portrait of Abraham Lincoln and gave her childhood piano pride of place.

And Marilyn was back in the kitchen, in her new role of housewife, in which she prepared her husband's breakfast every day and experimented with home-made noodles and bread. She relaxed by writing poetry, riding her bicycle along the East River, playing tennis and pottering around the household department of Bloomingdale's. 'I have no sales resistance when it comes to anything for the house – especially when there's a sale. I'll go absolutely berserk buying furniture, garden implements, seed for birds and clothes for Arthur.' She enjoyed seeking out Miller's favourite foods. Once overhearing two old ladies discussing the merits of a sausage shop on Third Avenue She rushed there only to find it replaced by a car park. As for her other role, of actress, Marilyn continued her classes with the Strasbergs – as she did her therapy sessions, now with psychiatrist Marianne Kris, recommended to her by Anna Freud.

Despite continuing her work with Milton Greene to build up a photographic portfolio, the gaps in their relationship were ever widening. The last straw was Greene's proposed credit as executive producer of *The Prince and The Showgirl*, about which she called an emergency meeting with the board of Marilyn Monroe Productions. On 11 April a statement followed to say she had never been informed about the credit. It also stated that Marilyn Monroe Productions had been created to make better pictures and improve her work, but instead she was finding herself having to defend her aims and interests. Greene had to quit, but he refused to believe that Marilyn could have had anything to do with it, blaming Miller. He surprised everyone by requesting only the return of his original investment of $100,000, but when the contract was finally dissolved, he was a broken man.

Speaking subsequently about a failed business relationship, Marilyn said: 'I went along with it as far as I could, but you get to a point where – well, enough is enough! At that moment I couldn't believe it was happening, but for the first time in my life I really yelled my head off!' She was not specific, but everyone knew what she was talking about. And it wasn't the only thing she had to deal with; speculation continued about her being pregnant, even supported by newspaper and magazine exclusives. On 22 March, following rumours that she had turned down the part in *The Brothers Karamazov* because she was pregnant, Marilyn released a statement: 'I have nothing to say at this time. I am sure that everyone will agree that some things are private matters.'

Other private matters were just as public. Two months later, head of Twentieth Century Fox, Spyros Skouras, flew to New York to try and convince Miller to name names in the course of his forthcoming court appearance. He was unsuccessful. Days later the Millers travelled to Washington, DC, to contest the Contempt of Congress charge, staying with Arthur's friend and lawyer, Joe Rauh, and his wife, Olie. While Miller and Joe Rauh attended court, Marilyn's days were domestic and low key. Eventually, Miller was found guilty on two counts of contempt, against which he launched an immediate appeal. Federal Judge Charles F. McLaughlin withheld sentencing, but Miller faced a potential year in prison and a $1000 fine on each count. Marilyn was up beat about it, telling the press she was: 'Pretty confident that in the end my husband will win this case.'

Back in New York, on 13 June, the Millers attended something much more pleasurable; the première at Radio City Music Hall of *The Prince and the Showgirl*. In early June, Marilyn had given a series of interviews to the media, including Herbert Kamm and Hal Boyle, who asked her, specifically, about *The Prince and the Showgirl* and, generally, about her New York life. There were three subjects off-limits; religion, politics and pregnancy. Though she was remarkably open and frank when she said: 'The thing I'm scared of most is myself. But I do feel I've grown both as an actress and a person, and I hope I'll keep growing.'

With husband Miller at the April in Paris Ball fundraiser, New York, 1957

The arrival of Mr and Mrs Miller and basset hound Hugo for their summer vacation in Amagansett, Long Island, sent the townspeople into a frenzy. Three teenagers who met them at the local petrol station requested autographs: 12-year-old Dicky Gosman made them laugh when he dared to say that he preferred Jayne Mansfield; Bob O'Brien, delivery boy for Toppings grocery store, who wanted to have his photo taken with Marilyn; and Roger Mattei, owner of the Corsican restaurant, who did a telephone survey of New York eateries asking about Marilyn's favourite food.

Most Amagansett residents were pleased to admire from a distance, but two enterprising youngsters, Stephanie Baloghy, and her cousin Maureen McArdle, had other plans, which they recalled some 50 years later:

Stephanie:'When I was a kid I spent every summer in Amagansett. My cousin Maureen, then 14, visited one particular weekend, and we set off on an adventure to see Miss Monroe. After a little detective work we discovered she was staying at a house at Stony Hill Farm about three miles north from where we were. My father wouldn't drive us so we set out, undaunted, on foot. It seems to me that we walked for ever, and though there weren't very many houses at Stony Hill we didn't find the right house right away, but a kind neighbour told us where she and Arthur Miller were staying.'

Maureen:'Stephanie and I went to her home and crawled on all fours, hidden from view by hedges, along a very long driveway to ask for her autograph. We finally reached our destination and discovered Marilyn, her husband and another couple on the front porch of her house. Marilyn wore no make-up but looked beautiful in an orange blouse with spaghetti straps, about 6 straps each shoulder. We jumped out from behind the hedges and asked for her autograph. She said she would have to check with her husband. She then said something to Arthur Miller and very sweetly told us that her husband said she could not do this, or everyone would be at their house trying to get an autograph. Stephanie and I were very disappointed, and when we just stood there, someone − I don't remember who − told us to leave. We were walking down the driveway, her dog was following us, and Stephanie called to Marilyn to tell her to call it, or it was coming with us. [After which] she called for the dog.'

Stephanie:'As I recall we waited outside the house for some signs of life and then the dog was released − presumably to frighten us − but we befriended it. I guess upon seeing that that ruse didn't work, Arthur came out along with another couple and sat down on some garden chairs and then, finally, Marilyn appeared. My recollection of her at that moment was of a beam of sunshine. She was so gorgeous, that she looked illuminated. Maybe it was the hair − maybe it was her complexion and the orangey top − maybe it

was just that she looked so fresh and delicate. Her whole being just said 'star'. I know we
asked – pleaded – for her autograph; told her we had walked so very far; but to no avail.
I do recall her saying in that breathy voice of hers that we were 'so sweet'. I do remember
the long walk back – empty handed but elated. And somehow I remember a good dose of
disbelief when we got back that we had actually seen her since we didn't have an autograph
to 'prove' it. We do have the memory though! Considering that we had barged in on her, I
think Miss Monroe was exceedingly kind to us!'

Marilyn and Miller settled into their holiday routine; a morning walk with Hugo then some errands for Marilyn, popping into Toppings and chatting sometimes with the local people she encountered there. In the afternoon, Miller liked to sit and write in the garden, while Marilyn did a bit of watering and tending, her green fingers surprising her: 'I planted some seeds that grew, and to my amazement I had flowers.'

For the first time, Marilyn was finding herself able to lead a quiet life, away from any career and business problems, and she must have relished that time to herself. She started to go horse-riding, wrote some poetry, did a little painting – watercolours, of which she gave one or two to the Strasbergs. There were hours on the beach with Miller, walking, holding hands and paddling in the surf – Marilyn once rescuing some fish stranded above the waterline, scooping them up in her hands and tipping them back in the sea. Other times were more sociable, when Miller's children and his parents or the Rostens would visit. Her time in Amagansett was joyful. She was taking things easy,

Happiness is splashing in the sea, captured by Sam Shaw, 1957

enjoying her privacy and most of all relishing a secret – she was expecting a baby. Although no announcement had been made, apparently two old ladies had noticed 'a look' about her when they saw her in the Post Office and went up to express their congratulations, at which Marilyn, embarrassed, made a hasty retreat. But it was enough already to fire up the gossip-mongers.

Marilyn was to make only a few public appearances during 1957. She attended two premières, the second being *Baby Doll*. She also kicked out the first football during a soccer match on 12 May. New York doormen remarked that the only time they saw the Millers was walking their dog. On 2 July, though she could be seen at an inauguration ceremony held at the construction site of the Time-Life Building – though she was late, as ever. Due to appear at 11 am in a scheduled encounter with Laurance S. Rockefeller, Marilyn didn't show up until 1.20 pm Rockefeller had gone by then, muttering furiously: 'I've never waited that long for

1957 publicity outing at Ebbets field baseball park, Brooklyn

anyone.' When she did turn up, she was worth waiting for. Beautiful as ever, in a pink and white dress; she was late, she said, because they'd had their first wedding anniversary the previous night. 'Oh, was I sick … We celebrated with champagne, but instead of it going to my head it went to my stomach.'

It was likely to have been this same day that Marilyn was given a grand tour of the *New York Times*, where author Carl Schlesinger then worked as a Linotype machine operator in the composing room:

'When tourists came through our department the foreman had designated me as the official 'explainer' as to how the complicated but fascinating Linotype typesetting machine worked. I gave Marilyn the 'gold-plated' demonstration of the machine, ending in my giving her a warm Linotype bar of type, freshly cast with her name on the surface. Marilyn seemed interested, so I explained and at the end of my demonstration she thanked me and leaned over me – I was seated and she was standing – and kissed me on top of my balding head. Several of my co-workers, who had been watching 'the show', broke out into applause. I didn't wash my head for a week!'

After their meeting, Schlesinger was regretful that he hadn't given Marilyn something more than a simple cast of her name. A few days later he bought an un-circulated 1926 penny and cast it into the side of a lead bar, on which, on the other side, he also cast her name again and then sent it off to her. 'Months passed, and I forgot all about the incident, then one day *The Times* mailroom sent me a letter addressed to me from Miss Monroe. She apologized for the long delay in answering my note and gift, and thanked me for thinking of her.'

Back in Amagansett, unfortunately, Marilyn's harmonious existence was about to be cruelly disrupted. On the morning of 1 August, she collapsed in the garden. Miller was in the house; an ambulance was called. Amagansett resident Edward Damiecki was with the ambulance crew; afterwards he told his brother that when they had tried to put Marilyn on the stretcher, she had spat in the driver's face. Such behaviour could be seen as vulgar and unnecessary, but it was more likely despairing; having suffered menstrual problems since childhood. Marilyn would have been only too well aware that something was badly wrong. By the time she arrived at the hospital, she was covered from head to toe in a blanket and in great pain.

She'd suffered from what is known as an ectopic pregnancy, in her case the foetus had been growing in a fallopian tube and had to be removed during a life-saving emergency operation. Her doctor, Hilliard Dubrow, announced she had been five or six weeks pregnant and that, if Marilyn wanted to try for a child again, she could certainly do so, no problem. But that wasn't top of Marilyn's agenda at that moment in the hospital, where she felt devastated and in great pain. The following day, 2 August, Arthur Miller released a statement that read in part, 'Marilyn wants as many [children] as she can get. I feel the same way.' It was over a week before Marilyn left the hospital, on 10 August, walking slowly and wearing the pink and white dress she had worn for her Time-Life appearance. It was a distressing departure to watch, with Marilyn in full make-up, smiling for the cameras and remarking: 'I'm feeling wonderful'. Asked about the future, she replied: 'I definitely still plan to have a large family. I'm going to rest, rest and more rest.' God knows how quickly the smile vanished in the privacy of the waiting ambulance.

Marilyn was reluctant to return to Amagansett, and when she did, she was quite different from the happy young woman she'd been earlier in the summer. She was uncommunicative and nervy, rumoured to be drinking heavily. Even Miller's mother found her distant and untrusting, consequently cutting short her visit. Local farmer John Damiecki remembered her at that time, noticing her as she passed him at work in his potato fields:

> 'Marilyn would ride her horse through the field. She was never in any hurry, and I would have to stop work in order to let her through. One time Marilyn was riding through the field, and she was drunk and fell off the horse. My brother and I had to catch the horse, and Arthur Miller walked it back to the house. He came back and invited us up to the house, and when we got there he said, 'Marilyn, John is here,' but she paid no attention – she was out of it by then.'

Marilyn was reported to have had tried to take an overdose, either in Amagansett or earlier in the New York apartment; luckily, Miller's presence most likely saved her from harm, but the emotional scars were apparent.

Back in their 57th Street apartment, she tried hard to pick up the pieces. There were distractions in the Millers' commission of Frank Lloyd Wright, to design them a family home on land connected to their Roxbury farmhouse. This was not, as is sometimes suggested, as a replacement for the original house. Wright's 'organic architecture' – the art of building round nature and incorporating it into the structure. – was a wonder. The plans drawn up by the then 90-year-old Wright were inspired by a home he had designed in 1949. They included a domed, three-tiered living room, with each tier slightly lower than

Sharing a quiet moment
with Arthur Miller;
photographed by Sam
Shaw

the other, with glass walls, a movie screen and a large crystal chandelier. There was also to be a large nursery.

When Marilyn talked to reporter Radie Harris about the house, she seemed bright and happy, although ultimately it didn't happen, and they opted simply to remodel the existing farmhouse, adding a garage and studio (for Miller) and a nursery. To Harris, Marilyn was to say: 'We do long so much for a child, but that will come I'm sure. I look at our house, and I know that it has been home for other families, back through all those years. And it's as if some of their happiness has stayed there even after they went away, and I can feel it around me.'

· · · · ·

Weekdays in New York and weekends and holidays in the country set the pattern for the following year. But, by 1958, Marilyn had also begun to think about work again. 'My Marilyn Monroe Productions company is all set to start things going in a big way,' she said, speculating about a remake of the Marlene Dietrich movie, *Blue Angel*. In the end though the decision was taken out of her hands when she read an outline of a screenplay from Billy Wilder. It was the start of *Some Like It Hot*, and he'd written it with Marilyn in mind. If she liked it, he said, he would finish the script especially for her. 'So I read it, and I loved it,' she said and agreed to do the film without even seeing the completed script.

Things moved fast, and while Marilyn made plans to fly to Los Angeles for filming, Miller stayed at home, preoccupied with his court appeal. It was at this

Around the time of *Some
Like It Hot* (1959)
complete with 1920s
hair-do

time that he wrote her a loving letter, in which he described how 'entirely alive' and at home he felt with her and expressed the joy that she gave him, calling her his dear baby girl and comrade. Without her, he said, he felt lonely; if they ever had children together, he would know what to do and how to be with them. Some believe the end of Millers' marriage had come when Marilyn discovered his notebook during *The Prince and the Showgirl*, but all evidence (including Miller's letter) seems to show that they were very much in love and trying hard to make their marriage work.

In early August, Miller received welcome news that his name had been cleared; he celebrated with the workmen at the Roxbury house, with a case of beer and bottle of whisky. Marilyn was thrilled by the result and called for Miller's lawyer,

Joe Rauh, to run for president. Even Fox's Spyros Skouras (or 'The Spiral Staircase' as Miller called him) sent a letter of congratulations. She was even more delighted when her husband joined her in California.

Shooting on *Some Like It Hot* had begun at Hollywood's Goldwyn Studios. It had started on a positive note: Tony Curtis and Jack Lemmon had fun being coached by a German drag queen; and rehearsals were a time of joking and laughter. The cast often ate lunch together at The Formosa, where Marilyn and Curtis, as Josephine, took trips to the ladies room together, to see if Curtis would be recognized. The whole set had a light-hearted feel to it. Discovering that Goldwyn Studios had banned smoking after the set of *Porgy and Bess* burned down, Wilder pinned a sign on the door that read, 'Come on the Billy Wilder set and smoke your little hearts out. Some Like it Hot!'

With Tony Curtis, one of Marilyn's co-stars in *Some Like It Hot*

But, inevitably, before long, problems arose on set, initially, with Marilyn, because of an ear infection (she had persistent ear and sinus infections throughout her life and a five per cent hearing impairment). Generally, though, she was finding it hard to adjust to be being back at work again, and away from home and all its comforts. 'Will you return to New York after the picture?' one reporter asked, to which she replied: 'Just as fast as the airlines can take me. This is nice but it isn't home.' As an antidote to missing her dog, hairdresser Sydney Guilaroff presented her with two parakeets. She chose the male bird, Butch, whom her secretary May Reis described as 'peachy and frothy' and trained him for Marilyn. She became attached to the parakeet and used to take him around with her whenever she could.

It was, though, a shoot that was dogged by Marilyn's familiar inability to be on time as well as drama-coach interference, absences and forgotten lines. Marilyn got to be called 'MM: Missing Monroe' by the press. The reports that were circulating that she was pregnant again were this time correct. Her husband's request to Wilder that his wife might be excused early starts bewildered him since Marilyn never arrived until at least 11.30 am, long after everyone else. Her chronic lateness was a source of tension on set. 'She doesn't know we're alive,' commented one member of the crew, while Lemmon later recalled that she would drive everyone crazy, locking herself in the dressing room, refusing to come out until she was psychologically ready. Anyone who knocked on her door before that moment was told, in no uncertain terms to: 'Fuck Off'.

But not everyone was annoyed by Marilyn's inability to be on time; indeed Peggy McQuigan, hired to play a trumpet player in the All Girls' Band, thought Marilyn:

'Adorable, very, very charismatic. The first time I saw her, she was walking down the street, just coming from the hairdressers. She had rollers in her hair and was wearing slacks, but still all the attention was riveted on her; she looked spectacular. Marilyn was always late on the set, but that was an advantage to me because I was originally contracted for two weeks, but that went up to four months.'

Perhaps her absence on set would not have been such a problem if Marilyn had been able to remember her lines once she got there. One scene, in which she had to walk into the room and ask: 'Where's that bourbon?', famously required some 70 retakes and for the lines to be pasted into a drawer so she could read them. Reporter, Peer J. Oppenheimer, says:

'I interviewed her several times [over the years], and gradually noticed a pronounced change in her. On the set of Some Like It Hot, I witnessed Billy Wilder and her co-stars becoming very agitated because Marilyn could never remember her lines. Billy always had to use her best take. But in the long run, no one held it against her.'

Oppenheimer also discovered a rule that female co-stars had to have their hair a darker shade than Marilyn's. When some of the girls rebelled and went lighter, they were immediately sent back for corrective colouring. It seemed that Marilyn was so cut-off and aloof from everyone on set, from reporters and cast and crew, that any

Enjoying a joke on the *Some Like It Hot* set with Belgian-French actor Maurice Chevalier

attempt at friendship with her felt unsafe and risked dismissal. Nobody wanted to upset her and risk losing their job. Yet, as far as Marilyn was concerned, she had never been happier.

When the production moved to the Hotel Del Coronado in San Diego, Marilyn did seem happier; perhaps because her husband was on set. Her fans were around to cheer her on during location filming on the beach (where she believed the sea air was good for her and the baby). But her initial euphoria turned to frustration at the huge number of photographers, so much so that she was once heard to scream: 'No pictures, no pictures'. Frequently, exterior scenes were disturbed by the roar of jets from a nearby naval base; exhausted, she was once seen carried off set by Arthur Miller. More disturbingly, following a love scene on 14 September, Miller drove her to the Cedars of Lebanon hospital, where she was treated for what was described as exhaustion but believed to be an overdose of drugs.

The shoot had been scheduled to last three months, but would clearly take longer. This was partly the consequence of days, like 18 October, when Marilyn was absent from set pleading she was 'just tired', though everyone knew she was pregnant. On 10 November, however, she collapsed on set and cast members remembered her concern that she might be losing her baby. She was taken back to her hotel room and from that point on didn't leave it until she was able to fly to New York for medical tests. By 17 December it was confirmed she had lost the baby, probably earlier that week.

One of Marilyn's gynaecologists, Dr Oscar Steinberg, adored her – and had done so from the moment they first met. He did all he could at that time to comfort her. Vanessa Steinberg, his daughter, remembered him speaking of her with great respect. Not so of Arthur Miller, whom he considered rude and dismissive of his wife's problems: 'He treated her like an inferior.'

In the lead-up to what was surely one of the most depressing Christmases of her life, on 22 December *Life* magazine published an article, with text by Arthur Miller and photos by Richard Avedon. Marilyn was made up to look like a series of film-star legends, such as Jean Harlow, Theda Bara, Clara Bow, Marlene Dietrich and Lillian Russell. A great deal of care and attention had been taken to recreate the sets and make-up. But that brief sighting of her was more than she gave the public in the year that followed. She confined her appearances to doing publicity for *Some Like it Hot*, receiving a couple of awards and a rather memorable meeting with Soviet statesman and prime minister, Nikita Khrushchev, at the Twentieth Century Fox studios. She would spend most of 1959

With director Billy Wilder on the *Some Like It Hot* set

trying to recover from the miscarriage that had sent her into a spiral of depression and prescription drug use. Norman Rosten remembered her during that time, on one occasion at a party, where she stared moodily at the street from an upstairs window, wondering if anyone would notice if she fell and complaining of sleep problems. On another occasion, the Rostens received a 3 am phone call from Marilyn's maid, begging them to come over to the apartment, where Marilyn was in recovery from an overdose of pills. When Rosten got to speak to Marilyn and ask how she was, she replied: 'Alive. Bad luck.'

⁕ ⁕ ⁕ ⁕ ⁕

Yet, although the walls seemed to be closing in on her, Marilyn still had moments of optimism, and, during 1959, underwent a series of gynaecological operations to improve her chances of having children. On 23 June 1959 an announcement was made that Dr Mortimer Rodgers had performed a corrective procedure at Lenox Hospital. Then, too, Dr Oscar Steinberg performed radical surgery intended to unblock her fallopian tubes and remove scar tissue, though he later told his secretary, Kae Turner, that Marilyn had a uterus of someone ten years older. 'She'll never have a child because her uterus is such a mess,' he said, adding that it was, he believed, the consequence of septic abortions.

'[Marilyn] had also had numerous pelvic infections that had gone untreated, which had contributed to the scar tissue and infertility problems,' Vanessa Steinberg recalled. Arthur Miller was present during the operation by Dr Steinberg. 'It was a dismal failure,' said Vanessa Steinberg. 'My father had the unfortunate task of telling her that she would never be able to have children. Apparently he walked into her room, she looked up at him and said: "Thank you, doctor, I already know." He told her that if he ever had a daughter he would name her after her, which he did.'

It must have been hard to reconcile to this. She continued her sessions with psychiatrist Dr Kris, and went on taking classes with the Strasbergs. She also went about her day-to-day life in New York, shopping at the 400 Cake Shop and Gristede Brothers Superior Market, browsing for antiques on Third Avenue and borrowing books from the Sutton Place Stationers. She gave the occasional interview: 'I'm sorry to report that I'm not pregnant again,' adding: 'I feel fine now, but it takes time to get over the feeling of loss.' She spoke of the strength of her relationship with Miller, insisting that marriage was a wonderful state and adding – perhaps to convince herself – that she didn't mind if her husband didn't remember anniversaries or send her flowers. 'I can buy my own flowers,' she said.

One thing that did keep her spirits up during 1959 appears to have been her relationship with the Miller children, Bobby and Jane. 'It's such fun for all of us to plan different things to do together. I really look forward to each visit,' she said. She appears to have got on particularly well with Bobby, supported by a letter he once wrote to her thanking her, touchingly, for her 'hostessing and hospitality' and, another time, a little note urging her to reach him, if ever she needed to, via the phone in his bedroom. He and Jane bought Marilyn a subscription to *Horticulture* magazine for her birthday, and when they travelled to Europe that summer, Bobby filmed his adventures and sent them back to New York for Marilyn to see. 'I have only been to England and Korea and Japan, and through Bobby I am now seeing Paris and the rest of Europe,' she said.

When Bobby and Jane were due back from Europe, Marilyn travelled from Roxbury to the New York apartment to retrieve a large television set for them to watch on their return. She was assisted by her agent, Joe Wohlhandler, and his friend

Hollis Alpert. When the TV wouldn't fit in the car, she was happy to accept help from Miller's friend Frank Taylor, who promised to take the set up to Roxbury that weekend. Taylor and Miller were discussing working together on a film, The Misfits, the screenplay of which had been written by Miller. It was also one of the many projects that Marilyn, eager to return to work, was considering (the others being Holly Golightly in Breakfast at Tiffanys and Paris Blues with Marlon Brando). It was with The Misfits production in mind that Miller invited Frank Taylor, his wife, Nan, and their three boys, to visit them in Roxbury. Son Curtice remembered how:

> 'I was fairly young – maybe nine or 11 – when I first met Marilyn. The whole family were taken to the Roxbury farm for a reading of Arthur Miller's play, The Misfits, which he was hoping my father would produce. Marilyn didn't come down right away – she was upstairs vacuuming, which is what she did when she was nervous. She eventually came down and she was very sweet. She liked children, and she was very drawn to my brother Mark, who had had the most problems out of all the children. She immediately recognized that and made an extra effort to reach out to him – she recognized people in trouble and would reach out to them in some way.
>
> My mother helped her make lunch; unfortunately, the script reading went on for ever and the lunch was burnt and had to be made again. There were no seats left after all the family had sat down, and Marilyn told me to come and swing on the hammock with her. I lay down on the hammock with Marilyn and all my brothers were jealous, although they all eventually got a turn.'

Smiling broadly for fans, mid-1950s, ringlets framing her face

On another occasion, Curtice got to see the soft, caring side of Marilyn, during a trip to the 57th Street apartment:

> 'Marilyn decided she had to go out to get some shopping, so she took me with her. She wore a crazy disguise – dark wig and dark glasses, and people were looking because of it. She walked like Marilyn but didn't look like her. There was a homeless man, and Marilyn walked right up to him, not at all afraid. "Things are not going well at the moment, are they?" she said. "No, they're not"' he said. She opened her purse and gave him $5 before walking on.'

But it was a side of her that could make life difficult to handle, at times in some unexpected ways. In an interview in 1959, Marilyn described how there was a working farm on their land at Roxbury. She didn't know much about what went on there, she said, though as Curtice Taylor recalled, on one occasion she found out:

'We [Curtice and his brother] were out in the field which belonged to Arthur but was managed by a farmer. While we were walking we saw a cow that had just given birth, and said, 'Wow, look at that'; we knew we had to go and get Marilyn because she would be thrilled. We got her, and she was thrilled and amazed. The farmer came, checked the sex and discovered it was male. This was not good because he bred milking cows and wasn't interested in males. He went to the van and came back with a bag to put the calf in. Marilyn went completely hysterical and shouted, 'You can't do that! You can't take it away from its mother!' She went absolutely crazy. She rushed back to the house and brought back money to try and buy the cow from the farmer. He wouldn't take the money and instead told her that he was the farmer, he had to do his job, and the calf was going to be veal. She just didn't understand.'

Adding to Marilyn's distress that day was a hawk circling above some swallow chicks nesting above her front porch; she spent ages throwing rocks at the hawk to chase it away and the rest of the day feeling upset. But the fact was that she was generally low and miserable, mostly because her marriage to Miller was heading towards the rocks. One friend described the 57th Street apartment as more like an office than a love nest and Susan Strasberg remembered Marilyn staying with them to avoid her husband. It was hardly a propitious time to consider working together, but once Miller had completed the screenplay for *The Misfits* that was what they would do.

The 1960 Golden Globes, by when the camera had begun to dominate

While still working on *The Misfits*, Miller accompanied Marilyn to Los Angeles for her new role in the Fox movie, *Let's Make Love*. It was a musical, in which a multi-millionaire, learning that he is to be burlesqued in a Broadway show, joins the cast as an actor. It was a lightweight role, and even before shooting started, the problems began, with Miller informally rewriting the script and co-star Gregory Peck deciding that he no longer wanted the part. With Marilyn ready and willing to shoot, Peck's departure was an unwelcome delay, fortunately curtailed by his replacement, French actor, Yves Montand. At the ensuing press party, Marilyn stood alongside Miller, Montand and Montand's wife, Simone Signoret, for photographs, declaring happily that, after her husband, Montand was the most handsome man she had ever met. It was a bad sign; with the Miller marriage crumbling, banter about his wife's attraction to another man was probably the last thing Miller needed.

But Marilyn had her own admirers on the set of *Let's Make Love*; indeed she proved popular with several members of the cast and crew, including dancer Bob Banas (in the scene in which Marilyn performs 'My Heart Belongs to Daddy'):

'She was very nice and comfortable but very childlike. She was not like some other big stars, with closed doors etc. She was very happy to talk, and when I brought people on to the set to get autographs, Marilyn was very nice about it and spent time with them. All the dancers asked her for an autographed picture at the end of the shoot, and they all got one.'

There were also light moments, particularly during the filming of 'My Heart Belongs to Daddy' when she had to pull two dancers (including Bob Banas) by the hair, before swinging round a pole:

'I had so much grease on my hair that when Marilyn went round the pole, she really flew round fast and was very alarmed. She went up to the director and jokingly said, 'I don't want to say but someone has too much grease on their hair!' after which I was sent to have my hair shampooed. Later, when we filmed the part of the song where Marilyn had to kiss me, she had lots of lip-gloss on, and I slid off her face! I went to the director and jokingly told him that she had too much grease on, and Marilyn laughed.'

But it wasn't all light-hearted. Marilyn was perennially late, leading Montand to leave a note under her door, chastising her for keeping him waiting. Tony Randall, who played Montand's sidekick, recalled, 'Marilyn would report to work around five in the evening. You've been in make-up since 8.30 in the morning waiting for her. That ceases to be amusing after about a week.'

Happy together with Arthur Miller during production of *Let's Make Love*, despite marital problems

Another problem was Miller's countless rewrites, which did nothing to improve marital relations. Things got so bad that, on 8 March, when Marilyn went to receive a Golden Globe award for her performance in *Some Like It Hot*, her publicist acted as her escort while Arthur Miller stayed behind at the Beverly Hills Hotel. After the rewrites came an actors' strike, which, coupled with Marilyn's usual illnesses and late arrivals, led to the shooting schedule falling way behind. Montand was due to leave for a 30-day tour of Japan on 15 May. Fox sent representatives to Tokyo to try and stall the tour, but despite offers of financial remuneration, the tour's producers refused to postpone it. When the Japanese threatened legal action, the *Let's Make Love* team moved into overdrive to try to complete filming by mid-May. But, ultimately, with Marilyn still phoning in sick and other delays, Montand had to pay $120,000 to be released from his Japanese tour; a sum that was reimbursed by Fox.

One person who witnessed that stressful time was Dorothy Jeakins, costume designer for *Let's Make Love*, who was later hired for *The Misfits*. Initially, relations between Jeakins and Marilyn were good. As time went on, though, Marilyn began to refuse to attend meetings about *The Misfits* designs. When she started insulting Jeakins in private and in front of other cast and crew, not knowing how to react, Jeakins would stare into space without saying a word. The situation began to feel hopeless; Jeakins wrote a heartfelt letter to Marilyn, apologizing if she had displeased her and admitting defeat. She would withdraw from *The Misfits*, requesting no payment or credit. There is no recorded response to any of this from Marilyn, though the episode does show her dark side; how she could take a dislike to people and be anything but an angel on set.

She may not have made a friend out of Dorothy Jeakins, but Marilyn did connect with some people during the production of *Let's Make Love*. The first was psychiatrist Dr Ralph Greenson, whom she met at the Beverly Hills Hotel on recommendation of her New York analyst, Marianne Kris. The second was Ralph Roberts, a massage therapist and actor who became her masseuse and friend while the third was Evelyn Moriarty, hired to be her stand-in. Moriarty worked with Marilyn for six weeks, without a word said between them: 'I didn't talk to her, and she didn't talk to me.' She told the Marilyn: Then and Now club: 'I had heard that she was difficult, and I wasn't going to go up to someone that I didn't know.'

Jack 'Waukeen' Cochran, hired to play an Elvis impersonator in the film, remembered that everyone was frightened to talk to Marilyn. This was probably not her intention and something that just added to her frustration and insecurity. He took matters into his own hands one day, though, when he greeted her on set with a huge hug. She was surprised but delighted, and so he continued the practice for the rest of his time on the film. But Moriarty was less sure how to approach her and pleased therefore when Marilyn eventually took the initiative and came up to introduce her to her pet cat, Serafina. 'It was a sweet, funny sort of thing to do,' recalled Moriarty, after which the two women became good friends. In later years she would always describe Marilyn in the most positive of ways, as demonstrated in a Marilyn: Then and Now interview: 'She was the most wonderful person that lived. I think that when she got up in the morning she used to wonder who she could help. You couldn't tell her that she had something nice on, because you got it the next day. She was very giving. She was fantastic.'

Someone else who was a fan was Simone Signoret, who, on leaving for a trip to Europe, had declared: 'I love Marilyn very much. She's clever. She loves her husband, which is a quality I like in women.' These were words she might have lived to regret, because, shortly after her departure, an affair began between Yves Montand and Marilyn. Arthur Miller was out of town too, working on *The Misfits*, nonetheless the affair was conducted with some discretion. But news of it did not take long to filter on to the set and into the media. Adding fuel to the flames were Marilyn's comments that Montand, as well as being a brilliant actor, singer and dancer, was 'very, very romantic'. Montand returned the compliment, declaring that he'd marry her if they were not already married to other people. Miller kept entirely quiet about the subject, though Simone Signoret remarked, with a certain restraint: 'If Marilyn is in love with my husband, it proves she has good taste, for I am in love with him too,' before adding, poignantly: 'She is a warm, delightful person … But this business could spoil our friendship.'

It would seem that the affair had run its course by the end of filming, although Marilyn made a much publicized trip to the airport to say goodbye. In fact, when Louella Parsons later asked if her marriage was breaking up because of Yves Montand, Marilyn retorted: 'Of course not! Just because Yves is a gentleman and treated me like a lady is no reason to say we are in love.'

But Marilyn did have strong feelings for Montand and was hurt when she read that he had accused her of having a schoolgirl crush on him, something Montand subsequently denied to columnist James Bacon. 'Even if it were true, which it isn't, no Frenchman would ever make such an ungallant statement.' But the damage was done. Marilyn never heard from Montand again, although she for ever retained what she described as, 'such a strong, tender, wonderful memory'.

· · · · ·

Although feeling totally drained by the end of filming *Let's Make Love*, Marilyn went straight into pre-production of *The Misfits* (and also gave a series of interviews to a variety of newspapers and magazines, from the *Sunday Times* to *Life* magazine and *Paris Match*). For anyone this kind of workload would be tough, but for someone like Marilyn, not in the most robust of health, suffering, specifically, at that time, from anaemia, it was a potential recipe for disaster. By 20 July, when she travelled to Reno for location shooting on *The Misfits*, she was physically and emotionally at the end of her tether.

The people of Reno and Dayton were excited about the arrival of the film's cast and crew, and when Marilyn touched down at the airport, she was met by assorted local dignitaries and attended a cocktail party and press reception at The Mapes Hotel. It looked like

Every inch a sweater girl, during production of *Let's Make Love*

a positive start, but the combination of Marilyn's fragile health and script problems soon shattered that illusion.

'*The Misfits* should never have happened,' declared Marilyn's make-up artist Allan 'Whitey' Snyder to the All About Marilyn fan club. 'She wasn't feeling well when they insisted on starting shooting, and there were so many script changes in her part that Arthur made so often, she became less and less happy with her role and character.'

The problem was that Marilyn was playing a character Miller had largely based on her. He had written the screenplay as a valentine to his wife, but it became so personal at times that it was too painful to watch. Roslyn, Marilyn's character, is a divorcee who becomes involved with a bunch of cowboys – Clark Gable, Eli Wallach and Montgomery Clift – gathered in the Nevada desert to rope wild mustang for use, ultimately, as dog food. At one point, Roslyn describes how she had never wanted children with her ex-husband, at which point Marilyn scribbled in her script that this was just like her feelings towards Joe DiMaggio. There were other parallels, including the heart-wrenching scene where Roslyn screams for the release of the captured horses, an echo of how Marilyn had reacted to plight of the bullock her farmer neighbour intended for veal and the caged pigeons she'd bought from some New York teenagers in order to release them back into the wild.

With childhood idol Clark Gable, 1960, gardening in *The Misfits*

Angela Allen was script supervisor on *The Misfits*, and on first meeting Marilyn at rehearsal found her charming and delightful. Unfortunately, she soon changed her mind when shooting commenced. According to Allen, Marilyn would sometimes arrive five hours late and then only work for an hour and a half before leaving. This observation is supported by Curtice Taylor, producer Frank Taylor's son, there with his family: 'She was late on the set every day – hours late – because she was recovering from the pills. It was like working with a hangover.' Her growing reliance on prescription pills was evident. With cast and crew shocked at how she sometimes staggered around the set, at one point the cameraman commented, 'I can't focus on her eyes, there's nowhere to focus.'

If her eyes were a problem, so was her hair, also an issue on the set of *Let's Make Love*. One of the things Dorothy Jeakins had suggested before her departure was that Marilyn should wear a wig to help with the wind, dirt and dryness of the desert. It was a good suggestion and saved time on hairdressing, but if only Marilyn's other problems were so easily solved. Her marriage was in terrible shape, not helped by the continuing speculation about her relationship with Yves Montand. There were no specific incidents on set but generally it was obvious that things were not going well, with one member of the crew describing Marilyn's treatment of Miller as 'appalling'. Both bore their own resentments, felt let down by the other, shared failed expectations, and although Miller told friends that he and Marilyn were planning a trip to Europe, in reality they could hardly bear the sight of the other.

With Miller and director John Huston, an exhausted Marilyn on *The Misfits* set

Friends recalled that even in the relative privacy of their hotel, neither would speak to the other, as if 'a barrier [had] come between them, going from professional to cool and eventually hostile,' remarked Snyder. As time went on Marilyn started to believe that anyone associated with her husband was against her, including producer Frank Taylor and script supervisor Angela Allen, whom Marilyn accused of having an affair with Miller. In fact, it was photographer Inge Morath, covering the shoot for Magnum, whom Miller was later to marry, though there is no evidence their enduring relationship began during production of *The Misfits*.

When Harry Brandon interviewed her and Miller for the *Sunday Times*, Marilyn said little, but for reporter, Peer Oppenheimer, her misery was only too evident:

> 'The last time I saw her was when she was making The Misfits. I was there to interview both her and Clark Gable, who became extremely upset with Marilyn's inability to get to the set on time and remember her lines. Gable was not the sort of man to become aggravated easily, but he was extremely upset with Marilyn. I think she realized there was a real problem with her career. I felt sorry for her because things were beyond her control.'

In Oppenheimer's article in *Family Weekly*, published on 11 December, he sets out Marilyn's continued determination to be a mother, describing how she intended to take her child with her on filming trips and hire a tutor. 'I realize it takes more thought to raise a child in show business, but it doesn't need to work out badly,' she claimed.

Children were very much on Marilyn's mind during the shoot. While filming a rodeo scene, she took great delight in walking some dogs with 13-year-old Bob Plummer Jr, while eight-year-old Gene Walmsley took his friends to the set to meet 'the prettiest lady I'd ever seen'. Dayton resident Edna MacDiarmid told *Lyon County Reflections* that Marilyn treated both her son Tom and the other children in town in a very special way, and this was extended to a fan who admired one of her diamond rings; Marilyn went out and bought her one. Marilyn still had similar, though perhaps not quite so wildly generous, moments of being friendly and giving, to her fans, particularly, and her 'group' or entourage; Whitey Snyder, Evelyn Moriarty, Marjorie Pletcher and Ralph Roberts. 'When *The Misfits* was going bad, it was her employees who rallied round,' remembered Curtice Taylor.

Still, despite her generosity and kindness and support from some quarters, Reno residents noticed an unhappy air about her, one describing her as lovely but

A vulnerable-looking Marilyn during a break from filming *The Misfits*, 1960

with a 'lost, scared look'. Another, a shop assistant at the Joseph Magnin store, said she was 'the saddest looking woman, really tormented'. During a scene filmed in Harrah's Casino, employee Mark Curtis noticed Marilyn seemed oblivious to everything, giving him, at one point: 'A smile from a sick bed ... Though she was adored by millions, I could not imagine a more pathetic or lonely creature,' he later told the *Reno Gazette-Journal*.

According to stand-in Evelyn Moriarty, Marilyn's state of mind was not helped by her sometimes harsh treatment on set. On one occasion, during the rodeo scene, she had had to sit for hours on end in the blazing sun during rewrites. Another time, in a scene that Moriarty was convinced could have been filmed without her, Marilyn was required to sit in a car for almost two hours in the 115-°F heat. Reporter Art Long, who visited the set, witnessed Marilyn 'so sad, so down in the dumps. She was not in a good way'. Massage therapist Ralph Roberts (who also appeared in the film as an ambulance driver), with whom she had become very close friends, got into the habit of massaging Marilyn to sleep. One night he was called to her room to find her barely conscious, something of which she subsequently had no memory.

A clause in Marilyn's contract allowed her to take time off at times of the month when she had her period, and it was at one such moment in late August that she flew to Los Angeles, determined to rest. On 29 August, following a consultation with her doctor Hyman Engleberg, she was admitted to Westside Hospital with extreme exhaustion. Roberts was shocked to learn that, effectively, Marilyn was having a nervous breakdown and together with Susan and Lee Strasberg, drove immediately to California, in the wake of Miller, Paula Strasberg and May Reis who had all flown there ahead of them. From Nevada, Clark and Kay Gable expressed their concern with a huge and elaborate bouquet of flowers and a heart-felt note.

In Reno, the set closed down. Cast and crew left, and unfounded rumours surfaced of Marilyn being taken from the set wrapped in wet towels and of *Misfits* director John Huston sending her to Los Angeles so he could concentrate on his gambling, retrieving money lost in local casinos. But the reality was that Marilyn's health had become increasingly worse as the shoot progressed. Huston had become ever concerned that if she continued to work in such a fragile state, she could die. As Whitey Snyder recalled: 'Marilyn got very ill up there during filming. She was under too much pressure with the situation with Arthur and all.'

After resting for more than a week, on 5 September, Marilyn returned to Nevada in fighting form, declaring: 'I'm looking forward to getting back to work. I'm feeling much better. I guess I was just worn out.' Filming carried on as before, but it was exhausting for everyone, especially Clark Gable, who at 59, though the oldest member of the cast, insisted on doing his own stunts.

The weekend before location filming ended, and the production moved back to the sound stages of Los Angeles, Marilyn and a few of the others, including Ralph Roberts, Paula Strasberg, May Reis and hair stylist Agnes Flanagan, travelled to San Francisco to see Ella Fitzgerald in concert. Marilyn had been a fan since the early 1950s, when she had made a deal with the manager of a Hollywood nightclub that she would attend each performance if he hired Ella as a singer. Marilyn kept her part of the bargain and sat in the front row for every performance. For Marilyn this trip was a chance not just to see the concert but also to renew her ties with the DiMaggios. Joe DiMaggio was not in town, but Marilyn spent time with his brother and sister, along with his good friend Lefty O'Doul, even finding time to visit the DiMaggio restaurant, where she had spent much of her time in 1954.

That weekend proved to be a turning point for Marilyn. Back in Los Angeles, at the Beverly Hills Hotel, where they were staying, Ralph Roberts witnessed the Millers engaged in a huge row, and while they kept up appearances on set, both knew that Miller had moved out of the hotel and out of her life. Whitey Snyder later summed it up during an interview with All About Marilyn: 'I felt extremely disappointed that Marilyn once again had lost something that she had cherished so much … The normality of a happy marriage and life of security with the one you love.'

'Arthur is a brilliant man,' Marilyn later told Louella Parsons. 'Maybe it wasn't his fault that he was a much better writer than he was a husband. I'm sure that his writing is the most important thing in his life.'

· · · · ·

The day before the film wrapped, Clark Gable saw a rough cut of the movie and declared it to be the best thing he had done since *Gone with the Wind*. When they said goodbye the following day, Marilyn told Gable he was her hero, but couldn't get up enough nerve to tell him just how much she idolized him. 'I don't know how he would have reacted if he had known how important he had been to me all those years,' she told *Family Weekly* magazine. Alas she was never to find out; on 5 November, Gable suffered a massive heart attack and died just eleven days later after suffering a second attack.

On 7 November, just over a week before Gable's death, Miller went home to Brooklyn to break the news of his marriage break-up to his parents, telling them there was no hope of a reconciliation and that he had left because 'it could not go on this way'.

'It hit us like a bomb,' his mother, Augusta Miller, later told *Motion Picture* magazine. 'We never interfered. They had their own lives to live. And we've always been very fond of Marilyn. She was just as fond of us too.'

Back in New York, on 16 November, Marilyn was awoken at 4 am to be told the news of Gable's death by a reporter. She was immediately grief stricken, and by the time she rang Ralph Roberts she sounded hysterical. Things were made even worse by rumours that Marilyn had been somehow responsible for Gable's death. Later she described how she was even confronted by people shouting 'Murderer' at her in the street, hardly tolerable given her already fragile state of mind. She had grown close to Gable, and his wife, during filming, and though the stories did not contain a kernel of truth, they hit her hard.

Refusing to believe that Gable's death had nothing to do with her, Marilyn spiralled into a depression, spending days alone in her bedroom, refusing to see any of her friends and playing sad songs on her phonograph. In *Marilyn: An Untold Story*, Norman Rosten described how when his wife, Hedda, eventually did get through to Marilyn, 'her voice was blurred, distant, unhappy'. It was a desperate situation, and no one knew how to help her. 'I was completely run down,' Marilyn later admitted; 'more unhappy than I remember being at any time in my life.'

During this period of turmoil, May Reis took charge of the practical aspects of the separation and packed up Miller's books and papers, sending them on to Roxbury and a nearby hotel. Miller was given custody of the Roxbury house and also Hugo, the basset hound Marilyn had adored so much. Marilyn remained in the 57th Street apartment they had leased at the beginning of their marriage. On 23 November, Miller resigned as a director of Marilyn Monroe Productions, and on 28 November, an emergency meeting held at the offices of Weissberger and Frosch, discussed the resignation not only of Miller but also of secretary John C. Taylor and advisory committee members John F. Wharton and Robert H. Montgomery.

With the realization that her company and marriage was in tatters, Marilyn found little to be happy about during the run-up to Christmas, but her New York publicist John Springer tried to cheer her with interview requests as well as sending her a recording of poet Robert Frost reading his own poetry. She even received a card from her mother, Gladys, addressed to Norma Jeane Miller, signed, quite bizarrely, 'Loving good wishes, Gladys Pearl Eley'.

Christmas Day was spent quietly with Patricia Newcomb, the publicist with whom Marilyn had worked briefly on *Bus Stop*. Newcomb had been relieved of her duties after a dispute with Marilyn but had returned to work with her at the end of 1960. Despite any problems they might have had in the past, Marilyn was happy to welcome Newcomb into her group, so much so that she even gave her a mink coat as a Christmas present. That night, Marilyn was surprised to receive a forest of poinsettias from Joe DiMaggio, sent, he said, because he knew she would call to thank him, and 'besides, who in the hell else do you have in the world?' Despite the fact that the two hadn't seen each other in a long time, Marilyn agreed to him visiting her on Christmas evening, later saying: 'I was bleary and depressed but somehow still glad he was coming over.'

On New Year's Eve, Patricia Newcomb returned to Los Angeles, and during the flight wrote Marilyn a heartfelt letter. She urged her to phone any time, day or night; sympathizing with what she was going through, asserting what she hoped would be a lifelong friendship. It was a genuine gesture, and one that Marilyn would appreciate during the bleak months ahead.

PHOTOGRAPHS

1956–1960

ABOVE

On 14 July 1956, Marilyn arrived in London to make The Prince and the
Showgirl with Laurence Olivier. Here she is seen with Olivier's wife, Vivien
Leigh, who had played Marilyn's role on stage and made frequent visits to the set
during the making of the film.

The day after her arrival in London, Marilyn attended a press conference at the
Savoy Hotel. Here she leaves the large Surrey mansion where she was staying, at
Englefield Green, en route to the hotel, her departure delayed by the vast crowd of
fans waiting to greet her.

ABOVE

Demurely dressed in a tailored suit, Marilyn attended a second press conference at
the Savoy Hotel on 16 July 1956, and afterwards enjoyed lunch with Miller at
Claridge's in London's Mayfair.

A lighter moment during the sometimes difficult UK visit in which Marilyn, husband Arthur Miller and friend Hedda Rosten (acting as Marilyn's secretary), all enjoy a joke in the back of their car.

A rare shopping expedition in London, 1956. The British public found Marilyn captivating and followed her wherever she went. Mobbed at one stage in Regent's Street, the police had to be called; Marilyn was left visibly shaken.

PART THREE: 'AUTUMN' 1956-1960

An electric Marilyn sparkling with life during a photo
session. The close-fitting, slinky design of her sparkly dress
was a favourite, and she wore this dress and others like it
for numerous publicity appearances.

Marilyn and the Oliviers – Vivien Leigh in fur coat,
gloves and pearls, Laurence Olivier next to her, talking to
Marilyn. They smiled on, but the press showed scant
regard, aside from a young Alan Whicker, in trademark
glasses with a cigarette dangling from his mouth, seen
busy taking notes.

With Miller, prior to her departure from the UK on 20 November 1956, following several months filming The Prince and the Showgirl with Laurence Olivier. Marilyn surprised everyone by arriving on time at the airport, where a scheduled press conference was held at 6.15 p.m. But compared to the excitement of her arrival in the July, her departure was low key.

RIGHT

With husband Arthur Miller on a trip to Washington in 1957, where Miller was required to appear in court on a Contempt of Congress charge. Marilyn went along for moral support, staying with lawyer Joe Rauh, and his wife, Olie, ironing her husband's shirts and reading books on psychology.

Enjoying a laugh with Arthur Miller at the annual *April in Paris Ball*, a
fundraiser for French charities, at the Waldorf-Astoria, New York, on 11
April 1957. Despite rumours that the marriage was a virtual non-starter,
Marilyn tried hard to make it work. For a time it looked as though she'd
succeeded, with Miller declaring he'd gained a few pounds thanks to
Marilyn's cooking and 'general contentment'.

ABOVE

A splash in the ocean with Miller, taken by Sam Shaw in 1957. Living on Long Island, New York, the Millers visited the beach almost every day; on one occasion Marilyn rescued fish stranded above the shoreline, tossing them back into the sea.

LEFT

During 1957, following a traumatic miscarriage, Marilyn made few publicity appearances, but on 12 May she kicked out the first ball at a soccer match at Ebbets Field, Brooklyn. Here she is seated in a car outside the park, surrounded by fans and spectators.

ABOVE

Around the time of Some Like It Hot (1959), sporting a hairstyle similar to the one she had in the film. Marilyn joined the cast after reading an outline from director and writer Billy Wilder. 'I read it, and I loved it,' she said, although she was ultimately disappointed by the way the film was edited. Her opinion was not shared by the film-going public, however: it was a box-office smash.

ABOVE

During her marriage to Arthur Miller, Marilyn threw herself into the role of housewife, spending almost every weekend in their country house in Roxbury, tending the garden and looking after her dog, Hugo. Here, in a stylised shot by Sam Shaw, she is seen enjoying time with her husband.

RIGHT

With actor Tony Curtis during the filming of Some Like It Hot.

With Some Like It Hot co-star Jack Lemmon. Both he and
Tony Curtis were driven to distraction by the delays in filming,
largely due to Marilyn, a situation made worse by having to sit for
hours in full make-up, high heels and women's clothing.

ABOVE

During the making of Some Like It Hot in 1958, with director Billy Wilder. Filming was beset with problems, particularly with Marilyn's regular late arrival on set, exacerbated by her pregnancy.

ABOVE

On the set of Some Like It Hot. Although Marilyn is
laughing, there wasn't much to be happy about, with her
constant lateness and absence. She shares a joke here
nonetheless with Belgian-French actor Maurice Chevalier,
famous for his signature tune 'Thank Heaven for Little
Girls', released in 1957.

RIGHT

By the late 1950s Marilyn seemed not to enjoy press
attention as much as she had done earlier in her career.
She had a list of subjects off limits for the media that
included pregnancy, religion and politics. In this photo of
her walking through a crowd, a camera dominates the
foreground, much as it did her life.

ABOVE AND RIGHT

Practising her dance moves for Let's Make Love in 1960 with Jack Cole.
Together they worked on the fun number 'My Heart Belongs to Daddy', one of
the film's few great moments.

In a scene from The Misfits in 1960, with Clark Gable, whom Marilyn idolised. When he died, just days after finishing the film, she blamed herself for exacerbating any stress he might have been under that may have contributed to his death and endured shouts of 'Murderer' from his fans, some of whom blamed her for his death.

ABOVE

Looking physically exhausted on the set of The Misfits, alongside director John Huston (left) and husband, Arthur Miller. This was a time of huge personal upheaval and heartache: Marilyn and Miller's relationship was unravelling, so much so that by the end of production their marriage was over.

PART FOUR:
'WINTER'
1960—1962

12

'I'M WORKING ON THE FOUNDATION'

'Believe me, no matter what the gossip columns say,' Marilyn told Hollywood columnist Louella Parsons, 'there is no spark rekindled between Joe and me.' During January 1961, Marilyn and Joe DiMaggio had begun seeing each other regularly, in a low-key way, but it was only a matter of days before the press had got wind of it, sparking talk of a reconciliation that led to her denial. So persistent had the rumours become that, on 11 January, Marilyn's publicist John Springer issued a statement to confirm the friendship but play down any romance. But the reality was a reconciliation of sorts. Time, it seemed, had done its usual healing and dampened the fire of their divorce, and Marilyn was to tell psychiatrist Ralph Greenson that in a heartfelt moment DiMaggio had even admitted that he didn't blame her for divorcing him. 'I'd have divorced me too,' he said, adding that he believed her advice that he should see a psychotherapist had saved his life.

With another divorce in mind, on 20 January – the day of John F. Kennedy's inauguration – Marilyn travelled with Pat Newcomb to Juarez, Mexico. Choosing that day to avoid publicity, at a special night session with Judge Miguel Gomez and her attorney Arturo Sosa Aguilar, Marilyn cited her differences with Arthur Miller as 'incompatibility of character'. She was spiralling into depression, but managed somehow to keep up enough reserve to continue her work at The Actors Studio. On one occasion she encountered W. J. Weatherby. He was a reporter she had met on the set of *The Misfits*. A Miller fan, he had not been impressed at first by Marilyn, but on seeing her again, he invited her for a drink with him at a bar on the corner of 8th Avenue. Over the next few weeks, they met some four times, discussing everything from literature and civil rights, to acting and personal issues – even touching on politics. When Marilyn declared that she thought Kennedy spoke a lot of sense she stated that she admired the Kennedy family's zest for life. Weatherby was struck mostly by her sadness, noticing on one occasion that she had a faint body odour and that her hair needed a wash. There were times too when she did not respond when he spoke, something she attributed to the pills that made her feel 'dopey sometimes'.

She was certainly in introspective mood and she had put Miller through a lot. She felt guilty about Clark Gable's death, but now accepted that he had died from a heart condition although she avoided the funeral because she'd been afraid of breaking down. But when subsequently she read a newspaper report that, erroneously, ascribed to Kay Gable a belief that Marilyn was implicated in her husband's death, she spiralled back into depression. In just two months, Marilyn reportedly visited psychoanalyst Marianne Kris, 47 times. None of the sessions was as disturbing as one towards the beginning of February, in which she confessed that after the Kay Gable comment, she'd opened her living- room window wide and considered throwing herself out, only stopped, she told Ralph Roberts, by the sight of a woman she knew walking past the building.

Kris was alarmed at this development, coupled with Marilyn's continuing drug problem, and was persuaded that she needed complete hospital rest. On 6 February, Marilyn telephoned Joe DiMaggio. The following day she checked into the Payne Whitney Hospital as Mrs Faye Miller for 'study and treatment of an illness of undisclosed origin'. Unbeknown to Marilyn, Payne Whitney was a psychiatric hospital. On arrival, Marilyn claimed a psychiatrist conducted a physical examination that included her breasts. Having had a physical with a doctor within the past month, Marilyn was understandably not pleased, but what pleased her even less was the depressingly cell-like room she was allocated, with bars on the windows and the markings on the walls of former patients. Everything was kept under lock and key, including the bathroom, closets and electric lights. The door to her room had an observation window and there was no way of buzzing for assistance.

In a letter dated 1 and 2 March 1961, Marilyn told Ralph Greenson that she had been encouraged to 'mingle' with other patients and take up such occupational therapies as sewing, knitting and playing draughts. Ever mindful of the mental illness that plagued her family, Marilyn was appalled to be there and said as much in reply to a question about why she wasn't happy there. 'I'd have to be nuts if I liked it in here.' When she asked to use the phone, hospital staff told her there wasn't one, though a fellow patient managed to locate a payphone.

Standing in line to use the phone, a security guard informed her that she was forbidden to make any calls. Back in her room, her part in *Don't Bother to Knock* in which she had threatened to self-harm with a razor blade inspired her. 'It took a lot of banging [on the door] to get even a small piece of glass,' she wrote to Ralph

Greenson. Threatening to harm herself, the doctors were called, and four medical staff arrived carried her, face down and sobbing, to the seventh floor that housed the ward for extremely disturbed patients. Told she was a 'very, very sick girl', Marilyn was forced to remain in Payne Whitney for four nights, during which time she was able to get a letter to Lee Strasberg, begging for help. But, the Strasbergs had no power to secure her release. This was arranged, thankfully, by Joe DiMaggio, who arrived at the hospital threatening to take it apart 'brick by brick' if they did not release her into his care. Later Marilyn took pride in telling friends of his rescue and via lawyer Aaron Frosch drew up a document that ensured DiMaggio, Frosch and Reis would all have to be notified before she could ever be locked up again.

Marilyn was driven back to her apartment to confront Dr Kris, 'like a hurricane unleashed', according to Ralph Roberts. Kris was shocked and deeply apologetic, but the damage was done. Marilyn never forgave her and in future relied on her Californian therapist Ralph Greenson. Still emotionally disturbed and exhausted, Marilyn was persuaded to enter Columbia-Presbyterian hospital on 11 February, admitted for 'a rest and check-up', according to a hospital spokesman. John Springer elaborated to reporters; 'She is here for a complete physical check-up. She's had a hell of a year. She had been exhausted, really beat down.'

Joe DiMaggio was a frequent visitor, and the waiting press were eager to hear his take on events. 'She went to the hospital for what amounted to exhaustion and nothing more. The girl has been working very hard with pictures she has done, and Clark Gable's death did not help matters,' was all he was prepared to say.

On Tuesday, 7 March, two days after leaving hospital, Marilyn attended the funeral of Augusta Miller, who had suffered a fatal heart attack. Arriving unexpectedly, she put her own problems on hold to comfort her ex-husband and his father, Isadore.

But, her problems soon resurfaced when more press reports of Kay Gable blaming Marilyn for her husband's death reached John Springer. Aware of Marilyn's fragile state of mind, the clippings were not brought to her attention, on 17 March, when Springer forwarded the comments to lawyer Aaron Frosch, Marilyn somehow managed to see the accompanying letter. She wrote a note to May Reis, demanding she get Frosch on the phone so that she could discuss the issue with him and expressing her anger at anyone who tried to keep 'this kind of thing away from me'. Knowing that she could be confronted about the article at any time, she told Reis: '[I] must know my own business, so I can protect myself. Keeping things from me is no protection.' This episode was just one example of how Marilyn felt her career was being taken out of her hands; by the end of 1961, she was to take steps to try to regain control.

• • • • •

In late March Marilyn accepted Joe DiMaggio's invitation to Florida, where he was to help with the spring training of the New York Yankees. On her arrival at the Tides Hotel at St Petersburg Beach she said: 'I came down here for some rest, some sun and to visit Joe,' though it was also an opportunity to regain her strength after the trauma of the past months. Always prepared to connect with people less famous than herself, Marilyn became friendly with Lynn Pupello, a teenage reporter who, in 1961, won an award for best writer for the American Newspaper Association.

Taking a short break with ex-husband Joe DiMaggio, Florida, 1961

As Pupello recalled: 'I sat near her [on the beach] and struck up a conversation as if she wasn't famous. At first she was shy but my enthusiasm won her over.'

For Marilyn, the friendship became a welcome diversion, though, according to Pupello, Joe DiMaggio at times seemed to resent it:

> 'I wasn't nervous being with Marilyn. She had a loving nature and ability to put you at ease. Joe DiMaggio was aloof with me; he said, 'Hello', but wanted to be alone with her, quietly talking. She smiled occasionally but told me she would not reconcile with him because of his bad temper during the night of the skirt-blowing scene in New York City.'

According to Pupello, in the course of their conversations, Marilyn admitted to having met John F. Kennedy: 'She said she had been in South Florida before, visiting the President. She lit up speaking of him and said: "He has always been very kind to me."' She did not suggest to Pupello or W. J. Weatherby, with whom she had also discussed Kennedy, that she thought of him in a romantic way but made no secret that she was a huge supporter of Kennedy, as both a person and a politician. What makes her comments all the more intriguing is a letter she wrote to Ralph Greenson on 2 March 1961, in which she admitted to a 'fling on a wing' with an un-named man whom she described as being unselfish in bed, but of whom she knew Greenson did not approve. Could this un-named lover be Kennedy? Possibly, though it is more likely she was talking of Frank Sinatra, whom Greenson had once treated. On her return to New York, rumours indeed began to circulate that Sinatra had been in Florida at the same time as Marilyn, and that she had fallen in love with him. Consequently, any plans DiMaggio might have had were put on hold, although they continued to see each other and even attended a baseball game at Yankee Stadium on 11 April.

Just days before, on 1 April, Kay Gable had written to Marilyn, asking when she planned to visit Los Angeles to meet her new baby, John Clark. She still missed her husband each and every day and would spend the summer at their ranch, where she hoped Marilyn and DiMaggio would visit. The letter was friendly and informal; as a result any thoughts that Kay blamed Marilyn for Gable's death were dispelled. With one less thing to worry about but still in need of a break, Marilyn travelled to Los Angeles in April and, despite a minor gynaecological operation on 24 May, enjoyed dating and lying on her private patio at the Beverly Hills Hotel. 'I like my freedom; I like to play the field,' she told columnist Earl Wilson.

Marilyn had lost weight, her hair was short, she'd bought some new clothes and made a new friend in poet (and idol) Carl Sandburg. She travelled to Palm Springs (where she spent time with Sinatra) then dashed to Las Vegas to see him perform with Dean Martin, Peter Lawford and Sammy Davis Jnr at the Sands Hotel, which was becoming something of a mascot for Sinatra's group, the Rat Pack. She spent time with Dean Martin and his wife in Newport Harbor, discussed making a film with Sinatra and found herself settling into LA life. 'I've never had such a good time ever – in Hollywood,' she confided to Louella Parsons. 'For the first time in many years I am completely free to do exactly as I please. And this new freedom has made me happier. I want to look for a home to buy here; I think I'll settle in Beverly Hills' were comments she repeated to columnists Bob Thomas and Hedda Hopper.

In June, Marilyn visited Kay Gable and met John Clark. Talking into the night, she later described the meeting as, 'Wonderful … kind of sad too', and declared John Clark: 'My real love; he's the big man in my life, even if he is a little young for me.' Shortly after she was honoured to attend the baby's christening, where she posed gleefully for the cameras and mingled with the other guests.

Marilyn seemed happy with her life in Los Angeles, but she decided to return to New York in late June to try and firm up negotiations with NBC to televise Somerset Maugham's *Rain*. Negotiations for her starring role (with Lee Strasberg as artistic co-ordinator) had begun in January 1961, and the shoot had been planned for March. But, with Marilyn's illness, NBC had refused to set a date for production; many heated meetings of lawyers, agents and the TV company followed until late May, when the final contract was received by agency MCA.

Another meeting held on 2 June, due to last-minute questions from lawyer Aaron Frosch, saw the contracts rewritten. A further hitch occurred when Marilyn decided she wanted specific co-stars, such as Richard Burton, and for Lee Strasberg to have more power. Yet although it has been said that the deal fell through because of Marilyn's wish to have Lee Strasberg as director, neither the request nor its rejection is noted anywhere in any correspondence or notes. Indeed, through to the very last day, Lee Strasberg was always referred to as either 'Artistic Co-ordinator' or 'Artistic Advisor'. On 27 June, NBC wrote to Aaron Frosch to inform him that the deal was off; the correspondence was filed away, and a statement prepared that Marilyn had been advised not to take part.

While Marilyn was undoubtedly disappointed about *Rain*, she had more pressing things with which to deal. On 28 June she was rushed to Polyclinic Hospital suffering from what her spokesman described as 'a mild intestinal disorder'. However, it was quickly determined that there was much more to her pain than that, and on the evening of the 29th she underwent a successful two-hour operation to remove her gall bladder. Marilyn required a long convalescence on her return to 56th Street. Joe DiMaggio was on hand almost constantly, as well as Marilyn's sister, Berniece, who had travelled from Florida to look after her. Sleeping in what had been Arthur Miller's study, Bernice helped around the house and walked Marilyn's new dog, Maf, a present from good friend Sinatra.

Berniece became aware that something was troubling Marilyn and worried on her behalf, not only about her intake of prescription pills but also the problems she continually seemed to encounter. There were money worries, anxiety over the will she had signed in January (but of which she, apparently, disapproved), concern for her career and stress over the complaining letters she was receiving from Gladys in Rockhaven Sanitarium. But there was also something else on Marilyn's mind; her father had been in touch, she said, and had visited her during a recent stay in hospital. A quite enjoyable though not particularly affectionate occasion, this was undoubtedly a major moment in Marilyn's life, though one she found hard to process.

Perhaps with her mind on family connections and relationships, Marilyn told Lynn Pupello, her reporter friend from Florida, whom she had invited to stay that summer in New York, something she would never forget:

> 'She said that if she could pick out someone to be her daughter that it would be me; she liked the fact that I was a professional writer on an important newspaper; someone interested in and knowledgeable about archaeology, art history, architecture, film, theatre, literature, and fine arts. She talked to me for hours about how depressed she was about her divorce [but also] talked about moving back to LA, so she gave me some of her nightgowns and jewellery, which she said I should wear whenever the time came later in life to marry.'

Other erstwhile close relationships came to the fore when, together with Ralph Roberts and Berniece, Marilyn travelled to Roxbury to sort out some personal items that had been overlooked during the separation and divorce. During what must have been a difficult and painful encounter, Marilyn smiled continually as if it had all been well rehearsed. Miller made tea and asked about her health; Marilyn took some delight in showing him her gall-bladder scar, as if to prove that she really had been ill all those years. On leaving, she almost seemed to stall then waved silently goodbye, to be driven away from the house for what would be the last time.

• • • • •

Fully recovered from the operation, Marilyn began to think about returning to work. Although she had expressed an interest in the George Axelrod film *Goodbye Charlie*, she changed her mind at the last minute, declaring: 'As far as I'm concerned

882 Doheny Drive: the three-room apartment where Marilyn lived,1953 and 1961

it's Goodbye, *Goodbye Charlie*.' There were no repercussions this time for turning down the role; Fox agreed that she was not required to accept it or, indeed, any part in it. What they did want her for, though, was *Something's Got To Give*, a remake of *My Favorite Wife* (1940); it was with this in mind, plus a desire to see her therapist, Ralph Greenson, that Marilyn returned that September to Los Angeles and the apartment at 882 North Doheny Drive, where she had lived before her marriage to DiMaggio.

On 22 September, on her way back to New York again briefly, Marilyn's plane encountered problems during take-off and had to return to Los Angeles. The episode rattled her, and as soon as the aircraft touched back down in LA she sent a telegram to Joe DiMaggio, confiding that during the incident the two things she'd thought about had been 'you, and changing my will', before adding, 'Love you, I think, more than ever'. But loving him was one thing; she still had no plans to remarry her 'slugger', telling reporter Helen Hendricks: 'I've always been able to count on Joe as a friend … Now I like being with him, and we have a better understanding than we've ever had.' And she repeated the claim that she'd made to Louella Parsons that there was no spark rekindled between them.

On 5 October, Patricia Newcomb sent an internal memo to her boss at the Arthur P. Jacobs Agency, informing him of Marilyn's new Los Angeles address. She requested all her mail should be marked for the attention of Marge Stengel, (Marilyn's assistant for a while), so that the name Marilyn Monroe did not appear on the envelope. Back in Los Angeles, Marilyn was determined to protect her privacy. However, one person she did not mind seeing was Ralph Roberts, whom she urged to join her in California as her masseuse and unofficial chauffeur. Roberts duly showed up, and they spent a lot of time together, having barbeques and talking into the night. But their companionship came to an abrupt halt when Marilyn told him that Greenson was urging her to drop old friends; Roberts found himself travelling back to New York.

This turn of events has been confirmed by Whitey Snyder, who told the 'All About Marilyn' fan club: 'Marilyn mentioned several times that Greenson often suggested there were many of her so-called friends that were only using her, and she should only trust him. She laughed and said that she often trusted her so-called friends more than him. I am sure Dr Greenson did everything to keep Marilyn under his thumb.'

Much has been said of Greenson's treatment of Marilyn during her last few months, yet it remains shrouded in mystery. Marilyn was to become Greenson's most famous client, and the full extent of his control over her life may never be known. But what is known is that he did something very few doctors have done before or since — welcomed her into his home and into the bosom of his family (who still refuse to talk about her forty-five years after her death). The children of Marilyn's former therapist Marianne Kris, in New York, were not involved with Marilyn in any way, but Greenson's children, Joan and Daniel, did become friends, sharing walks and friendly chitchat with her. It was an unconventional way of working as a therapist, but Greenson was hopeful of a successful outcome and confided to friends that she was showing some improvement. (Though he admitted to Anna Freud that he had improvised her treatment, feeling that was the best option for her, although often wondering where he was taking her.) Greenson had discovered that Marilyn took a variety of pills including narcotic analgesic Demerol and barbiturates Phenobarbital HMC and Amytal. She had a developed the knack of being able to obtain prescriptions and large doses of drugs from a variety of different doctors, none of whom knew about the other. Greenson was concerned about this and about her drug intake, especially about her use of Demerol. It was believed to be dangerous if used on a regular basis, leading to addiction and an inability to function without it. Withdrawal accompanied by severe anxiety and insomnia and a host of other symptoms also followed.

Greenson described Marilyn to Anna Freud as a sick, borderline paranoid, addictive personality. It was hard, he said, to treat such severe problems in anyone, let alone someone as famous, yet alone, as Marilyn Monroe. To this end he hired some help for Marilyn in the form of housekeeper, Eunice Murray, a middle-aged woman whom he had known since he had bought her former home on Franklin Avenue in Santa Monica and whom he believed would be an ideal companion for her. Murray seems to have been a bit of a 'jill' of all trades, turning her hand to a variety of different skills, including dressmaking and cooking, landscaping and interior design, bookbinding and even dabbling in psychology. She had worked with several psychiatrists and their patients, helping with whatever home support was required. In November 1961, Murray began work at Doheny Drive, chauffeuring Marilyn around town, helping with the groceries and performing simple housekeeping errands such as washing and cleaning. 'I was everything Marilyn needed,' Murray later said.

But Murray's sentiment was not one echoed by Marilyn's friends, many of whom wondered why she was there and what her real motives were. 'My impression of Eunice Murray was that she couldn't be trusted and that every move Marilyn made was reported immediately to Dr Greenson,' Whitey Snyder remarked to the 'All About Marilyn' fan club. 'She was extremely quiet, secretive, and always hovering around Marilyn.' He also wondered if Greenson's treatment was at all beneficial: 'As the months went by it was obvious his influence was becoming stronger and stronger,' he said. He also felt that the frequency of Greenson's visits, at his suggestion, and his 24-hour availability to Marilyn was 'unprofessional and greedy'.

But her therapeutic work did not take up all her time. There was film work looming with preparations in progress for the next Fox production. This included supportive publicity via her contribution to articles for magazines including *Paris Match*, *Tempo*, *Look* and *Redbook* as well as interviews with Vernon Scott, Joe Hyams and Henry Gris. And there was one more key project; photographer Douglas Kirkland's portrait assignment of Marilyn for the twenty-fifth anniversary special edition of *Look* magazine. Kirkland's first impressions of Marilyn were positive. On arriving at the small Doheny Drive apartment he found her:

> '*Amazingly pleasant and playful like a sister and not at all intimidating as I had imagined her to be ... She sat beside me, laughed easily and made small talk, putting me at ease. I was young and did not know how to ask her to pose for the sexy images I hoped to get, but she simplified it all by suggesting, 'I should get into bed with nothing on but white silk'. We discussed the details and Marilyn said she wanted Frank Sinatra music and chilled Dom Perignon.'*

On the day of the photo shoot, she arrived very late, and when she stepped into the room Kirkland was amazed to discover that she was now Marilyn Monroe, the superstar:

> '*It was an extraordinary photo session. She was wonderful; luminous as she floated under that semi transparent silk sheet. She arrived with her hair and make up already done and an assistant carrying various changes of clothes although they were not really needed. She told everyone in the room, "I'd like to be alone with this boy. I find it usually works better that way." There was sexual tension in the air and it reflected in the resulting photos.'*

However, the next afternoon when Kirkland took the transparencies to Marilyn's department, there was a distinct difference in her demeanour: 'She seemed depressed. She was wearing dark glasses and might have been crying, but she eventually brightened up and decided she loved the pictures.'

Another photographer who had the opportunity of working with Marilyn in late 1961 was Eric Skipsey, who took photos of her with Maf, her small, white puppy.

'Marilyn was a friend of mine, but I only had one occasion to do a portrait sitting which was a success. It was a bit complicated in that the publicist was three quarters of an hour late in arriving, during which time we talked and joked and even had a small taste of champagne to pass the time away. When the female publicist finally arrived she turned to me and said, "You have ten minutes, Mr Skipsey", and Marilyn immediately said, "You have as long as you wish, Eric, they are my pictures, not hers." We worked together for another hour, and in fact Marilyn said I could have more time if I wished. This attitude was typical of her: she did not behave like a superstar; she was a nice and considerate person.'

With her career and psychological well-being in mind, and in the spirit of Greenson's desire to get her working and studying again, Marilyn wrote to Lee Strasberg on 19 December, informing him that in the absence of his coaching she felt as if she were only half functioning. She had big plans for the future and was desperate for him to move to California to work as part of a new independent production unit she was hoping to form. So determined was she that she even wrote to Marlon Brando asking his opinion on how best to get her coach to Los Angeles, declaring, 'time is of the essence'.

* * * * *

Marilyn had once told reporters that: 'I seem to be a whole superstructure without any foundation', but as 1961 rolled into 1962, it appears she was making every effort to 'work on the foundation'. At her side again was Joe DiMaggio, shopping for Christmas presents on Olvera Street, buying a little tree for her apartment and even attending a seasonal dinner with the Greenson family and friends. But the event wasn't altogether successful, when, as the men gathered around DiMaggio and bombarded him with baseball questions, someone remarked that no one was paying any attention to Marilyn; she laughed, but, in truth, did not find it funny.

Another friendship under pressure was Marilyn's relationship with Frank Sinatra. The trigger for the decline was the moment he said: 'Oh, not that again', when he heard her talking about her orphaned past. His honesty stunned her but did not make her warm to him. On coming across photographs taken during a boat trip with him in 1961, she determined not to send him any, declaring that she'd 'already given him enough'. Marilyn could be warm-hearted to people she liked, but, by her own admission, to W. J. Weatherby the previous year, she could also be something of a 'monster'. One person who did see this side of her was Michael Selsman, who worked with her through the Arthur P. Jacobs agency:

> 'She was Pat Newcomb's client, but Pat was frequently busy with some of her other clients, so I was detailed to cover certain PR functions for her. It was always difficult to work with Marilyn – sometimes unpleasant. I had other 'difficult' clients but they were also kind and generous, which Marilyn was not. She made it hard for me (and others around her) to do our jobs – just because she could. It's tempting to say she was a spoiled brat, but it went deeper than that. She could be mean, spiteful, threatening and duplicitous; to the point I dreaded having to see her.'

On one occasion in January 1962, Selsman and his wife, Carol Lynley, travelled to the Doheny Drive apartment for a meeting with Marilyn.

> 'Carol was nine months pregnant, due any moment now. I couldn't and didn't want to leave her at home by herself, so I took her along to Monroe's apartment, where Marilyn was to look at negatives from a photo shoot she had just done with the hot new photographer, 21 year-old, Doug Kirkland, for Look magazine. I knocked on her door, as Carol stood shivering beside me. Marilyn opened the door and looked at Carol, whom she knew, since they had adjacent dressing rooms at the studio, and said, 'You come in,' motioning to me, 'but she can wait in your car.' This was unexpected, and I was momentarily stunned. Carol and I exchanged glances, and I assured her I'd be out in 15 minutes. I was frankly scared. Monroe was one of our biggest clients and I did not want to confront her, or lose my job.
>
> Every other actor I worked with would use a red grease pencil to put an X through the negatives they didn't like, but not Monroe. She took scissors and cut out every one she did not like, then cut those into tiny splinters and threw them in the wastebasket. This laborious process took three hours, during which I repeatedly got up to leave. Marilyn kept ordering me to sit down. To be young is to be stupid, someone said, and if I were ever in a situation like that again, I might be out of a job, but I might still have a wife. It was my first evidentiary [sic] of Marilyn Monroe's capacity for cruelty.'

Another less endearing side of Marilyn was her occasional ruthlessness, evidenced on the occasion Richard Merriman, interviewed her for Life magazine. According to memos from the Arthur P. Jacob's agency, Marilyn reacted well to Merriman, though less so with another reporter who was there and apparently a little drunk. Constantly interrupting both Marilyn and Merriman, she spoke to the actress as if she were 'underprivileged' and became absolutely hysterical when told that all photos not approved by Marilyn would be destroyed. 'How can you dare such a thing?' she demanded, to which a surprised Marilyn replied: 'You're giving me a fishy-eyed stare, but I love you anyway.'

She was not shy of giving official liaisons the snip too. At that point she was intent on getting out of her contract with MCA and hiring a new lawyer, 'Mickey' Rudin – Greenson's brother-in-law. But on a personal level, at that moment, Marilyn wanted to forge rather than cut links. She'd become tired of hotels and rented apartments and wanted her own home, ideally near the coast and in the Mexican style of the Greenson home that she liked so much. Eunice Murray was pleased to help and, eventually, found the ideal property in 12305 Fifth Helena Drive, Brentwood, tucked away down a short side street. It was a bungalow with good, thick walls, heavy beams and security bars on the front windows. Four decorative floor tiles cemented into the ground by the front door read *Cursum Perficio*: 'I've finished my journey'. At the back of the house a large garden, with a terrace and kidney-shaped pool, cascaded down the hillside with a magnificent view of the streets below; Marilyn loved it. 'It's the first house I've ever owned, and I bought it because it reminded me so much of the orphanages I was brought up in as a child.' This seems a strange comment in the light of everything she had ever said about orphanage life, but perhaps shows how her memories and feelings were mellowing with time.

After asking Joe DiMaggio to look over the house for her, Marilyn decided to remodel the kitchen and otherwise just redecorate the rest of the house in a Mexican style. Among the variety of people hired to help with the restoration, was Twentieth Century Fox electrician, James A. Gough, whose son, Jim Gough, went with him to the home one Saturday afternoon:

Fifth Helena Drive, the tucked-away street where Marilyn bought her first and last house

'Marilyn and Mrs Murray were delighted as they had just discovered the original fireplace with Mexican tiles, under a layer of plaster, and they were happily cleaning the tiles when we arrived. Marilyn showed us around the home and the garden, and I was surprised to discover that the house wasn't grand. It was a simple, 1930s Spanish-renaissance style, and Marilyn had found that she loved gardening, although she had never had the opportunity to do it before.'

Lawyer Milton Rudin drew up the purchase papers, and, although saddened at buying a home on her own, the experience was largely a positive one, enabling her to start to make plans and put down roots for the future. 'The house was important for Marilyn,' recounted Eunice Murray: 'her doctor thought it would take the place of a baby or husband.'

In early February Marilyn set off for Mexico to buy furniture for her new home, going, briefly, via New York then Miami, where she visited her ex-father-in-law, Isadore Miller. On 19 February, after a poignant few days with 'Dad', she flew to Mexico with Pat Newcomb and other members of her staff. She met up with Eunice Murray who had travelled down the week before, researching places of interest and visiting her brother-in-law, Churchill Murray. Despite the fact that the trip was basically a shopping expedition, it captured the attention of the FBI, as their files, now in the public domain, make clear. It appears the Federal Bureau of Investigation had been keeping a discreet eye on Marilyn since the mid-1950s (after she expressed a desire to visit Russia, and then began dating Arthur Miller). From Mexico an un-named informant sent snippets of information to Washington about how Marilyn had been seen to be associating with members of the American Communist Group in Mexico (ACGM).

The FBI were particularly interested to hear of a mutual infatuation said to be developing between Marilyn and one Fred Vanderbilt Field, a man who had served nine months in prison for refusing to name his communist friends, before finally moving to Mexico in 1953. Although Field's name is blanked out on most of the FBI documents, there remains one instance where his name has been mistakenly left in, making it almost certain that Field is the man to whom they are referring. According to the documents, Marilyn spent a great deal of time with the married Field, causing 'considerable dismay' among her entourage and members of the ACGM. Whether there was any substance to the romance between Field and Marilyn is not known, but they do seem to have spent time together, such as on 21 February, when he was said to have visited her in suite 1110 of the Hotel Continental Hilton. Whoever the informant was for this and other information remains unclear, but it was someone with access not only to Marilyn but also to her entourage – particularly Eunice Murray (who is falsely identified as Eunice Churchill in the FBI files). The informant seems to have spoken with Murray, quoting her as saying that Marilyn was disturbed by Miller's recent marriage to Inge Morath and how she felt like a 'negated sex symbol'.

Intriguingly the informant also mentions that Marilyn had spent time previously with Attorney-General Robert Kennedy at the home of the Peter Lawford and his wife, Patricia, Robert Kennedy's sister, and had challenged him on some points proposed to her by friends. This meeting probably took place in October 1961, when she also bombarded the Attorney-General with questions supplied by Dr

Greenson's son, Daniel, and allegedly became so drunk that Kennedy and his assistant Edwin Guthman had to drive her home. But, primarily, the informant is concerned by the relationship with Field, declaring that she travelled to a native market in Toluca with him on 24 February, after which she spent time with him and others at an undisclosed location.

Beach house of Peter Lawford and his wife, Patricia, sister of Jack and Bobby Kennedy

If the informant is to be believed, the friendship did cause distress to friends of both parties, particularly Eunice Murray who felt that Marilyn, vulnerable because of recent rejections was becoming increasingly dependent on him. The nature of the relationship with Field will probably never be known, but he was married at the time. His wife, Nieves, was present during the Mexico trip and later travelled with her husband to New York, where they stayed in Marilyn's apartment for three weeks while she was in Los Angeles. So unless the relationship was carried out with Field's wife's approval, it would seem to have been more of a mutual attraction than a full-blown affair.

On 25 February, Marilyn had cancelled a date with a furious Field just five minutes before he was due to collect her. Hardly the behaviour of a love-struck woman. Indeed another person who was touted as boyfriend material was José Bolanos, a Mexican fan/scriptwriter. How they met remains a mystery, but Bolanos showed Marilyn around local nightspots and at the end of the visit gave her every photo he could find of them together. 'She was the most funny person I have ever met,' he later told reporter Glenn Thomas Carter. 'She had one quality that really delighted me – the ability to demolish verbally anyone who proved to be obnoxious to her.'

Bolanos also escorted Marilyn to the Golden Globe Awards in Los Angeles – where she received an award for the World Film Favourite – but there is no sign of a serious romance. What there is, however, is evidence that he may have helped her with something more important – the possible adoption of a child. It is speculation supported by an article in *Motion Picture* magazine, in which reporter Glenn Thomas Carter tells of how he accompanied Marilyn on a night out in Acapulco, where she encountered an eight-year-old boy entertaining customers. According to Carter, Marilyn was intrigued by the boy and his background, which turned out to be deprived. His parents were dead, and he had been fostered out to people who had taught him how to dance and pick-

With date Jose Bolanos at the 1962 Golden Globes

pocket tourists. Marilyn broke down in tears at his story, and the boy joined her, crying and asking if he might be able to live with her in California. Impulsively, Marilyn said yes, and the next day went to visit his foster parents, informing them that her friend José Bolanos would arrange all the details of the adoption for her.

Whether the story of the adoption is entirely true is not known, but it does make sense when reading newspaper reports of Marilyn's trip to a Mexican orphanage, where she turned down the opportunity of adopting a baby and gave a donation of $10,000 instead. Furthermore, at a farewell party held at the end of the Mexican trip, Marilyn talked about adopting a Mexican child. Her occasional stand-in, Evelyn Moriarty, recalled: 'It was around this time that I first heard talk of Marilyn trying to adopt a child ... that her trip to Mexico was for more than buying furniture.'

13

CURSUM PERFICIO

In early March 1962, on her return to Los Angeles from Mexico, Marilyn enrolled Joe DiMaggio's help with her move into 12305 Fifth Helena Drive, still being remodelled and with virtually no furniture. But, Marilyn didn't care. 'I just want to live in my own house,' she told friends, as she busied herself with gardening and decorating. Among the one or two items lost in the move was a list of questions to Marilyn from *Paris Match*, the answers to which were due to run alongside photographs by Willy Rizzo. These photos showed a very different Marilyn; her hair is rumpled, her clothes are plain, and she looks thin and exhausted. Still, she loved them, and on 9 March Pat Newcomb wrote to Rizzo to say so, adding that Marilyn looked forward to working with him again.

Work of a different nature preoccupied Marilyn. This was costume tests for *Something's Got to Give*, for which she had fittings at Fifth Helena with designer Jean Louis, while hosting a champagne and caviare party for the seamstresses and fitters. She seemed happy to be starting a new movie, even though the script was still undergoing rewrites. Indeed, from 1960 to 1961 five writers worked on the screenplay. Edmund Hartman wrote at least three versions of it; Gene Allen, Nunnally Johnson and Arnold Schulman all tried their hand at it, and Walter Bernstein did final rewrites of a script that was shaky at best.

One Fox executive dismissed it as old-fashioned, full of hokum and just not funny, saying there was nothing to suggest the light bedroom comedy had the makings of a successful film. As late as February 1962, the leading man had yet to be found. Somewhat bizarrely, Fox studio chief Peter Levathes got Ralph Greenson involved in the production. His remit; to keep Marilyn on an even keel. Then Greenson's friend Henry Weinstein somehow replaced producer David Brown, much to director George Cukor's dismay. The net result was a production over budget early on. Not a good sign, especially given Fox's already dire financial straits, partly the result of their production of *Cleopatra*, then being filmed in Rome. Fox employees were told they had to engage in some cost cutting, with instructions to water their own plants and bring their own lunch to the studio, since the gardeners and cafeteria staff had been laid off. 'The place was like a ghost town,' remembered one.

Still, plans continued to ensure *Something's Got to Give* would soon be ready to begin shooting and actress Edith Evanson was to help Marilyn with the Swedish accent for her role as Miss Tic. She found her at times in philosophical mood. 'Isn't it a terrible thing about life that there always must be something we have to live up to?' On one occasion, Marilyn invited Evanson to accompany her to New York for the weekend. 'She was so pleading,' recalled Evanson, 'but I couldn't leave my husband and my home. She understood.'

That spring, Marilyn was happy to hear from old friend, Norman Rosten, based in California for six weeks. He visited her often during his trip, and she showed him around her new house, urging him to use her pool and laughing at things that had gone wrong in her life. She was optimistic about the future, but Rosten couldn't help worrying about her, sensing she was 'tired to her soul'. When the time came for him to leave for New York, Marilyn seemed afraid to see him go and berated him before he left for not using her pool.

April had the beginnings of a busy month. On the 6th, Marilyn heard news of someone who had once meant a lot to her – Milton Greene – when *Glamour* magazine invited her to take part in his photographic portrait of a group of famous women with hairdresser Kenneth (Battelle). Although she could probably have made the time for it, she asked Pat Newcomb to send her regrets. On 9 April she became a founder-member of the Hollywood Museum, sending her (tax-deductible) fee of $1000. The next day, she attended costume tests at Fox, followed by a discussion the next morning with photographer Bert Stern about a shoot for *Vogue*. She expressed her delight at his ideas, added her suggestions of which designers they might use, then said she'd be happy to dedicate a weekend to him, to give him 'all the time you need'. There were also plans afoot to film a Christmas Seal trailer, for charity stickers sold in aid of sufferers from TB. This Newcomb considered an important public service for Marilyn, and on 11 April urged Henry Weinstein to film it whenever possible.

But there was a shadow over what was largely a hopeful time. One day Henry Weinstein, concerned by Marilyn's non-appearance at a production meeting, had gone to Fifth Helena Drive and, he claimed, discovered her unconscious, almost naked and sprawled across her bed. She had apparently taken an overdose, though she was saved from harm by Weinstein's prompt summoning of Dr Greenson and Dr Engelberg. Both doctors had long been concerned with Marilyn's sudden mood swings and her habit of mixing sleeping pills with champagne, to the extent that Engelberg had kept a key to Doheny Drive, and both had access to keys at Fifth

Helena. When Weinstein returned to Fox that day, his pleas to postpone production were met with refusal.

On 23 April, the first official day of shooting, Marilyn did not turn up. She had gone to New York after the overdose episode to work with the Strasbergs and see friends. There, she had caught a cold, and by 19 April when she returned to Los Angeles with Paula Strasberg in tow, she had sinusitis verging on a bronchial infection. The schedule was quickly rearranged to shoot scenes featuring co-stars Dean Martin and Cyd Charisse. They worked around her for a full week, until on 30 April Marilyn arrived on set, greeted by a friendly telegram from agent Arthur Jacobs, wishing her luck and signing off love and kisses, 'The Right Arthur'.

Looking over her shoulder during the making of *Something's Got To Give*

Despite running a temperature, Marilyn worked a full day. The next day, 1 May, she turned up again with a temperature, only this time studio physician Lee Seigel examined her and declared it unwise to expose the children in the cast to her contagious virus infection and sent her home. Marilyn was absent for the rest of the week, while shooting continued at Fox, up to the point at which studio executives declared no more could be done without her.

As if this weren't enough, an article about her, told with the co-operation of her erstwhile coach Natasha Lytess, was about to appear in *France-Dimanche*. Lytess had been paid $10,000 for her memories of Marilyn, some of which were so intimate that they could not publish them. But although the Arthur P. Jacobs agency offered to buy the article, the magazine refused, convinced it could make at least $200,000 if they ever decided to publish. But, for the moment, Natasha Lytess was the least of Marilyn's worries.

At the beginning of production of *Something's Got to Give*, Marilyn had received permission to travel to New York to perform at President Kennedy's birthday party on 19 May. She was committed to the appearance and had been specially invited to perform. In May, during her absence from set, press reports circulated that she was 'knocking herself out' to rehearse for it. On 11 May studio chief Levathes, informed Marilyn's lawyer, Milton Rudin that since the film was so far behind schedule, he could not consent to Marilyn attending the celebration. However, when she returned to the set on 14 May, Marilyn either did not know of this withdrawal of consent or did not care. Either way, on 17 May she left Los Angeles for New York, telling reporters: 'I told the studio six weeks ago that I was going. I consider it an honour to appear before the President of the United States.'

Pat Newcomb added that Marilyn had not wanted to break her promise on such an important occasion, but, back on the set, no one could believe she had gone: 'It was like the roof caving in. It was awful,' remembered Evelyn Moriarty.

·　·　·　·　·

Rumours of an affair – between Marilyn and Jack Kennedy and between Marilyn and his brother Bobby – have been rife since the 1960s. The general consensus is that she was romanced by Jack then later passed to Bobby when the President had become bored. There is no evidence to prove or disprove these rumours, but there are witnesses to Marilyn being in the presence of one or both brothers. Whitey Snyder drove Marilyn to the Lawfords, in February 1962, to attend a party held for President Kennedy. While Ralph Roberts was said to have received a call from her, on 24 March 1962, from Bing Crosby's home, where she was spending time with Jack Kennedy.

Vanessa Steinberg, daughter of Marilyn's gynaecologist Oscar, remembered her father sharing with her what he knew of the Kennedy relationship. 'By the time my father saw Marilyn at Cedars hospital in Los Angeles [c. 1961] she was well and truly having an affair with Robert Kennedy. According to him it was Bobby Kennedy whom she was madly in love with and she had no intention of returning to a relationship with DiMaggio.' Interestingly, Steinberg also told his daughter that Marilyn had fallen for Kennedy while she was still with Miller.

Press representative Michael Selsman firmly believes Marilyn was involved with both Kennedy brothers at different times. 'Of course she was, and everyone knew it, but in those days, the press had a different relationship with celebs, both in showbiz and in politics. I usually gave reporters inside stuff on other clients to assuage their desire to publish something about Marilyn and the Kennedys.'

In the 1980s Eunice Murray affirmed that both brothers were important in Marilyn's life, and certainly we know that she was friends with Patricia Kennedy and her husband, Peter Lawford, meeting the Kennedy brothers on a variety of occasions at their home.* Certainly a friend of Kennedy's later told reporters that there was not even the faintest romantic interest on either side, and that all the relationship consisted of, was Bobby providing a friendly ear for Marilyn's numerous problems. Not everyone in Marilyn's circle trusted the rumours either: "I never

The celebrity look of dark glasses and headscarf, New York, 1962

*On one particular occasion, she was seated to Robert Kennedy's left, while Kim Novak was to his right. Marilyn monopolized him by asking political questions, while Novak apparently had hardly any chance to talk at all.

believed 90 per cent of what was written about the involvement with the Kennedys", remarked Whitey Snyder some 30 years later.

Regardless of that, Marilyn certainly caused a stir at President Kennedy's Birthday party, when she arrived with her ex-father-in-law Isadore Miller. Wearing a skin-tight, sparkled dress, designed to give a nude look, Marilyn shimmered her way onto the stage, after being introduced by Peter Lawford as: 'The late Marilyn Monroe'; the running joke of the evening being that Marilyn was never on time. She stood for a moment, looking around her, before breathily reciting 'Happy Birthday, Mr President' and a reworking of 'Thanks for the Memory'.

The event was televised on news programmes around the world, including the UK, where viewer Michael Finn remembered: 'My parents and I were watching it on the news and on walked Marilyn. We were shocked because she looked so drunk.' She was extremely nervous on the evening of the party, and certainly the grainy footage seems to show her a little 'tipsy', but she got through it fine. It prompted John F. Kennedy to announce: 'I can now retire from politics after having had "Happy Birthday" sung to me in such a sweet, wholesome way.'

When Marilyn returned to Los Angeles, she spoke with reporters about her experience at Madison Square Garden: 'I liked it. I like celebrating birthdays. I enjoy knowing that I'm alive; and you can underline alive.' However, she was sad that she had lost a good luck charm – a pawn from her chess set – and felt extremely fatigued, which once again affected her work on the film, preventing close-ups and forcing filters to be used to hide her exhaustion.

On 22 May, Marilyn refused to work with Dean Martin as he had a slight cold and she was afraid to catch it, but on the 23rd everyone's spirits were raised when she filmed a nude swim scene, the first by a major US actress. Marilyn was supposed to wear a flesh-coloured swimsuit, but after a few takes it was decided that it could be seen on camera, and she removed it. Suffering from ear-ache, Marilyn did not take the scene lightly; she banned most people from the set and demanded Whitey Snyder should look through the lens to make sure it was not too risqué. She was happy with the results, though, delighted that the photos would 'knock Liz Taylor off the front pages'.

That weekend Henry Weinstein tried but failed to contact her and on Monday she phoned in sick. When she turned up on Tuesday, 29 May, she was unfocused and repeatedly forgot her lines. On the morning of 1 June, her thirty-sixth birthday, Evelyn Moriarty went to Farmer's Market to pick up her birthday cake. Arriving back on set, she was shocked to be told that under no circumstances must she bring it on to the set until 5.30 pm. 'She's got to do a full day's work first.'

By the end of the day, the sparkle-decorated cake was wheeled out, along with a personalised 'Happy Birthday (suit)' card, which everyone had signed. Marilyn loved the gesture and stayed for a while to enjoy a small celebration, before heading to Dodger's Stadium to attend a charity baseball game. For once all seemed to be well, but again, it was a misapprehension. On 2 June, the Greenson children were shocked to find Marilyn depressed and inconsolable at her home in Brentwood, so much so that they called Dr Leon Uhley who was standing in for their father, while Greenson and his wife holidayed in Europe. Uhley was so shocked to see Marilyn in such a state that he promptly confiscated her pills. The next day she gave Mrs Murray a list of urgent questions and instructed her to phone Greenson in Europe to find out the answers.

By Monday, Marilyn was again not able to work, which, according to one crew member, caused everyone on set to: 'tear our hair out. There was no logic to what she did.' By this time it was clear Marilyn was in a terrible state, requiring Dr Greenson to return to Los Angeles from his holiday in Rome. He arrived at Marilyn's house to find her heavily drugged but feeling better and went straight on to a meeting with Fox executives, assuring them he could get her back to work. Although he did not want his relationship to be seen as Svengali-like, he could persuade her to do 'anything reasonable'. But Fox had had enough. Already reeling from the huge overspend on *Cleopatra*, they refused to believe Marilyn would complete the film without incident; on 8 June, they announced that she had been fired. Almost immediately they took out a $500,000 lawsuit against their star for her failure and refusal to perform in *Something's Got to Give*, and she even found herself lumbered with an invoice for $5000 from the set photographer Don Ornitz. The situation so infuriated Pat Newcomb that she called in Milton Rudin.

Meanwhile she began to be blamed for the loss of 104 jobs. 'In my opinion, Marilyn cannot face reality,' commented one crew member, while an extra was quick to tell the press that Marilyn took hours to get to the set, stumbled on her lines then had lunch in her dressing room. Marilyn tried to counter this bad press with telegrams hand-delivered to cast and crew on 11 June, explaining how what had happened was not her fault and that she had looked forward to working on the picture. She also confided to staff at the Arthur P. Jacobs agency her belief that the studio was in a panic, because they had over-extended themselves on *Cleopatra* and were choosing to blame her. She pointed out that there were still scenes to be shot that didn't involve her, that had not even yet been written. Marilyn was angry and for good reason; she had worked at the studio for 16 years and was by far their most major player. 'Remember, you're not a star,' they had told her in 1952, a philosophy to which some Fox executives apparently still adhered ten years on.

Marilyn's representatives were keen to get the film back on track and wrote to Fox to say so, suggesting 23 July as a restart date. The studio responded with a stern letter setting out a number of strict rules that would have to be adhered to if production were to resume. There would be no consultation or approval of co-stars, other players, director, script, number of takes, photos, crew (including make-up, hairdresser or wardrobe). Marilyn would have to arrive on time taking lunch breaks specified by Fox; neither Paula

1506 Blue Jay Way, where Marilyn posed for George Barris, summer 1962

Strasberg nor any PR representatives, agents or associates of her lawyer were to be allowed on set. In short, Marilyn was to have no control over any aspect of the film but, in return, Fox would drop their lawsuit against her. This letter would have done nothing to improve relations between studio and star, but fortunately for Marilyn, she still had her allies on set. One player declared he could not feel bitter towards her: 'I can't forget the sadness I saw in her eyes,' he said. Dean Martin also proved to be a true friend; when Fox announced they were replacing Marilyn with Lee Remick, he handed in his resignation and walked off set, much to Marilyn's delight.

Eager to keep herself in the public eye, Marilyn embarked on a series of PR exercises, one of which was the long-awaited *Vogue* photo spread with Bert Stern, on 23, 24 and 25 June. Then shortly after that she undertook a variety of sessions for *Cosmopolitan* magazine with friend and photographer George Barris, during which he took hundreds of photos of her on the sand behind the Lawford house and in a privately owned home in the Hollywood Hills. On the surface at least, it appeared that Marilyn was taking control of her life and career. She attended several meetings to get *Something's Got To Give* back into production and she went to a party for Robert Kennedy at the Lawfords' beach house and enjoyed the numerous photo sessions. But not everything was rosy, as press representative Michael Selsman remembered: 'She was upset about various things – always. It was clear she was unhappy 24/7.' A potential overdose was high on the list of concerns about her mental health: 'It was a problem for her friends,' confided one associate. Meanwhile, she was not in the best of health physically, still addicted to pills and now undergoing a series of liver injections from Dr Engelberg in an effort to strengthen her system.

During her interviews with George Barris, Marilyn spoke about adoption, declaring that no single person should ever adopt a child, as, 'there's no Ma or Pa there'. Considering her earlier plans, these comments are intriguing and raise the possibility that her own plans had fallen through. Unfortunately, there is nothing to confirm how or why her views changed. Shortly after her death, Mexican press reports claimed Marilyn had become depressed by a sudden coldness from José Bolanos, though this seems an absurd notion, since the relationship never appeared anything but casual. But what might be closer to the truth is that she became depressed when she realized Bolanos was no longer able or willing to help her adopt. In 1963, reporter Glenn Thomas Carter asked Bolanos for his version of events, but said only that it was a matter between him and Marilyn. If, simply, Marilyn had changed her mind or encountered legal problems, Bolanos would have had no reason not to comment. But if he had decided not to help, perhaps the fear of her disappointment at this had pushed her over the edge was enough to ensure his silence.

Carter found Marilyn's intended adoptive son a year after her death in Mexico City. Describing her as a 'beautiful friend', he said: 'I was sad for many months because the beautiful blonde senorita did not come for me as she promised.' He has never been traced since.

A further complication to Marilyn's life in 1962 concerns the rumour that sometime that summer she either had an abortion or suffered a miscarriage. There is no documentary evidence either way, but Michael Selsman insists that he heard the story at the time: 'Marilyn didn't directly tell me,' he recalled. 'Arthur [Jacobs] and I were told by Pat [Newcomb], in that we had to know to counter any rumours – since the two major Hollywood columnists, Louella Parsons and Hedda Hopper, had paid spies in the hospitals and labs, so they knew pretty much what was happening.' Selsman believed the pregnancy to be a product 'of either Jack or Bobby, he didn't know which, since the switch had taken place recently'.

Added to the mystery is an invoice for $25 dated 7 June 1962, from the office of doctors Steinberg and Conti, which states Marilyn underwent an 'X-ray of nasal bones'. This is an intriguing document, not least because Dr Steinberg was one of Marilyn's gynaecologists, while Dr Conti was his anaesthetist. Steinberg's daughter Vanessa Steinberg has a clear view on the matter:

> 'I can say, with some certainty, that the procedure most likely had nothing to do with X-raying of nasal bones … [it] would have been performed at Cedars hospital in Los Angeles. [My father] saw her many times in Los Angeles, and I am certain that the procedures did not involve X-raying of nasal bones. My father was not a nasal surgeon, and I have no idea what the actual procedures where – I assume follow-on routine dilate and curette procedures for her gynaecological ailments, or else perhaps a termination or dilate and curette after a miscarriage? Apparently she suffered from severe endometriosis, and this may have been a procedure in relation to that, which was written down as X-ray of nasal bones. I can only speculate that the procedure you refer to was something that she wanted to remain a secret,

and this is not an uncommon practice in medicine, particularly if the patient was a celebrity.
I know that in New York she was treated and admitted to Mount Sinai under a pseudonym.'

The discovery of this document not only fuels the abortion-miscarriage rumour but also a persistent story of a visit Marilyn made to plastic surgeon Dr Gurdin, after what was described by Dr Greenson as a 'fall in the shower'. Dr Gurdin, who had performed the minor plastic surgery on Marilyn's chin years earlier, examined her during summer 1962 to determine if she had broken her nose. She hadn't, but the appointment has been tied in with the 'X-ray of nasal bones' procedure over the years, although a link is unlikely.

During these various upheavals and health problems, Pat Newcomb tried to keep Marilyn upbeat with a letter dated 11 July that listed the 19 magazine and newspaper articles in which she had appeared over the past few weeks, along with a variety of others to anticipate. She also sent her a copy of *Redbook* magazine on 19 July, in which Marilyn had done an interview. There was disappointment that the article did not contain the human insight they had wanted, but Newcomb felt it was the first positive story she'd read in a while.

Newcomb was trying hard to keep Marilyn's spirits up, but it came at the price of gossip about their friendship; that it was more than platonic. 'They were very close friends,' remembered Michael Selsman. 'I never saw them do anything of an intimate nature together, but there were rumours.' Selsman remembered the speculation coming principally from Marilyn's inner circle, from people whom she trusted and who should have known better.

On 19 July Marilyn hosted a dinner party for Greenson's children at Fifth Helena, then, on 21 July, reportedly, underwent a gynaecological procedure at Cedars, from where she was driven home by Joe DiMaggio. She rested for several days then resumed her summer of interviews and photos. Her lawyers continued their negotiations with Fox and pressure on the studio was even rumoured to be coming from the White House and in particular from Robert Kennedy. One of the interviews Marilyn gave during that time was with *Life* magazine's Richard Meryman. It was the last one she ever gave, and in it she complained magnificently about the studio and its treatment of their stars, declaring for the first time in her career that fame was a burden. By the time the interview ended, Marilyn was beginning to worry about her comments and asked Meryman not to make her appear a joke. He promised he would not and kept his word; when the article was published on 3 August it showed her as a mature, sensible woman, who had obviously learnt much from the hand she'd been dealt.

On the weekend of 28–29 July, Marilyn travelled to Cal-Neva Lodge in Lake

Tahoe, where she stayed with Frank Sinatra, Peter Lawford and his wife, Pat. Much has been said about this weekend, ranging from the depressing – Joe DiMaggio followed Marilyn but was not allowed on the premises, leaving her to stand silently and watch him as he stood on a hill opposite the complex. To the distressing – she was drugged and photographed in states of undress to ensure her silence regarding her relationship with Kennedy. There is virtually no factual information on the weekend, only a few photos that appear to show Marilyn at the lodge and give some insight into the mood surrounding her at the time. Much has been said about Frank Sinatra not being happy with his former girlfriend, and the photos show that most probably to be true. Singer Buddy Greco was performing at the lodge and seen in one photo sharing a friendly embrace with Marilyn, in which both are smiling broadly. However, Sinatra is also in the photo, looking up at the couple disapprovingly.

Generally, the Cal-Neva weekend is seen as a miserable couple of days. Marilyn was said to be depressed and, some say, almost overdosed in one of the bungalows; saved only by the fact that she had kept a telephone line open to the casino operator. There is also talk of Frank Sinatra being so wound up by her

9730 Wilshire Boulevard: office of Dr Hyman Engelberg

drugged and drunken behaviour that he asked Marilyn and the Lawfords to leave. Peter Lawford and Marilyn flew back to Los Angeles, while Pat Lawford travelled to the Kennedy compound at Hyannis Port. However, if it were as bad as rumoured, it doesn't fit that Marilyn returned home on the Sunday and did not call out either Drs Greenson or Engelberg. Instead, she attended Greenson's office the next day for a routine appointment and did not see Engelberg again until two days later, on 1 August.

If we are to believe some accounts, 1 August was a big day for Marilyn – Peter Levathes had visited her at home and, consequently, Twentieth Century Fox had renewed her contract with a large pay rise and a promise that shooting would be resumed. However, there is no trace of it in either the Fox or Arthur Jacobs archives, and no copies have ever been made public. However, on 1 August, Marilyn did speak on the phone to Evelyn Moriarty, who remembered she was happy because negotiations were going well with Fox. And, she was sure they would be back in production soon: 'That's how close they were to settling their differences,' said Moriarty. George Barris remembers a telephone conversation with Marilyn on 3 August in which she was very excited as the studio were going to give her an increase and start the film again in a month. So certainly negotiations did seem to have been progressing, though Twentieth Century Fox never confirmed the contract renewal, and the film continued to be described as 'shelved' in the newspapers.

On 3 August Marilyn received an injection, possibly a liver shot, from Dr Engelberg then filled a prescription for 25 Nembutal capsules, (barbiturates) issued by the doctor. That evening she went to La Scala with Pat Newcomb, who was suffering from bronchitis. Concerned when Newcomb told her she was planning to book into hospital for a rest, Marilyn invited her to stay at Fifth Helena to 'bake it out' next to the pool. Newcomb agreed, and the two returned to Marilyn's home. On 4 August, Newcomb slept late, while Marilyn pottered around and lounged in bed in her white towelling robe. 'She wasn't ill,' said Eunice Murray, 'she was just resting.' She drank fruit juice and spoke to Murray about household matters, such as the three shipments of furnishings expected from Mexico and a carpet that was being specially woven there. 'The development of the house was so important to her,' said Murray. 'In the past few weeks Marilyn had everything to live for. The plans we made were so wonderful.'

It has been claimed that when Newcomb eventually rose, an argument broke out between the two women, a result, it is said, of an insomniac and depressed Marilyn being angry that her friend had been able to sleep for so long. However, peace must surely have been restored, since Newcomb stayed for hours afterwards, leaving around 6 pm During the course of the day, Marilyn received several phone calls and visitors. One guest, photographer Larry Schiller, came to talk about shooting a cover for the December issue of Hugh Heffner's *Playboy* magazine. She had been aware of Heffner's request since July, but had still not decided whether to do it and told Schiller that she would give him an answer later.

In the afternoon she telephoned Norman Rosten who found her 'rambling but pleasant' as she talked of the future and anticipated her visit to New York that autumn; reminding him that he had not yet used her pool and urging him to come visit. 'Let's all start to live before we get old,' she told him, in words that stuck with him for the rest of his life.

Several workmen came and went, among them Murray's nephew Norman Jefferies and local mechanic Henry D'Antonio, who had been working on Mrs Murray's car and who returned it sometime that day. He had been to the Fifth Helena property many times to undertake work for Mrs Murray and Marilyn, and would sometimes take along his eight-year-old son, Tony. On such occasions, remembered Tony:

> 'They would discuss the work that was done, and Marilyn would thank him and of course pay for the repairs. Sometimes Marilyn would ask dad to do some handiwork, which he did and would never accept any payment for his time. He liked her and enjoyed doing little

things for her. I remember one time she asked him to replace some outdoor light bulbs and while he was doing that, she played catch with me in the backyard, asking all sorts of questions. As I recall she was a very unassuming person, always had a smile; generous, athletic and would slip some loose change into my pocket, holding her finger to her lips as this was our secret. Dad would not have approved.'

These were happy memories, but on 4 August, when Tony's father returned to Fifth Helena, he found Marilyn 'looking tired, not well groomed and as though she might have been crying'.

Dr Greenson was called to the house at 4.30 pm, arriving at 5.15 pm to find Marilyn in a 'somewhat drugged' and depressed state. He telephoned Dr Engelberg to ask him to come over, but he refused; he was in the midst of separating from his wife and understandably had other things on his mind. Concerned for her welfare, Greenson suggested to Marilyn that Mrs Murray should drive her to the beach then stay at the house that night. Mrs Murray later told reporters that she had stayed at the house several times in the past week, because Greenson did not want Marilyn to be on her own.

At around 7 pm, Peter Lawford phoned to invite Marilyn to a dinner party with several friends; this wasn't the first time they had spoken that day – Marilyn had earlier phoned to ask him for Pat Lawford's telephone number in Hyannis Port. 'She picked up the phone herself on the second ring,' he remembered, 'which leads me to believe that she was fine. She did sound sleepy, but I've talked to her a hundred times, and she sounded no different.'

While Marilyn was in session with Greenson, Ralph Roberts had called but had not been able to speak to her. Shortly after Greenson's departure, her stepson Joe DiMaggio Jnr telephoned to say he had called off his engagement to a girl of whom she did not approve. 'If anything was amiss, I wasn't aware of it,' he later said. Mrs Murray told reporters that Marilyn had been in bed at the time of the phone call, and she had woken her to ask if she wanted to talk with him. She had then listened in to the conversation, remembering how pleased Marilyn had been by DiMaggio Jnr's news, so much so that she had called Greenson to tell him.

For the rest of the evening, Marilyn stayed in her bedroom while Mrs Murray settled down in front of the television, noticing during this time that Marilyn received another phone call that seemed to upset her, although she was not able to say who the call was from or what it was about. Marilyn then spoke with Peter Lawford again, who became concerned when her voice started to 'fade out' but when he called back, the line was busy. At 8.30 pm a call was placed to Milton Rudin's exchange from Milton Ebbins, vice-president of Lawford's production company, who was concerned by what Peter Lawford had just told him. Rudin rang Marilyn's home at 9 pm but was assured by Eunice Murray that Marilyn was fine. Although Murray stated that this conversation took place around 9 pm, it is more likely that it happened after the DiMaggio Jnr call, but before the second call to Peter Lawford. Murray's memories have always been sketchy, even subsequently described as vague and evasive. At approximately 9 pm Marilyn appeared at her bedroom door and called out, 'I think we'll not go to the beach, Mrs Murray. I think I'll turn in now,' and she closed the door.

14

'SAY A PRAYER FOR NORMA JEANE'

At 4.25 am, the emergency services received a call from 12305 Fifth Helena Drive: 'Marilyn Monroe has died. She's committed suicide. I'm Dr Engelberg, Marilyn Monroe's physician. I'm at her residence. She's committed suicide.' When Sergeant Jack Clemmons arrived at the scene, he discovered Eunice Murray operating the washing machine, and doctors Greenson and Engelberg in the bedroom, where Marilyn's body lay on the bed, alongside which was a bed-stand covered in empty pill bottles.

From the start, the story Mrs Murray told of her discovery of Marilyn was patchy. She informed police officers that she had awakened at around 3 am and noticed a light on under Marilyn's door. Apparently, Marilyn had taken the phone into her room, as the cord trailed on the floor and beneath the door. She phoned Dr Greenson, who instructed her to pound on the door, which she had said was locked, and look through the bedroom window from outside. She received no response to her pounding but through the window she saw Marilyn, who 'looked strange', lying on the bed with the phone in her hand. As Greenson got up and dressed to come over, Mrs Murray phoned Dr Engelberg. Greenson arrived at 3.40 am and broke into Marilyn's room via the window. As he approached Marilyn to remove the phone from her hand, he discovered that rigor mortis had set in. Engelberg arrived ten minutes later and declared her dead.

By 4.30 am, employees at the Arthur P. Jacobs agency had been told of Marilyn's death and summoned to an emergency meeting at Fifth Helena Drive. Michael Selsman remembered: 'It was panic, of course. Events were already out of control, and now she was dead the press didn't feel constrained to hide what they knew – except of course, for the Kennedy stuff, which came later. I fended off the media by saying we didn't know what the cause of death was, because we didn't.'

By the time Marilyn's body had been picked up by the coroner, the news was flying around the world with tragic results. In England, 28-year-old actress Patricia Marlowe told friends that she understood why Marilyn had died and promptly took her own life with a concoction of sleeping pills. then 38-year-old dancer Gerdi Marie Havious repeatedly asked her husband: 'Why did she do it?', then leapt to her own death from their third-floor window. In Mexico three teenage girls gathered together their photos of Marilyn, then tried to take their own lives, thankfully, without success.

Closer to home, Marilyn's three husbands were told of the news. Jim Dougherty received a message from his colleague Jack Clemmons and turned to his wife: 'Say a prayer for Norma Jeane,' he said. 'She's dead.'

Arthur Miller refused to comment to reporters, but later revealed his feelings in a letter to friend Joe Rauh, confessing that he was stunned at the news. He had always worried she'd step over the edge, but didn't believe she meant to do it. His father, Isadore Miller, heartbrokenly told reporters: 'She was like my own. She was a kind, good girl. I'm so sorry I was not out there to be with her. She must have been very lonely and afraid.'

Meanwhile Joe DiMaggio flew into Los Angeles from San Francisco. He had been increasingly worried about Marilyn's well-being. On 1 August he had resigned his $100,000-a-year job as a representative for a military-goods supply company and travelled back to San Francisco. According to *Where Have You Gone, Joe DiMaggio?*, his biography by Maury Allen, DiMaggio told colleague Sid Luckman that he was leaving his job because he had decided to ask Marilyn to marry him again. There is some suggestion that Marilyn and he had already decided to remarry and had fixed the date for 8 August. That Marilyn had had a dress made for the occasion seems highly unlikely, judging by Luckman's comments. What is more likely is that DiMaggio was planning to ask Marilyn to marry him when he returned to Los Angeles; the dress she had ordered was probably for the opening night of the Irving Berlin musical, *Mr President*, which Marilyn was due to attend that autumn. The dress was never worn, and the marriage proposal never made. DiMaggio, Berniece Baker Miracle and former business manager Inez Melson arranged Marilyn's funeral for 8 August instead.

Sealing the crypt at Marilyn's funeral

They were all concerned to avoid a Hollywood spectacle and released a statement to that effect. The funeral would be a private affair, 'so that she can go to her final resting place in the quiet she has always sought'. They could not invite one personality without offending many others and so urged everyone to 'remember the gay, sweet Marilyn and say a prayer of farewell within the confines of your home or church'.

But not everyone was pleased by this decision. Frank Sinatra was apparently turned away from the gates at Westwood Memorial Park, while Peter Lawford told reporters: 'I am shocked. Pat flew in Monday night from Hyannis Port, where she had been vacationing with the kids, to just attend Marilyn's funeral. But we were not invited. I don't know who's responsible but the whole thing was badly handled.' Even Arthur Jacobs got in on the act when he declared that if Marilyn had been in charge of the invitations, half the people on the guest list would not have been invited and more of her friends would have been included.

Almost immediately, Abbott and Hast were brought in to provide help with the funeral arrangements, including hearses, flowers and other services. Both Allan Abbott and Ron Hast were pallbearers, and Abbott assisted the embalmer to dress Marilyn in a green Pucci dress and blonde wig before carefully placing her in the velvet-lined coffin.

According to Hast, Joe DiMaggio was 'noticeably heart broken', during arrangements, while Abbott remembered that on the night before the funeral, DiMaggio spent four or five hours with Marilyn's body, although what he said during his vigil will for ever remain private.

On 8 August, fans and the curious queued at the gates of Westwood Memorial Park to try and gain access. Inside, some thirty friends and associates said goodbye beside Marilyn's open casket, while Lee Strasberg read a heartfelt eulogy. DiMaggio bent to kiss the forehead of the woman he had never stopped loving and whispered: 'I love you, I love you, I love you' before finally the coffin was sealed.

Grieving family and friends,

8 August 1962

Marilyn's body was entombed in the Corridor of Memories section of Westwood Memorial Park, where DiMaggio sat for several moments after the other mourners had left. After he'd finally gone, hundreds of onlookers stormed in, knocking bouquets to the ground, crushing flowers, taking ribbons and stealing roses from the giant floral-heart tribute sent by DiMaggio. Two guards had to prevent people from attacking the tomb itself, and by the time they went most of the flowers had gone. They behaved like that, they said, because of their love for Marilyn, oblivious to the fact that it was not Marilyn Monroe who was buried in the crypt that day, but Norma Jeane Baker, the girl whose only desire in life was to be loved, respected and cared for, who, in the words of close companion Bill Pursel:

'From a very humble beginning … really blossomed into a legend, and along the way she met many men who could have – would have – given her the lasting fulfilment of womanhood. But, like the beautiful flower she was, she bloomed and died … and so the cycle of life goes on. The Lord giveth, and the Lord taketh away.'

PHOTOGRAPHS

1960–1962

ABOVE

In early 1961, Joe DiMaggio came to Marilyn's rescue after a stressful few
months with an invite to Florida for a break in the sun. Their marriage had
ended in 1954 after some nine months, but the friendship remained;
DiMaggio never stopped loving her.

At the Golden Globe awards in Los Angeles, 1962, with date for the evening, Jose Bolanos, whom she had met just before during a trip to Mexico. The relationship was never a serious one, though it is believed she tried to enlist his help with adopting a Mexican child.

On the set of Something's Got to Give, a romantic comedy directed by George Cukor, and Marilyn's last film. Marilyn was plagued by viral infections from the start of the shoot.

ABOVE

RIGHT

Unmistakably Marilyn in dark glasses and a fur coat. During the making of Something's Got to Give, Twentieth Century Fox forbade their star to leave Los Angeles. But here she is seen in defiance of the ban, returning briefly to New York to sing Happy Birthday to President Jack Kennedy at Madison Square Garden.

The mood on set deteriorated when, in defiance of orders from the film studio, she took time off to entertain President Kennedy at his birthday party in New York on 19 May 1962. She was fired shortly thereafter, and despite protracted negotiations she died before she was officially reinstated or the film ever finished.

Marilyn 'off duty': she would often go out wearing old clothes, no make-up and with her hair unstyled. It was a disguise that often worked, although the evidence of these photographs indicates that she was occasionally still recognized.

Marilyn's death at the age of 36, on the night of 4 August 1962, sent shockwaves around the world and triggered copycat suicides. Her coffin is glimpsed here, at the funeral arranged by Joe DiMaggio and her half-sister, Berniece Baker Miracle, which controversially excluded some of her Hollywood friends, such as Frank Sinatra and Peter Lawford.

POSTSCRIPT

Given the innumerable theories over the years about how and why Marilyn Monroe died, it's quite possible that among them the truth of her death has already been told. But the manner of her passing still attracts myriad questions and answers, though some people, including her many fans, would rather an open ending to her life than yet another theory presented as fact about her death.

The official verdict on Marilyn's death was probable suicide, although many of her fans dispute this: why would someone take their own life when they had so many plans for the future? Eunice Murray was about to leave on a six-week vacation, and Marilyn was looking forward to the arrival of a former housekeeper; the Arthur P. Jacobs agency had advised her that Billy Wilder wanted her for his next movie, and Arthur Jacobs had himself bought the rights to the movie I Love Louisa and scheduled a meeting about it for 6 August with Marilyn and director J. Lee Thompson; a Jean Harlow biopic with Sidney Skolsky was in the offing, as was an appearance in a hour-long TV special, a meeting on 9 August to discuss a musical version of A Tree Grows in Brooklyn with Jules Styne, plus renewed negotiations over Something's Got to Give.

Summer 1962 had been busy, and it looked as if autumn was going to be too, certainly when it came to Marilyn's career: it all looked hopeful. On a personal level, however, there are pointers to the possibility that Marilyn may have been struggling emotionally and possibly unhappy enough to consider suicide. Friendship was always an issue, and Marilyn had few people in whom to confide: she had virtually no friends who were not employed by her in some way. There was no relying on family, either; certainly not her parents, with whom she was never going to enjoy a close and supportive relationship. There were various bumps in the road that year, including the cooling of her allegedly close friendship with the Kennedy brothers and her dismissal by Fox being spun to depict her as a has-been, her career in free fall. To cap it all, Arthur Miller had recently remarried, and his wife was expecting a baby – news of which might have served bleakly to highlight Marilyn's own childlessness. Connected to which was the apparent collapse of any plans Marilyn may have had to adopt. Was this somehow linked to the mysterious phone call Marilyn had received shortly before she died?

Jose Bolanos told the press that he had called Marilyn on the night she died and that she had told him something that 'would one day shock the whole world'.

While this might seem a tad dramatic on Bolanos's part, was there something he said in the course of their telephone conversation that might have tipped Marilyn over the edge? She had planned a trip to Mexico for 15 September, perhaps a last-ditch attempt to fulfil her plans for adoption. Had Bolanos's phone call put paid even to that? It all remains speculative.

But if Marilyn didn't kill herself, was she murdered? And, if so, by whom and for what reason? The possibility that she was killed is awash with conspiracy theories that range widely. There's talk that she may have been killed to stop her publicly discussing her relationship with the Kennedys, rumours of mafia involvement and CIA plots and even the absurd notion that she had to be silenced because she'd found out that aliens had landed in America. Speculation is incessant; the so-called expert witnesses never ending; the stories ever more outlandish. Without exception, they each raise questions of credibility.

If Marilyn didn't take her own life, if she wasn't murdered, then was her death accidental, either a deliberate overdose with the hope of rescue or a genuine mistake? Maybe Marilyn wanted people to know how desperate she felt, possibly by taking an overdose then calling for help? Or did she just have lose track of how many pills she'd taken and take too many? Apparently, Marilyn used enemas, even for prescription pills, and might have overmedicated, which could account for Eunice Murray operating the washing machine in the middle of the night? Each question invites further answers, on and on, like an endless hall of mirrors.

Over the past sixty years, much has been written about how Marilyn Monroe died; David Marshall and a panel of Monroe experts tackled the subject most thoroughly, in 2003, in a painstaking examination of the months leading up to her death. Marshall and his team looked at every theory, story and aspect of Marilyn's demise, her medical and mental health, creating a vast database of files, photographs and e-mails. The results of their year-long labour is available in a 500-page book, The DD Group: An Online Investigation into the Death of Marilyn Monroe. It is the best exploration of Marilyn's death to date and comes closest to establishing exactly what happened that night of 4 August 1962.

But regardless of how or why Marilyn died, it is important to remember that beneath all the rumour and gossip – talk of suicide, murder and conspiracy – Marilyn Monroe was Norma Jeane Baker, a little girl who once dreamt of becoming an actress. The appeal of her life – its fire and its magic – is overwhelmingly more captivating than raking over the embers; with this in mind, Marilyn Monroe, Private and Undisclosed has determined to do justice to her, to the pleasures and the pains of the life of an extraordinary woman who not only brought joy to millions but also succeeded beyond a little girl's wildest dreams.

LAMENTING MARILYN MONROE

Paul 'Wes' Kanteman – Norma Jeane's nephew by marriage

I do remember when she died as Uncle Jim had been given the word by an old partner of his who was investigating the case. It was early in the morning when he called and told my mother what had happened. I was sad and wished more then ever that I had tried a little harder to get in touch with her. I do believe that she and Uncle Jim would still be together if she hadn't have become famous. They were very much in love and were really meant for each other. She never did achieve the happiness with the others that they had together – at least from what I have read she was a pretty unhappy lady. A lot of years have now passed, and I guess all I can do is keep the thought that she was my Aunt Norma, and I really thought a great deal of her.

Bill Pursel – friend and early boyfriend

She didn't find the little cottage and white picket fence; the three children and loving dog she sought. She loved the publicity and attention she attracted, but she was not happy. She sank into the quicksand of Hollywood like many others have done, but placing blame for the inevitable is folly. I was surprised at her death. What a tragedy. To me she was like a dream, and that is what she really was. Raising this past has brought melancholy to a very private part of my life, and if Norma Jeane is looking down on all this, I hope she is smiling.

Bob Cornthwaite – actor, *Monkey Business*

I always felt nothing good could happen to her. She had an aura about her that nothing good could happen. Of course good things happened to her career, but she was so vulnerable. There were so many things she didn't know, and she knew that, but she always said, 'I'm going to do it.' Her stubbornness was her strength and also her weakness. Perhaps she couldn't help her behaviour, she was so disturbed emotionally and psychologically and just couldn't help it.

George Chakiris – dancer, *Gentlemen Prefer Blondes*

When Marilyn died, I was in Japan making a movie, and I remember being so sad because it seemed to be our loss. But she lives for ever on film; she gave so much; she had a deep caring for her work and cared a great deal. Actors care about the parts they play, but Marilyn cared even deeper. She was glorious, something else. She stands alone and is incredibly unique. When I need cheering up, I watch 'Diamonds' or the opening number of *Gentlemen Prefer Blondes*, and it lifts my spirits. Marilyn was a lovely, kind person who wouldn't hurt a fly; she was adorable, but that isn't even a good-enough word. She was so gifted.

A. C. Lyles – film producer and friend

I join all her friends in Hollywood who had the privilege of knowing her; we remember her with devotion and love. Each of us felt a personal loss, and the industry was deprived of a great talent at an early age. As time goes on she becomes more legend. One has only to say 'Marilyn' and everyone knows that means Marilyn Monroe.

Alan Young – actor and friend

When Norma Jeane died I was very annoyed. I was saddened, of course, but very annoyed at how she was used – or misused – by people. She was so sincere and wanted more than anything to have a nice home with a nice family.

Peer J. Oppenheimer – press reporter

I have always believed her death was a mistake. I am convinced she simply picked up the wrong bottle or took too many pills. It didn't occur to me then – and doesn't now – that there was any foul play.

Jim Gough – son of a Fox electrician and friend

The memories I have of Marilyn are of a friendly person, full of attention for everyone, from bricklayers to painters and artists. She was far from being a snob, an eccentric or a manic-depressive during the times I spent with her. Marilyn was slender and full of energy, at peace with herself and concerned about other people's well-being. She was eagerly facing the future and anxious to see what might happen next. She was in full control of her life and seemed to be looking forward to her career as a mature actress. She was excited to harvest the fruits of her labour; her two most precious possessions were her house and her little white dog, Maf, whom she adored so much.

Lynn Pupello – journalist and friend

When Marilyn bought her house in Brentwood, LA, she invited me for the grand tour. She had little furniture, and the house was so modest it surprises people. Many trips to LA for business and pleasure have brought me to the tiny, lovely cemetery behind a movie theatre, where she reposes for all to see. It is one of the most beautiful spots on earth, which is appropriate.

Joe Coudert – photographer

It was a surprise when she passed away, since she was so young. That made it even more tragic for us, and we were greatly saddened. I often wonder what Ms Monroe would have been like if she was alive today … Clearly, she would be the Queen of Hollywood.

SOURCES

The following resources were utilized during the research and writing of this book:

Interviews/Reminiscences

Abbott, Allan
Allen, Angela
Anderson, Daphne
Baer, Richard
Baker Miracle, Berniece
Baloghy, Stephanie
Banas, Bob
Belmont, Beryl
Bolender Jeffrey, Nancy
Brennan, Pat
Cardiff, Jack
Carey, Harry Jr
Carroll, William
Casson, John
Chretien, Jeanne
Clark, Colin
Cohen, Nelson
Corner, Samantha
Cornthwaite, Bob
Coudert, Joe
D'Antonio, Tony
Damiecki, John
Day, Vera
Dougherty, Jim
Finn, Michael
Finnegan, Nanciele
Foot, Donald W. J.
Franklin, Joe

Fredendall, Bill
Gielgud, Sir John
Gierasch, Stefan
Gillon, Margaret
Gilmore, John
Godfree, Bryan
Gough, Jim
Grant, Mayor Johnny
Haspiel, James
Hast, Ron
Henderson, Timothy
Hyman, Earle
Jackson, Joyce
Jacob, Joseph L.
Jones, Karla
Kanteman, Paul 'Wes'
Kent, Jean
Kingston, Kenny
Kirkland, Douglas
Loraine, Don
Lyles, A. C.
Mankowitz, Wolf
McArdle, Maureen
McGuiggan, Peggy
McKay, Dick
Miracle, Mona Rae
Obermeyer, Don
Oppenheimer, Peer J.
Packham, PC
Page, Charles H
Pearson, Geoff
Pemberton, Allan R.
Porter, Brenda

Pupello, Lynn
Pursel, Bill
Reid, Elliott
Robertson, Dale
Rosette, Win
Rosten, Patricia
Rubin, Kathleen
Rubin, Stanley
Schaefer, Hal
Schlesinger, Carl
Searle, Gerald
Selsman, Michael
Shaw Marcus, Edith
Sheehan, Howard Jr
Skipsky, Eric
Steinberg, Vanessa
Stiles, Dolly
Swain, Harry
Taylor, Curtice
Thome, Nancy
Truax, Lisa
Turner, Kae
Van Buren, Tobias M.
Vannucci, Bob
Weston, Mark
Whitehead, Annabel (on behalf of
    Princess Margaret)
Williams, Frank
Wilson, Colin
Wimer, Albert
Wisdom, Norman
Young, Alan
Zernial, Gus

Documents

The majority of the letters and documents that follow were available in catalogues from these auction houses: Bonhams, Butterfields, Christie's, Hunt Auctions, Julien's Auctions, Sotheby's and Swann Galleries.

1930 Census: Atkinson family; Bolender family; Monroe–Martin family
Agreement Marilyn Monroe/Milton H. Greene, 26 Feb. 1958
Agreement Norma Jeane Dougherty/Marilyn Monroe and Twentieth Century Fox, 11 June 1947
Baggage declaration and entry form for Marilyn Monroe and Joe DiMaggio,
Bill from the Beverly Hills Hotel, dated 13–15 Mar. 1954
Birth certificates: Berniece Baker; Norma Jeane Mortenson
Cable from Frank Taylor to John Huston, 9 Oct. 1959
Certificate of conversion to Judaism, 1 July 1956

Contract between Marilyn Monroe and Twentieth Century Fox, 24 Aug. 1946
Death certificates: Della M. Monroe; Grace Goddard; Marilyn Monroe; Robert Jasper Baker; Tilford M. Hogan
Desk-diary entry from Harry W. Briden, manager of the Palace Theatre
Divorce papers: Gladys Baker and Jasper Baker; Gladys Mortensen and Martin Mortensen; Lillian M. Gifford and C. Stanley Gifford; Norma Jeane Dougherty and James Dougherty
Divorce summons delivered to Joe DiMaggio on behalf of Marilyn Monroe
Elyda Nelson manuscript, courtesy of Paul Kanteman
Emerson Junior High School year book
Eunice Murray transcript from 'Legend of Marilyn Monroe'
Excerpt from a draft of 'Memories of a Famous Composer – Nobody Ever Heard Of' (autobiography of Earle Hagen)

FBI documents re. Marilyn's trip to Mexico

Guardianship records for Norma Jeane Baker

Initial notes on Marilyn Monroe from Rupert Allen,
11 Mar. 1960

Inscribed photograph of Norma Jeane and friends,
25 Feb. 1940

Insurance document for Marilyn Monroe and Arthur Miller,
c. 1958

Jane Wilkie notes on Jim Dougherty

Joe DiMaggio note(s) re.: his friendship with Marilyn,
1955; Marilyn's dispute with Fox, no date

Lee Strasberg transcript from 'The Legend of Marilyn
Monroe'

Legal documents related to Marilyn Monroe's business
manager, Inez Melson

Letters/documents re. Terence Rattigan party, 1956

Letter(s) from:

Arthur Miller to: Joe Rauh, 9 Aug. 1958, 5 Aug. 1960,
13 Aug. 1962; Kermit Bloomgarden, 20 Sept. 1956;
Marilyn Monroe, 25 May 1956, c. 1958; Marilyn
Monroe Productions, 23 Nov. 1960; Mr and Mrs
Louis Untermeyer, 9 Aug. 1957

Bebe Goddard to Norma Jeane Dougherty,
26 Oct. 1942

Ben Hecht to: Ben Orlin, 5 June 1954; Loyd Wright,
19 May 1954

Ben Hecht, Mrs, to: Greg Bautzer, 23 Sept. 1962;
Ken McCormick and Doubleday, 7 June 1954;
Loyd Wright, 2 June 1954

Berniece Baker Miracle to Marilyn Monroe and Joe
DiMaggion , no date

Buddy (unidentified surname) to Spyros Skouras,
6 Apr. 1960

Columbia Pictures Corporation to Maurice Zolotow,
19 Oct. 1959

Dewey, Mrs, to Grace Goddard, 6 Dec. 1935

Dorothy Jeakins to: Marilyn Monroe, 3 May 1960;
C. O. Erickson, 3 May 1960; Frank Taylor,
12 Apr. 1960, 4 May 1960, undated

F. L. Metzler, Mr, to A. W. Deweese, Mr, 26 May 1952

Frank Taylor to: his mother, 13 Oct. 1959, 10 Nov.
1959; John Huston, 3 Feb. 1960, 25 Mar. 1960;
Leslie A. Fiedler, 12 Apr. 1960

Gladys Baker to Berniece Baker Miracle, 7 Oct. 1944

Gordon Mosley to Marilyn Monroe: 22 Oct. 1956, 29
Oct. 1956

Grace Goddard to: Los Angeles Orphans Home, no
date; Mrs Van Hyming, 15 Aug. 1935

Greenson, Dr, to Anna Freud: 4 Dec. 1961, 22 June
1962, 20 Aug. 1962, 13 Jan. 1963

Gregson Bautzer to Ben Hecht, 11 Aug. 1954

Hollywood Studio Club to Maurice Zolotow,
18 Sept. 1959

Isadore Miller to Marilyn Monroe, 8 Feb. 1962

Joe DiMaggio to Marilyn Monroe, c. 1961

Joe Rauh to Arthur Miller, 20 Nov. 1957

John Carroll to Marilyn Monroe, 4 Dec. 1947

John Morris to Marilyn Monroe: 7 Aug. 1956;
15 Aug. 1956

John Springer to: Aaron Frosch, 17 Mar. 1961;
Marilyn Monroe, 19 Dec. 1960

Johnny Hyde to Marilyn Monroe, various dates

Kay Gable to Marilyn Monroe, 11 Apr. 1961

Kermit Bloomgarden to Arthur Miller: 11 Sept. 1956;
1 Oct. 1956

Louis Untermeyer to John and Harriett Weaver,
11 July 1956

Marilyn Monroe to Dr Greenson, 2 Mar. 1961; Joe
DiMaggio, 28 Feb. 1954, undated 1954; Joseph
Papp, 17 Feb. 1962; Lee and Paula Strasberg, 1961;
Lee Strasberg, 19 Dec. 1961; Marlon Brando, no
date; Sidney Skolsky, no date; Twentieth Century
Fox, 29 Mar. 1962; well-wishers, after her
miscarriage , c. 1956–7; William Morris Agency,
8 May 1951

Michael Gill to Marilyn Monroe, 27 Aug. 1956

Miller children to Marilyn and Arthur Miller, c. 1958–9

Milton Spitz to Marilyn Monroe, no date

Natasha Lytess to Marilyn Monroe, 5 May 1951

Norma Jeane Dougherty to: Berniece Baker Miracle:
2 Feb. 1944; c. 1947; Cathy Staub, no date; Grace
Goddard, 16 Feb. 1943, June 1943, 15 June 1944,
3 Dec. 1944, 1945; unidentified friend,
27 Oct. 1946

Pat Newcomb to Marilyn Monroe, postmarked
31 Dec. 1960

Paula Strasberg to Marilyn Monroe, 16 Jan. 1962

Robert Miller to Arthur Miller, 24 July 1959

Stephen W. Bonarjee to Marilyn Monroe, 19 Oct. 1956

Tom Pryor to Mr A. W. Deweese, 11 June 1952

Twentieth Century Fox to: Marilyn Monroe, 10 Feb.
1947, 11 May 1950, 13 Oct. 1952 (giving Marilyn
Monroe permission to appear on the Edgar Bergen
Radio program), 8 Apr. 1953, 20 Jan. 1954, 2 June
1960, 15 June 1962; Marilyn Monroe Productions,
15 June 1962; Maurice Zolotow, 29 Sept. 1959

Wooster, L. A. C, to Marilyn Monroe, no date

Letter(s) from (transcripts): Elia Kazan to Marilyn
Monroe, c. 1951; Marilyn Monroe to Dr Rabwin,
April 1952

Letters, from and to, the Hollywood Museum
Associates, 1962

Marilyn Monroe: bank statement, 27 Sept.–25 Oct.
1951; movie contract, 11 Apr. 1951; pages of script
from *Gentlemen Prefer Blondes, How to Marry a Millionaire*;
personal script from *Something's Got to Give*

Marriage certificates: Gladys Baker and Martin
Mortensen; Marilyn Monroe and Joe DiMaggio

Maurice Zolotow, notes on Marilyn Monroe; notes on
Inez Melson; notes relating to Marilyn's fan mail
and Marilyn Monroe Productions

Memo(s) from:

Arthur Jacobs to Rupert Allen, 16 June 1960

Buddy (unknown surname) to Spryos Skouras,
27 Apr. 1960, no date

Darryl F. Zanuck to Spyros Skouras, 29 Jan. 1955

Frank Taylor to Eliot Ryman and John Huston,
29 Sept. 1959

Glenn Norris to Spyros Skouras, 19 Aug. 1960

John Springer to several Arthur Jacobs staff, 8 Dec. 1960

Marilyn Monroe to Marilyn Monroe Productions board of
directors, no date

Rupert Allen to Arthur Jacobs: 17 May 1960, 8 Aug. 1960

Memo to stockholders of Marilyn Monroe Productions,
2 Apr. 1957

Memos and letters between employees of the Arthur Jacobs
Agency, various dates; re. *Something's Got to Give* from
Spyros Skouras, 1962

Model release form signed by Norma Jean [sic] for M. O.
Schwartz, 18 May 1945

Model release form signed by Norma Monroe for Tom
Kelley Studio, 27 May 1949

Natasha Lytess, 'My years with Marilyn', unpublished
manuscript, no date

Notes made by Marilyn Monroe in connection with the
Twentieth Century Fox dispute, 1954

Passport, Norma Jeane DiMaggio/Marilyn Monroe

Person to Person transcript, 8 Apr. 1955

Petition to establish the presumption of Death of Marion
Otis Monroe

Postcard from Norma Jeane to: Catherine Staub,
28 Oct. 1944; Jim Dougherty, 15 Dec. 1945

Press release from Arthur Jacobs Agency, no date

Production records and letters related to *The Prince and the
Showgirl* from the Laurence Olivier Archive, 1956–7

Programme for *A View from the Bridge*, Oct. 1956

Questions and answers between Maurice Zolotow and
Milton Greene, 1956

Receipt for after-hours treatment at Elizabeth Arden, Beverly
Hills, 27 Apr. 1961; from Saks Fifth Avenue,
20 Mar. 1962

Report cards for Norma Jeane Baker, 1942

Surveillance report from City Detectives and Guard Service
– commissioned by Joe DiMaggio,
20 Oct.–5 Nov. 1954

Telegrams: Arthur Miller to Maurice Zolotow, 24 Oct. 1956;
Dorothy Jeakins to Frank Taylor, 8 Oct. 1959; Karl
Knust to Spyros Skouras, 20 Apr. 1960; Marilyn
Monroe to Joe DiMaggio, 22 Sept. 1961; Marlon
Brando to Marilyn Monroe, 27 Feb. 1961; Maurice
Zolotow to Arthur Miller, 23 Oct. 1956; Spyros Skouras
to Buddy (unknown surname), 28 Apr. 1960; Spyros
Skouras to Darryl F. Zanuck, 17 Mar. 1955; Spyros
Skouras to Karl Kunst, 21 Apr. 1960

Telephone messages from Marilyn Monroe to Joe
DiMaggio, various dates

Transcripts: interview with Marilyn Monroe for *Look*
magazine, 1961; interview with Harry Lipton, from
'Legend of Marilyn Monroe'; Jack Benny Show, 1953;
radio-news broadcast of Marilyn's arrival at the *Some
Like It Hot* première, 1959

Twentieth Century Fox: biography of Marilyn Monroe,
1954; legal records re. *Something's Got to Give*, 1962

Vaccination records for trip to Tokyo, Marilyn Monroe,
January 1954

Wedding announcement for Norma Jeane Baker and James
Dougherty, June 1942

Television/Radio

The Martin and Lewis Show (Dean Martin and Jerry Lewis),
radio broadcast, 24 February 1953

Marilyn Monroe talks to Sidney Skolsky, radio broadcast,
c. 1954

Marilyn Monroe talks to Dave Garroway, radio broadcast,
1955

Interview with Marilyn Monroe, unidentified interviewer,
not broadcast, *c.* 1960

The Legend of Marilyn Monroe, narrated by John Huston, 1964

Marilyn Monroe: Beyond the Legend, narrated by Richard
Widmark, 1987

Remembering Marilyn, narrated by Lee Remick, 1987

Marilyn Monroe: The Final Days, 2001

Marilyn on Marilyn, BBC, 2001

BBC Press Office, unseen Marilyn Monroe footage, no date

Newspaper/Magazine Articles

'260,000 minutes of marriage', Sidney Skolsky, *Photoplay*,
Aug. 1954

'Above all else Marilyn Monroe wanted to act', *Daily News*,
17 Aug. 1962

'Actress Marilyn Monroe attends Miller funeral', *Brainerd
Daily Dispatch*, 8 Mar. 1961

'Actress wanted baby', Maurice Zolotow, *Lima News*,
12 Sept. 1973

'All About Yves', *Idols* magazine, no date

'Am I too daring by Marilyn Monroe', *Modern Screen*, July
1952

'An afternoon with Marilyn Monroe', Hollis Alpert, *Woman's
Day*, Nov. 1959

'And the Lord taketh away', N. Polsky, *Modern Screen*,
Nov. 1957

'Anna Christie Scene, The', David Marshall, *Forever Marilyn*, no
date

'Another Lana?', *Long Beach Press-Telegram*, 13 Aug. 1950

'Are budgets necessary', *Movieland*, July 1951

'Arthur Miller likes a movie at last', *Nevada State Journal*,
8 Feb. 1962

Bebe Goddard interview, *All About Marilyn Magazine*, Jan. 1994

'Because of Joe', Shirley Emerson, *Motion Picture and Television*
magazine, July 1954

'Behind the scenes in Hollywood', Harrison Carroll,
Monessen Daily Independent, 21 Oct. 1952

Ben Ross interview, www.asmp.org

Bob Thomas memories, *Oakland Tribune*, 8 Aug. 1962

Bob Well's column, *Long Beach Independent*, 12 Apr. 1957

Carl Sandburg talks about Marilyn Monroe, *Cavalier*, no date

Cast/crew list for *The Misfits*, *Reno Evening Gazette*, 20 July 1960

'Conflict of careers', *Jerry Giesler's Hollywood* souvenir pubn, 1962

Coshocton Ohio Tribune (quotes from the news), 4 Sept. 1960

'Court dates up "Calendar girl" LA Judge calls Marilyn Monroe,' unidentified newspaper article, 26 June 1952

'Crawford aims barbs at Monroe', Bob Thomas, *Syracuse Herald Journal*, 3 Mar. 1953

'Creative agony of Arthur Miller, The', Allan Seager, *Esquire*, Oct. 1959

'Crowds trample Marilyn's flowers', *San Francisco Chronicle*, 10 Aug. 1962

'Darlin' Eileen: an appreciation of the life and career of Eileen Heckart', Michael Buckley, 7 Jan. 2002, www.theatermania.com

'Data sought on phone call just before actress died', *Chicago Tribune Press Service*, 8 Aug. 1962

'Day I became Marilyn, The', Una Pearl, *You*, 24 Nov. 2002

'Day I met Arthur Miller, The', Michael St John's Confidential File, 27 Feb. 2005

'Dead from his own hands', unidentified newspaper, 1933

'Did she try to call DiMaggio', *Oakland Tribune*, 6 Aug. 1962

'DiMaggio visits Marilyn in new hospital', *Oakland Tribune*, 11 Feb. 1961

'DiMaggio weeps over Marilyn at funeral', *San Francisco Chronicle*, 9 Aug. 1962

'Do you want to see her?', Robert Stein, *American Heritage*, Dec. 2005

Don Murray interview, www.americanlegends.com

'Don't call me a dumb blonde', Alice Finletter, *Modern Screen*, Apr. 1955

'Don't drink – it won't bring back the baby', Hedda Hopper, *Motion Picture*, July 1960

'Dozens drown as Floods sweep California', *Lima News*, 3 Mar. 1938

Drew Pearson footlight reflections, *Portsmouth Herald*, 30 Aug. 1954

Earl Wilson column: *Reno Evening Gazette*, 24 June 1961; *Daily Intelligencer*, 25 Jan. 1972; *Lima News*, 24 June 1956

'Earthquake ruins give up 130 dead; 5000 injured', *Syracuse Herald*, 12 Mar. 1933

'Empty crib in the nursery, The', Radie Harris, *Photoplay*, Dec. 1958

Erskine Johnson column, *Hollywood Today*, 29 Oct. 1953

Eunice Murray interview by George Carpozi, *Ladies Home Journal*, no date

Evelyn Moriarty interview, *Marilyn and then International*, vol. 1, no. 3, July 1997

'Failure was my spur', Marilyn Monroe, *Filmland*, Jan. 1953

'Film star happy but tired after eluding newsmen', *Coshocton Tribune*, 30 June 1956

'Friendship in Mexico may be a clue to Marilyn's death', *Chicago Tribune*, 8 Aug. 1962

'Gable christening is howling success', *Oakland Tribune*, 12 June 1961

'Gable discloses wife expecting', *Nevada State Journal*, 1 Oct. 1960

George Barris interview with Merja Pohjola, Oct. 2002

'Ghost materialized: Ben Hecht finally credited on Marilyn Monroe's memoir, A', *Ben Hecht, Story and News*, vol. 3, no. 1, 2001

'Girl with three blue eyes, The', Ezra Goodman, *Cavalier Magazine*, Aug. 1961

'Girl's love-happy, The', *Movieland*, Apr. 1957

'Hello Norma Jean: Would you believe Marilyn Monroe was named after a Louisvilian?', Ward Harrison, *Leo Weekly*, 15 Jan. 2003

'Hello Normal Jeane: Marilyn Monroe's unpublicized happy Hawthorne childhood', Corey Levitan, *Daily Breeze*, June 2003

'Here there and Hollywood', *Winnipeg Free Press*, 6 Dec. 1950

History of the SGTG scripts e-mail, Eric Woodard

Hollywood diary column, *Family Circle*, no date

'Hollywood happenings', Armand Archerd, *Van Wert Times Bulletin*, 9 Mar. 1953

'Hollywood's Marilyn Monroe: Blond, saucy, the new Harlow', Erskine Johnso, *Lima News*, 5 Aug. 1952

'Hollywood's most famous rear view', *Photoplay UK*, Sept. 1961

'Home life of a bachelor girl', *TV and Screen Guide*, Aug. 1951

'Hot not to cool down', *Movieland*, Dec. 1954

'House that dreams built, The', *Photoplay*, Nov. 1949

'How Marilyn Monroe rejected her secret dad in his dying days', Anthony Summers, *Star*, 1 Dec. 1987

'How Marilyn Monroe took London', Fleur Cowles, *Glamour*, Dec. 1956

'How Marilyn spends her nights', Merry Louis, *Movie Play*, Sept. 1955

'How much time and trouble is Marilyn Monroe worth?', Lloyd Shearer, *Independent Press Telegram*, 7 Dec. 1958

'How true is Arthur Miller's portrayal of Marilyn Monroe?', Ward Morehouse, *Daily Gleaner*, 5 Mar. 1964

'I don't owe Hollywood a thing by Del Wrightson', *Movie Secrets*, Aug. 1956

'I dressed Marilyn Monroe', Herbert Kamm, unidentified magazine, no date

'I know Marilyn's secret', Gitta Palmer, *Movie Secrets*, Oct. 1956

'I love you, I love you', *Newsweek*, 20 Aug. 1962

'I taught Marilyn how', Emmeline Snively, *People Today*, Apr. 1954

'I was an orphan', Marilyn Monroe, *Modern Screen*, Sept. 1951

'I won't be catty about Marilyn', Vera Day, *Picturegoer*, 12 Jan. 1957

'I'll always be alone', *TV and Movie Screen*, Mar. 1955

'I'll never be the same', Elsa Maxwell, *Modern Screen*, July 1956

'If Marilyn has a little girl', Isabel Moore, *Photoplay*,
  Oct. 1954

'If you were Marilyn Monroe's friend', Jack Holland, *Movies*,
  June 1955

'In defense of Marilyn Monroe', Earl Wilson, *Modern Screen*,
  June 1955

Inez Melson interview, Maurice Zolotow notes

'Inside story of the Marilyn-Jane feud, The', Jon Bruce,
  Screenland Plus TV Land, Apr. 1953

Interview with Marilyn Monroe by Louella Parsons, *Sunday
  Pictorial Review*, 1 Apr. 1951

Interview with Roy Turner by Jill Adams, *Book Club*, 2001

'Is Marilyn Monroe ruining her life?', *Movie Mirror*, Aug.
  1960

'It seems to me', Jane Dietzel, *Progress*, 29 Oct. 1960

'It's your fault, Olivier', Derek Walker, *Picturegoer*,
  13 Oct. 1956

'Jack "Waukeen" Cochran', Ray Campi,
  www.electricearl.com

'James has never said good bye to Norma Jeane', *Sunday Post*,
  4 Aug. 2002

'Jane Russell knows answer to Marilyn Monroe's problem',
  Erskine Johnson, *Sunday Tribune*, 29 Mar. 1953

'Jane, Marilyn get along well on set', Gene Handsaker for
  Bob Thomas, *Austin Daily Herald*, 20 Jan. 1953

Jim Dougherty interview with Lisa Arsenault, *Portland
  Monthly*, Nov. 1999

Joan and Marilyn talk to Louella Parsons, *Modern Screen*,
  July 1953

'Joe DiMaggio and Marilyn Monroe stir talk of a second
  marriage', *Lowell Sun*, 23 Mar. 1961

'Joe DiMaggio story, The', Joe DiMaggio as told to John M.
  Ross, *True*, 1954

'Joe DiMaggio visits Marilyn', *Odessa American*, 13 Feb. 1961

'Joe DiMaggio weds Marilyn Monroe at City Hall', Art
  Hoppe, *San Francisco Chronicle*, 15 Jan. 1954

'Joe Marilyn off to Tokyo', *San Mateo Times*, 29 Jan. 1954

'Joe quit $100,000 year job to be near Marilyn', *Salisbury
  Times*, 14 Aug. 1962

'Joe tries to patch up marriage to Marilyn', Aline Mosby,
  Oakland Tribune, 6 Nov. 1954

'Journey into paradise', *Photoplay*, Apr. 1954

Julius Caruso Obituary by Eric Wilson, *New York Times*,
  14 Aug. 2005

'Lawford tells of call to Marilyn', *San Francisco Chronicle*, 1962

'Lessons I've learned in Hollywood', *Movieland*, May 1951

'Life devoted to a lost cause, A', Robert Sherrill, *New York
  Times*, 16 Oct. 1983

'Look who's back: Marilyn', Peer J. Oppenheimer, *Family
  Weekly*, 22 Feb. 1959

Los Angeles Mirror, 27 June 1952

Louella Parsons column: *Galveston Daily News*, 28 Oct. 1949;
  Lowell Sun, 17 Apr. 1950, 2 Sept. 1950, 24 Nov. 1950;
  Modesto Bee and News-Herald, 7 Nov. 1950; *Charleston Gazette*,
  8 Feb. 1951; *Sunday Pictorial Review*, 1 Apr. 1951; *Modern
  Screen*, 1961

'Love and learn', Steve Cronin, *Modern Screen*, May 1953

'Love hungry', *Hollywood Life Stories*, no. 5 1955

'Lyons den', *Post Standard*, 8 Oct. 1955

'Magazine gets bum steer and apology from Marilyn
  Monroe', Erskine Johnson, *Daily Register*, 12 June 1952

'Make it for keeps', Marilyn Monroe, *Photoplay*, July 1951

'Marilyn and friends hint', *Waukesha Daily Freeman*,
  5 Jan. 1954

'Marilyn and Joe's wedding night in Paso Robles', Gary
  McMaster, privately published, 2006

'Marilyn and The Misfits', *Reno Gazette-Journal*, 23 Feb. 1997

'Marilyn arrives', unidentified newspaper clipping, 1960

'Marilyn attempted suicide four times', *Oakland Tribune*,
  7 Aug. 1962

'Marilyn back to work after NY sojourn', *Brainerd Daily*,
  25 May 1962

'Marilyn', Ben Ross', unidentified magazine, no date

'Marilyn', Ed Rees, *USA1*, July 1962

'Marilyn calls herself one-man-woman', Aline Mosby, *Ames
  Daily Tribune*, 15 Jan. 1954

'Marilyn changes hospitals seeking rest, checkup', *Lincoln
  Sunday Journal and Star*, 12 Feb. 1961

'Marilyn denies nude photo notes', unidentified newspaper,
  June 1952

'Marilyn doesn't impress Judge', *Wisconsin Rapid's Daily Tribune*,
  1 Mar. 1956

'Marilyn doesn't live here anymore', *All About Marilyn
  Magazine*, Apr. 1992

'Marilyn enters a Jewish family', *Modern Screen*, Nov. 1956

'Marilyn forms her own film company', *Great Bend Daily
  Tribune*, 10 Jan. 1955

'Marilyn gets last laugh in attempted blackmail scheme',
  Hy Gardner, *Oakland Tribune Daily magazine*,
  11 Nov. 1954

'Marilyn goes back to work', *Kingsport News*, 20 Oct. 1958

'Marilyn has minor corrective operation', *Oakland Tribune*,
  8 Nov. 1954

'Marilyn hospitalized for fourth time in five minutes', *Lowell
  Sun*, 29 June 1961

'Marilyn hospitalized The Misfits delayed', *Nevada State Journal*,
  30 Aug. 1960

'Marilyn in Korea', Forever Marilyn discussion list, no date

'Marilyn in the house', Helen Bolstad, *Photoplay*, Sept. 1955

'Marilyn keeping her books', *Indiana Evening Gazette*,
  18 Dec. 1952

'Marilyn leaves hospital', *Lima News*, 11 Aug. 1957

'Marilyn looked to future to pay debts', *Chronicle-Telegram*,
  8 Aug. 1962

'Marilyn may be pregnant', *San Mateo Times*, 18 Oct. 1958

'Marilyn may get divorce decree today', *Odessa American*,
  23 Jan. 1961

'Marilyn may lose her public by holding out', Aline Mosby,
  Great Bend Daily Tribune, 23 Jan. 1955

'Marilyn Missions', Jill Adams, transcript of Forever Marilyn
  website articles, no date

'Marilyn Monroe', *Life* magazine, 22 June 1962

'Marilyn Monroe "art" photo sellers convicted', *LA Times*, 27 June 1952

'Marilyn Monroe answers 33 intimate questions', *Stag*, Aug. 1953

'Marilyn Monroe back in town, late for work', *Daily Courier*, 29 Aug. 1958

'Marilyn Monroe collapses on set, fears miscarriage', *Fresno Bee Republican*, 14 Nov. 1958

'Marilyn Monroe comfortable after surgery', *Valley Independent*, 30 June 1961

'Marilyn Monroe confined to bed with influenza', *Sheboygan Press*, 18 Sept. 1954

'Marilyn Monroe has gall bladder operation', *Lowell Sun*, 30 June 1961

'Marilyn Monroe has her eye on Movie Oscar', Aline Mosby, *Lowell Sun*, 24 Nov. 1952

'Marilyn Monroe in hospital', *Lowell Sun*, 15 Sept. 1958

Marilyn Monroe interview by Helen Hover, *Motion Picture*, Jan. 1954

'Marilyn Monroe is buried, 100 guards keep crowd outside chapel', *Fresno Bee*, 8 Aug. 1962

'Marilyn Monroe left a child', *Motion Picture*, no date

'Marilyn Monroe loses baby after operation', *Hammond Times*, 2 Aug. 1957

'Marilyn Monroe loses her baby', *Ironwood Daily Globe*, 2 Aug. 1957

'Marilyn Monroe loses her baby', *Daily Courier*, 2 Aug. 1957

'Marilyn Monroe receives visitors in hospital room', *Florence Morning News*, 25 June 1959

'Marilyn Monroe resting at home', *Oakland Tribune*, 25 July 1961

'Marilyn Monroe rests comfortably', *Nevada State Journal*, 4 Sept. 1960

'Marilyn Monroe Story, The: Hamburgers and Cheesecake', Emmeline Snively, *Art Photography*, Oct. 1954

'Marilyn Monroe takes Whiteway by storm', Earl Wilson, *Lima News*, 15 Mar. 1955

'Marilyn Monroe talks about herself', unidentified magazine, no date

'Marilyn Monroe tells: I remember Clark Gable', Victor Sebastian, *Family Weekly*, 26 Feb. 1961

'Marilyn Monroe views Clift in unique light', *Reno Evening Gazette*, 3 Sep 1960

'Marilyn Monroe was a thin, unloved orphan 14 years ago', *Sheboygan Press*, 24 Nov. 1952

'Marilyn Monroe was my wife', Jim Dougherty, *Photoplay*, Mar. 1953

'Marilyn Monroe, Joe DiMaggio date again; just friends', *Nevada State Journal*, 16 Nov. 1954

'Marilyn Monroe, will new love give her a baby?', unidentified magazine , Oct. 1960

'Marilyn Monroe: Star at a turning point', Joe Hyams, unidentified magazine, no date

'Marilyn Monroe: That soul doesn't belong in that body', Hank Fardell, *Movie Fan*, Apr. 1953

'Marilyn Monroe's beauty biography', Joe Hyams, *This Week* magazine, 11 Dec 1960

'Marilyn Monroe's figure is tops at book auction too', *Pottstown Mercury*, 5 Dec. 1952

'Marilyn Monroe's hidden fears', Louella Parsons, *Modern Screen*, Mar. 1962

'Marilyn Monroe's honeymoon', Alice Hoffman, *Modern Screen*, Apr. 1954

'Marilyn Monroe's marriage', Robert J. Levin, *Redbook*, Feb. 1958

'Marilyn Monroe's secret tragedy', *Screen Stories*, Feb. 1961

'Marilyn Monroe's strange interlude', *Screen Mag*, Dec. 1955

'Marilyn Monroe's twin', Marcia Borie, unidentified magazine, no date

'Marilyn Monroe's voice secret recalled', Aline Mosby, *Lowell Sun*, 25 Nov. 1952

'Marilyn nearly 35 – and bouncy as ever', *Press-Telegram*, 12 May 1961

'Marilyn on Marilyn', Rita Garrison Malloy, *Motion Picture*, Nov. 1954

'Marilyn on middle age', Gan Gourlay, c. 1960

'Marilyn owes me everything', Natasha Lytess, *Movie Mirror*, 1957

'Marilyn plans rest before Reno Flicker', unidentified newspaper, 26 May 1960

'Marilyn protests as picture jumps from calendar to glassware', *Lima News*, 18 Dec. 1952

'Marilyn really agog over GI reception in Korea', *San Mateo Times*, 19 Feb. 1954

'Marilyn says she offered to give up film career', *Lincoln Star*, 28 Oct. 1954

'Marilyn says she's happy but has not changed', Vernon Scott, *Middlesboro Daily News*, 23 Oct. 1958

'Marilyn seeks divorce from Joe', *Bridgeport Telegram*, 5 Oct. 1954

'Marilyn set for surgery', *Lincoln Star*, 6 Nov. 1954

'Marilyn silent on stork talk', *Charleston Gazette*, 22 Mar. 1957

'Marilyn still hopeful she will become a mother', *Lima News*, 3 Aug. 1957

'Marilyn talks about Joe and babies', Sheila Graham, *Modern Screen*, Sept. 1954

'Marilyn talks of lost baby, new movie', *Independent Press-Telegram*, 15 Mar. 1959

'Marilyn to let Reinhardt son place manuscripts', *Newport Daily News*, 6 Jan. 1953

'Marilyn upset by phone call', *Independent*, 7 Aug. 1962

'Marilyn will fly to town for Centennial', *Oshkosh Daily Northwestern*, 6 Aug. 1955

'Marilyn, Joe leave for Japan', *Albuquerque Journal*, 30 Jan. 1954

'Marilyn's acting seen improved', *Hayward Daily Review*, 29 Oct. 1958

'Marilyn's children tell what they thought about her', *Marilyn Monroe: Her Last Untold Secrets* magazine, 1962

'Marilyn's death was inevitable', unidentified newspaper, 1962

'Marilyn's dream is coming true', *Modern Screen*, May 1957
'Marilyn's fight against insanity', Anthony Ashley, *Inside Story*,
    Oct. 1956
'Marilyn's last coach tells of starlet's unusual philosophy',
    Ada Evening News, 18 Nov. 1962
'Marilyn's the most', Harry Lipton, *Motion Picture*, May 1956
'Medical test for Marilyn', *Daily Review*, 14 Nov. 1958
'Memorable meal', *Gourmet*, Feb. 2001
'Memories of Marilyn', Earl Wilson, *Times Recorder*,
    15 Apr. 1973
'Memories of *The Misfits* in Nevada', *Nevada State Journal*,
    23 Oct. 1977
'Men who interest me by, The', Mrs Joe DiMaggio, *Pageant*,
    Apr. 1954
Michael Chekhov, 'Trivia of the Week', *Forever Marilyn* fanzine
'Mike DiMaggio drowning victim', *Oakland Tribune*,
    30 May 1953
Miscarriage, reports of Marilyn's, 18 Dec. 1958: *Fitchburg
    Sentinel*; *Odessa American*; *New Mexican*; *Lawton Constitution*
'Misfits filmed here with cast in harmony', *Reno Evening
    Gazette*, 2 Sept. 1960
'MM files in Mexico', *Nevada State Journal*, 22 Jan. 1961
'MM invited to pose for calendar', *Independent Press Telegram*,
    23 Aug 1959
'M-m-my M-m-m-m-marilyn', Earl Wilson, *Silver Screen*,
    April 1952
'Monroe and the wild life', *Modern Screen*, Nov. 1953
'Monroe doctrine, The', Sgt Robert A. Suhosky, unidentified
    magazine, no date
'Monroe gets role in *Cold Shoulder*', *Charleston Gazette*,
    18 July 1950
'Monroe prepares for long vacation', *Coshocton Tribune*,
    13 Nov. 1954
'Monroe–DiMaggio discord rumours persist', Louella
    Parsons, *Mansfield News Journal*, 12 Sept. 1954
'Monroe's gotta have that dress', *Picturegoer*, 29 June 1957
'Mr Hollywood Mike Connolly add Marilyn Monroe',
    Independent, 6 Mar. 1956
'My greatest portrait', *Screen Album*, Nov. 1955
'My love affair with Marilyn Monroe', Jim Henaghan,
    Motion Picture, Jan. 1955
'My wife Marilyn', Arthur Miller, *Life*, 22 Dec. 1958
'Mystery of Marilyn Monroe, IV, V, VI & VII', transcripts
    from the Maurice Zolotow archives
'Myth about Marilyn Monroe's death, The', Ben Hecht,
    Salisbury Times, 29 Sept. 1962
'NACA to give Xmas party for orphans', *Arcadia Tribune*,
    Dec. 1935
'New Marilyn, The', *Screen Stories*, Oct. 1961
'New Marilyn Monroe, The', Pete Martin, *Saturday Evening Post*,
    pt 1, 5 May 1956; pt 2, 12 May 1956
'New Marilyn Monroe has yen to produce her own
    movies', *Galveston Daily News*, 8 Jan. 1955
'New Monroe to come out of two weeks rest', *Chronicle-
    Telegram*, 6 Jan. 1955

'New Monroe, The', Jon Whitcomb, *Cosmopolitan*, Mar. 1959
'No leading man for Marilyn Monroe', *Long Beach Press
    Telegram*, 18 Dec. 1959
'Now Marilyn can talk', as told to Fred Harris, *Screen*,
    Nov. 1956
'On again off again', Earl Wilson, *Motion Picture*, Jan. 1955
'One man woman', James Wandworth, *Motion Picture and
    Television Magazine*, Sept. 1953
'Patient Lover, The', *Motion Picture*, Aug. 1961
Paul Kanteman interview, *Immortal Marilyn* magazine, no date
'Peeking in on Marilyn as a housewife', Ben Maddox,
    Screenland and TV Land, May 1954
'Police fear mob at Marilyn Monroe's funeral', *Manitowoc
    Herald-Times*, 8 Aug. 1962
Prince and the Showgirl news items: *Daily Mirror*, 1956; *Daily Mail*,
    1956; *Daily Express*, 1956; *Daily Sketch*, 1956; *Sunday
    Dispatch*, 1956; *Evening News*, 1956; *News Chronicle*, 1956;
    Daily Record, 1956; *Sunday Mail*, 1956;
    Evening Standard, 1956
'Prince and the Showgirl, The', *Picturegoer*, 29 June 1957
'Private life of Marilyn Monroe, The', Natasha Lytess, *Screen
    World*, Nov. 1953
'Prospect of audience scares Grable', Bob Thomas, *Portsmouth
    Herald*, 12 Nov. 1953
Radioplane Static, 15 July 1944
Ralph Roberts interview with *All About Marilyn* magazine,
    Apr. 1993
'Real Marilyn Monroe, The', Bob Thomas, unidentified
    magazine, no date
'Rebellion of Marilyn Monroe, The', *New York Post*,
    28 Sept. 1955
'Remembering *The Misfits*', *Lyon County Reflections*, 1994
'Remembrances of Marilyn', *Reno Gazette Journal*, 23 Feb. 1997
Richard Avedon photographs Marilyn Monroe, Forever
    Marilyn discussion list
'Riddle of Marilyn Monroe, The', I, II & III, transcript of
    articles from the Maurice Zolotow archive
'Rockefeller walks out on Marilyn', *Lima News*, 3 July 1957
'Role I most wanted to play, The', Peer J. Oppenheimer,
    Family Weekly, 11 Dec. 1960
Rose Post column, *Salisbury Post*, Rose Post, 23 Oct. 2006
Roxbury Historical Society News, spring 2005
'Saturday's Child', Roy Turner, website transcript
'Secret life of Marilyn Monroe, The', Steve Cronin, *Modern
    Screen*, Sept. 1952
'Secret Marilyn's life as a model, The', Emmeline Snively,
    Modern Screen, July 1954
'Sees Ex Hubby', *Herald Press*, 11 Jan. 1961
Sheila Graham column, *Monessen Daily Independent*,
    12 Oct. 1950
'Shocking facts behind Marilyn Monroe's crisis, The',
    unidentified magazine, no date
'Shooting Marilyn', Philippe Halsman, *Photography*,
    June 1953
'Simone meets Marilyn Monroe', *Lima News*, 20 Mar. 1960

'Simone Signoret likes Marilyn – but may change', *Newark Advocate*, 15 Nov. 1960

'Skyrocket a star is born', *Screen Fan*, Oct. 1952

'Small town girl covers The Misfits', *Lyon County Reflections*, 1994

'So far to go alone', *Redbook*, June 1952

Some Like It Hot at the Hotel Del Coronado, Hotel Del Coronado fact sheet

'Standing in for Monroe', *Picturegoer*, 18 Aug. 1956

'Star solves mystery of Marilyn Monroe's missing father', Anthony Summers, *Star*, 24 Nov. 1987

'Star turns', Norma Meyer, *San Diego Union-Tribune*, 25 Feb. 2002

'Stars marriage solid despite gossip', *Sunday Gazette-Mail*, 8 Jan. 1961

'Still together', *Morgantown Post*, 3 Apr. 1961

'Story behind Marilyn Monroe, The', Grady Johnson, *Coronet*, Oct. 1952

'Strange new life of Marilyn Monroe, The', Gene Houseman, *Movie Life*, Mar. 1956

'Studio suspends Marilyn Monroe for not showing up', *Portsmouth Herald*, 5 Jan. 1954

'Summit at Las Vegas', Earl Wilson, *Times Recorder*, 14 June 1961

'Symbol of success, The', Hal Boyle, *Lowell Sun*, 10 June 1957

'Tantrums and tiaras', *Times Magazine*, 21 July 2001

'Temptations of a bachelor girl', *Photoplay*, Apr. 1952

'That kiss from Marilyn Monroe's lips', Logan Jenkins, *San Diego Union-Tribune*, 4 Oct. 1999

'They really liked me', Joan Copeland, *Modern Screen*, Jan. 1957

'Things she said to me, The', Earl Wilson, *Photoplay*, May 1956

'Three encounters with a love goddess', *Hollywood Dream Girl*, 1955

Ticket to Tomahawk news items, *Silverton Standard & Miner*, 1949

'Time Marilyn Monroe hid out at our house, The', unidentified magazine, no date

Tony Randall interview with Theresa Hyde, www.houstontheatre.com, 11 March 2000

'Too hot to handle', *Modern Screen*, Mar. 1952

'Top Hollywood make-up artist tells all in book', *Lima News*, 31 July 1977

'Top stars 1955 resolutions', *Oakland Tribune*, 2 Jan. 1955

'Traffic judge fines Marilyn Monroe $56', *Sherboygan Press*, 1 Mar. 1956

'Tragedy of a sex goddess', *San Francisco Chronicle*, 6 Aug. 1962

'Truth about Marilyn Monroe's death, The', Ben Hecht, *Family Weekly*, 30 Sept. 1962

'Truth about me by Marilyn Monroe, The', as told to Liza Wilson, *American Weekly*, 16 Nov. 1952

'Two faces of Marilyn Monroe, The', Yves Montand as told to Bob Willet, *Liberty Magazine*, Oct. 1960

'University appeals to Marilyn Monroe for book generosity', *Pottstown Mercury*, 6 Dec. 1952

'Very private life of Marilyn Monroe, The', William Barbour, *Modern Screen*, Oct. 1955

'Victim of crash-in aimed at Marilyn Monroe tells story', *Bennington Evening Banner*, 20 Mar. 1957

'Voice of Broadway, The', Dorothy Kilgallen, *Pottstown Mercury*: 29 Aug. 1952; 18 Sept. 1952

'We knew Marilyn extremely well', *The Leader-Courier*, no date

Wedding announcement, Norma Jeane Baker and James Dougherty, unidentified newspaper

'What I saw in Marilyn's palm', Stephanos, *Modern Screen*, July 1959

'What Joe did for Marilyn', Lee Benedict, *Movie Stars Parade*, Oct. 1954

'What they don't tell you about Marilyn Monroe', Richard Vale, *Inside Story*, May 1959

What was Marilyn Monroe doing at 685 Third Avenue by Evan Michaels, *Photoplay*, Aug. 1959

'What's wrong with American men?', *Look*, 30 Nov. 1951

'What's wrong with sex appeal?', Leon Constantine, *Movieland*, Jan. 1952

Whitey Snyder interview with *All About Marilyn* magazine, Jan. 1994

'Who'd marry me?', Marilyn Monroe, *Modern Screen*, Sept. 1951

'Why Marilyn and Joe couldn't wait', Helen Hover Weller, *Movie Stars Parade*, May 1954

'Why Marilyn can't hold on to love', Helen Hendricks. *Screenland Plus TVland*, July 1962

'Will new love give her a baby?', *Untold Secrets*, Oct. 1961

'Witnesses say Monroe visited the Tri-State', *Herald-Dispatch*, no date

'Wolf-whistling Japanese mob Marilyn Monroe, DiMaggio', Frank Jordan, *Nevada State Journal*, 2 Feb. 1954

'Wolves I have known as told to Florabel Muir', *Motion Picture*, Jan. 1953

'Woman Arthur Miller went to when he walked out on Marilyn Monroe, The', *Photoplay*, Feb. 1961

'Woo Marilyn Monroe – for book collection', *Indiana Evening Gazette*, 13 Dec. 1952

'World stunned over death of Marilyn Monroe' by Bob Thomas, *Progress*, 6 Aug. 1962

'You don't really know Monroe, says Clifton Webb', interview with Ernie Player, *Picturegoer*, 11 June 1955

'Yves Montand's one-man show', Earl Wilson, *Lima News*, 23 Sept. 1959

Untitled articles: *Altoona Mirror*, 31 Dec. 1959; *San Rafael Daily Independent Journal*, 20 May 1950; *Greeley Daily Tribune*, 25 Nov. 1958; *Portsmouth Herald*, 24 June 1959; *San Mateo Times*, 1 June 1953; *Time*, 18 Oct. 1954; *Movie Spotlight*, Aug. 1955; *Nevada State Journal*, 6 Sept. 1960; *Picture Week*, 2 Apr. 1955; *Reno Evening Gazette*, 5 Sept. 1960; *Lima News*, 15 June 1957; *The News*, 12 Apr. 1956; *Time*, 16 Jan. 1956; *Traverse City Record Eagle*, 27 Feb. 1956; *Oakland Tribune*, 6 Dec. 1953

Bibliography

Allen, Maury: *Where Have You Gone, Joe DiMaggio?* (Dutton, 1975)

Arnold, Eve: *Marilyn Monroe: An Appreciation* (Hamish Hamilton, 1987)

Bailey, George: *Marilyn Monroe and the Making of Niagara* (Bailey & Co., 1998)

Barris, George and Steinem, Gloria: *Marilyn: Norma Jeane* (Gollancz, 1987)

Barris, George: *Marilyn: Her Life in her Own Words* (Headline, 1995)

Beauchamp, Anthony: *Focus on Fame* (Odhams, 1958)

Belmont, Georges: *Marilyn Monroe and the Camera* (Bloomsbury, 1989)

Black, Lendley: *Michael Chekhov as Actor Director and Teacher* (Umi Research Press, 1987)

Buskin, Richard: *Blonde Heat: The Sizzling Screen Career of Marilyn Monroe* (Billboard Books, 2001)

Cardiff, Jack: *Magic Hour* (Faber & Faber, 1996)

Carpozi, George jr: *Marilyn Monroe: Her Own Story* (Belmont Books, 1961)

Carroll, Jock: *Falling for Marilyn: The Lost Niagara Collection* (Virgin, 1996)

Carroll, William: *Norma Jean: Marilyn Monroe, 1945* (Coda, 2004)

Christie's: *The Personal Property of Marilyn Monroe* (Christie's, 1999)

Clark, Colin: *The Prince the Showgirl and Me* (HarperCollins, 1995)

Conover, David: *Finding Marilyn: A Romance* (Grosset & Dunlap, 1981)

Cunningham, Ernest: *Marilyn People* (self-published, 2003)

De Dienes, Andre: *Marilyn Mon Amour* (Sidgwick & Jackson, 1986)

Dougherty, James: *The Secret Happiness of Marilyn Monroe* (Playboy, 1976)

Dougherty, James: *To Norma Jeane with love Jimmie* (Beach House Books, 2001)

Feingersh, Ed, and LaBrasca, Bob: *Marilyn: Fifty Five* (Bloomsbury, 1990)

Ferber, Edna, and Kaufman, George S.: *Stage Door* (Dramatists Play Service, no date)

Finn, Michelle: *Marilyn's Addresses: A Fans' Guide to the Places She Knew* (Smith Gryphon, 1995)

Freeman, Lucy: *Why Norma Jean Killed Marilyn Monroe* (Global Rights, 1992)

Goode, James: *The Making of The Misfits* (Limelight Editions, 1986)

Gottfried, Martin: *Arthur Miller: A Life* (Faber & Faber, 2003)

Greene, Joshua: *Milton's Marilyn* (Schirmer/Mosel, 1998)

Guiles, Fred Lawrence: *Legend: The Life and Death of Marilyn* (Scarborough House, 1992)

Haspiel, James: *Marilyn: The Ultimate Look at the Legend* (Smith Gryphon, 1991)

Haspiel, James: *The Unpublished Marilyn* (Mainstream, 2000)

Haspiel, James: *Young Marilyn* (Smith Gryphon, 1994)

Hutchinson, Tom: *Marilyn Monroe* (Galley Press, 1982)

Jasgur, Joseph, and Sakol, Jeannie: *The Birth of Marilyn* (Sidgwick & Jackson, 1991)

Kazan, Elia: *Elia Kazan: A Life* (Knopf, 1988)

Leaming, Barbara: *Marilyn Monroe* (Weidenfeld & Nicolson, 1998)

Marshall, David: *The D D Group: An Online Investigation into the Death of Marilyn Monroe* (IUniverse, 2005)

Miller, Arthur, and Toubiana, Serge: *The Misfits* (Phaidon, 2000)

Miller, Arthur: *Time Bends: A Life* (Minerva, 1990)

Miracle, Berniece Baker, and Miracle, Mona Rae: *My sister Marilyn: A Memoir of Marilyn Monroe* (Weidenfeld & Nicolson, 1994)

Monroe, Marilyn, with Hecht, Ben, *My Story* (Taylor Trade Publishing, 2007)

Murray, Eunice, with Shade, Rose: *Marilyn: The Last Months* (Pyramid, 1975)

Peary, Danny: *Close-ups (Patricia Rosten on Marilyn)* (Workman, 1978)

Riese, Randall, and Hitchins, Neal: *The Unabridged Marilyn* (Corgi, 1988)

Rosten, Norman: *Marilyn: An Untold Story* (Signet, 1973)

Ryerson, Florence, and Clements, Colin: *Glamour Preferred* (Samuel French, 1940)

Shaw, Sam, and Rosten, Norman: *Marilyn among Friends* (Bloomsbury, 1987)

Shaw, Sam: *Marilyn: The New York Years* (Lardon, 2004)

Spoto, Donald: *Marilyn Monroe: The Biography* (Chatto & Windus, 1993)

Stern, Bert: *The Last Sitting* (Schirmer Art Books, 1993)

Strasberg, Susan: *Marilyn and Me: Sisters Rivals Friends* (Doubleday, 1992)

Summers, Anthony: *Goddess: The Secret Lives of Marilyn Monroe* (Gollancz, 1985)

Victor, Adam: *The Complete Marilyn Monroe* (Thames & Hudson, 1999)

Vitacco-Robles, Gary: *Cursum Perficio: Marilyn Monroe's Brentwood Hacienda;* (Writers Club Press, 2000)

Wagenknecht, Edward: *Marilyn Monroe: A composite view* (Chilton Book Co., 1969)

Weatherby, W. J.: *Conversations with Marilyn* (Sphere, 1987)

Wolfe, Donald: *The Assassination of Marilyn Monroe* (Little Brown, 1998)

Woodard, Eric: *Hometown Girl* (HG Press, 2004)

Zolotow, Maurice: *Marilyn Monroe* (Perennial Library, rev. edn, 1990)

no author, *Marilyn Monroe: The Life, The Myth* (Rizzoli, 1996)

Archives

Ancestry.com

Anna Freud Archive, Library of Congress

Arthur P. Jacobs Collection, Dept of Archives and Special Collections, Charles Von der Abe Library, Loyola Marymount University

Ben Hecht Archives, Newberry Library, Chicago
David Marshall Archive
DD Group Archive
Eric Woodard 'Rain' Collection
FBI Freedom of Information section
Foursquare Church Heritage and Archives Department
Frank Taylor Archive, Lilly Library, Indiana University
Hollywood Bowl Museum
Internet Movie Database (imdb.com)
Joe Rauh Archive, Library of Congress
Kent State University Special Collections and Archives
Kermit Bloomgarden Archive, Wisconsin Historical Society
Kris Peterson, San Juan County Historical Society Archives
Laurence Olivier Archives, The British Library
Maurice Zolotow Archives, Harry Ransom Humanities
    Research Center, The University of Texas at Austin
Merja Pohjola Archive
Michael Chekhov Studio, London
MPTV image vault
Natasha Lytess Archives, Harry Ransom Humanities
    Research Center, The University of Texas at Austin
Nevada State Library and Archives
NewspaperARCHIVE.com
Roy Turner Archives
Savoy Hotel Archive
Spyros Skouras Archives, Special Collections, Stanford
    University Libraries

Terence Rattigan Archives, The British Library
The BBC Written Archives Centre
Twentieth Century Fox Archive, UCLA
UCLA, Student Records section
University of Delaware Library
Whyte Museum of the Canadian Rockies
www.marilynmonroe.ca
www.marilynmonroecollection.com

Further Information

The Marilyn Lives Society: www.michellemorgan.co.uk
Forever Marilyn: www.forevermarilyn.com
Immortal Marilyn: www.immortalmarilyn.com
Marilyn Remembered: www.marilynremembered.org
The Official Marilyn Monroe website:
    www.marilynmonroe.com
Norma2Marilyn: www.norma2marilyn.com/frame.html
Marilyn Monroe Pages:
    http://marilynmonroepages.com/March.html
Marilyn collector:
    www.marilyncollector.com/legend/clubs.html
Marilyn Monroe Collection:
    www.marilynmonroecollection.com/
Milton's Marilyn (official website of Milton Greene):
    www.miltonsmarilyn.com
Marilyn Monroe and the Camera: www.marilynmonroe.ca
The Marilyn Pages: www.ellensplace.net/marilyn.html

Photo Credits

Jill Adams: 48; **George Bailey:** 121, 122, 123 top, 124 bottom, 160, 161, 162, 163, 164; **William Carroll:** 57, 58, 106, 107, 287; **from the collection of April and Jim Dakis:** 31 bottom, 44; **William M. Davies:** 138 bottom, 167; **from the collection of Henry Doody:** 174; **from the collection of George and Evan Finch:** 22, 24, 25, 26; **Hollywood Bowl Museum:** 17, 39; **Milton H. Greene © 2007 Joshua Greene www.archiveimages.com :** 154, 177; **from the collection of Paul Kanteman:** 52 bottom, 52 top, 54, 96, 97, 98, 99, 100, 101, 102, 103, 104; **Kobal:** 91; **Melissa Melgosa:** 72; **Mirrorpix:** 190 bottom, 191, 193, 206, 232, 233, 234, 235; **Don Obermeyer:** 2, 115, 169, 170, 171, 172; **from the collection of Don Obermeyer:** 139; **Photofest:** 68, 84, 112, 117, 147 bottom, 159, 175, 190 top, 209, 217, 224, 231, 240, 247, 252, 255, 259, 286, 289, 293; **Andrea Pryke:** 19; **from the collection of Bill Pursel:** 62, 66, 108, 109, 110; **Rex Features:** 155, 185, 196, 211, 212, 214 top, 214 bottom, 215, 216, 220, 221, 223, 225, 226, 236, 239, 241, 242, 243, 244, 245, 246, 248, 249, 250, 251, 253, 269 bottom, 273, 285, 290, 291, 295; **Win Rosette:** 133, 165; **Greg Schreiner**: 13 top; **used with permission from the Stars and Stripes a DoD publication:** 138 top, 140 top, 140 bottom, 141, 168, 173; **from the collection of Roy Turner:** 33 bottom, 43; **Horace Ward:** 187, 202, 207 top, 207 bottom, 237, 238; **Albert Wimer:** 150, 152 bottom, 178, 179, 180, 181, 182, 183; **Eric Woodard:** 13 bottom, 14 top, 29, 31 top, 32, 51, 59, 73, 74 top, 74 bottom, 86, 89, 119, 128, 130, 146, 147 top, 153 top, 156, 208, 262, 267, 269 top, 277, 280,; **from the collection of Alan Young:** 67, 111; **from the collection of Gus Zernial:** 118

INDEX